FAY WELDON'S WICKED FICTIONS

FAY WELDON'S
WICKED
FICTIONS

Edited by

REGINA BARRECA

UNIVERSITY PRESS OF NEW ENGLAND

Hanover and London

Published by University Press of New England, Hanover, NH 03755
© 1994 by Regina Barreca
Printed in the United States of America   5   4   3   2   1
CIP data appear at the end of the book

TO FAY WELDON,

whose wicked fictions
lead her readers to better lives

CONTENTS

Acknowledgments

In addition to thanking Fay Weldon, not only for her work but for her generosity of spirit and willingness to support this project through all its phases, I want to thank Fay's assistant and my lifeline in London, Jane Wynborne, who helped every inch of the way. In my own office, the work of two extraordinary research assistants, Julie Nash (who saw the manuscript through from the beginning) and Valarie Smith (who added essential finishing touches), allowed me to focus on the business of creating a better book rather than frantically searching for yet another misplaced footnote. In addition, agent Diane Cleaver, editors Jeanne West and David Caffry, and the Research Foundation at the University of Connecticut—especially the office of Dean Thomas Giolas—all contributed their support and encouragement in essential ways. My thanks, too, to the various publishers who have allowed material initially or partially printed elsewhere to be published here, including *Allure* magazine (where "Infidelity" first appeared), Wayne State University Press, and Gordon and Breach, Publishers.

CONTRIBUTORS

REGINA BARRECA is an Associate Professor of English at the University of Connecticut. She is the author of *Perfect Husbands and Other Strangers: Demystifying Men, Marriage, and Romance* (1993), *They Used to Call Me Snow White, But I Drifted: Women's Strategic Uses of Humor* (1991), and *Untamed and Unabashed: Essays on Women and Humor in English Literature* (1993). She is the editor of several volumes of essays. Barreca is Fay Weldon's designated biographer.

ELISABETH BRONFEN is an Associate Professor at the University of Zurich (Switzerland). She has written extensively on "the dead woman as muse" in women's literature, and her most recent book is *Over her Dead Body: Death Femininity and the Aesthetic* (1992).

RACHEL BROWNSTEIN, who teaches at the Graduate Center, CUNY, is the author of *Becoming a Heroine: Reading About Women in Novels* (Viking, 1982), and *Tragic Muse: Rachel of the Comedia Française* (Knopf, 1993). She believes in the importance of novels and novelists.

MARGARET ANNE DOODY, Andrew W. Mellon Professor of Humanities and Professor of English at Vanderbilt University in Nashville, Tennessee, is the author of two novels, *Aristotle Detective* and *The Alchemists*, as well as other books, including *Frances Burney: The Life in the Works*. She is completing a book-length study of prose fiction in the West from antiquity to the 1990s. At present she is Director of the Comparative Literature Program at Vanderbilt.

JOHN GLAVIN is a playwright and Associate Professor of English at Georgetown University. He has published on a variety of literary figures and topics from the nineteenth and twentieth centuries. His current projects include the pilot script for a television series "Remnants" and a book-length study of Dickens's theatricality, *A Book in Company.*

LEE A. JACOBUS is an Associate Professor of English at the University of Connecticut. He has written on Milton, Shakespeare, and modern Irish literature. Jacobs has edited several books, including *The Bedford Book of Drama.*

PAMELA KATZ is an award-winning filmmaker and screenwriter. She has worked in the world of motion pictures for 14 years and her career spans documentary, television, and feature films. Katz is the author of the screenplay *Angel, All Innocence,* a film adaptation of Fay Weldon's short story by the same title. She co-authored the screenplay *Lenya* with Steven Bach and is currently working on an adaptation of the novel *Simulacron III.*

SUSAN JARET McKINSTRY is an Associate Professor of English and Film at Carleton College, where she teaches on the nienteenth-century British novel, literary theory, and film narrative. She has written on Emily Brontë, Ann Beattie, Margaret Atwood, Toni Morrison, Emily Dickinson, and Jane Austen, and she co-edited *Feminism, Bakhtin, and the Dialogic* with Dale Bauer.

SIÂN MILE is currently finishing up her dissertation, "Slam Dances: Collisions/Collusions between the Theories and Practices of Feminism and Punk," at the University of Colorado at Boulder. Her work is grounded in an ongoing fascination with feminist theory and its place in and out of the academy, twentieth-century British literature, and popular culture. She has published articles on Marilynne Robinson's *Housekeeping* and on Roseanne Arnold, and hopes, in the future, to produce work that is as revolting as possible.

JULIE NASH is working on her Ph.D. in English at the University of Connecticut, where she teaches literature and composition. She is also an instructor at Eastern Connecticut State University. Nash has published on James Baldwin and has delivered papers on *Frankenstein, Jane Eyre,* James Baldwin, and David Mamet. She specializes in contemporary literature and feminist archetypal theory.

ROSE QUIELLO, who considers herself to be a "late bloomer," holds a Ph.D. in literature. She has been involved in women's and children's issues, in life and in literature, by her active work as an English professor and a registered nurse.

ROBERT SULLIVAN is a senior writer and editor at *Life Magazine.*

NANCY A. WALKER is a Professor of English and Director of Women's Studies at Vanderbilt University. She is the author of *Feminist Alternatives: Irony and Fantasy in the Contemporary Novel by Women* (1990), and *A Very Serious Thing: Women's Humor and American Culture*. She is also the editor of *Redressing the Balance* (1989).

FAY WELDON'S WICKED FICTIONS

REGINA BARRECA

Introduction

Reader, I *know* it isn't easy. But if I can write it, you can read it.
—Fay Weldon, *The Shrapnel Academy*

I picked up a copy of *Remember Me* at the Kings Cross railway station
bookstall on my first trip to Paris when I was twenty-two. Going to Paris
should have in itself been interesting enough to fully occupy my time, but
the journey paled in comparison to discovering Fay Weldon. I didn't look
up until we reached the Gare du Nord, and by then I was hooked. I was
speaking in short sentences, punctuated by satiric aphorisms which were
almost always softened by brief bits of wisdom; reading Fay Weldon made
me talk with her inflection the way that you might pick up a foreign accent
when traveling. As soon as I returned to my studies in England, I bought
every book she'd written and began doing my academic work on her prose.

After several years, I was back in New York and teaching at Queens
College, home to the prestigious Queens College Evening Readings Series.
Encouraged by Joe Cuomo, director of the series, I gathered all my nerve
and invited Weldon to give a reading. I spent more time revising the letter
I sent than I'd spent on many a graduate paper. Finally, I quite simply
began, "I've been told that you can never meet your heroes," and asked
her if she would consider making the trip over. I told her that part of my
dissertation on hate and humor in contemporary women writers was
based on her novels. I didn't want to seem presumptuous so I reassured
her that my writing my thesis on her work didn't mean I'd be digging up
her garden to look for unfinished manuscripts or anything, but that I hoped
for her benediction. I mailed the letter feeling like I was entering the Irish
Sweepstakes; I hoped against hope that she would reply. Weldon wrote

back the following week, saying "By all means dig up the garden. You can keep the manuscripts. We shall plant bulbs."

Weldon came to do her first American reading to a room packed with eager listeners who made the pilgrimage to Flushing driven by the shared belief that Fay Weldon is one of the most significant writers of today. Perhaps some of the audience were drawn by a blurb that announced that the writer of the initial episodes of "Upstairs, Downstairs" was appearing, but most of those who showed up on that May evening were there with Weldon's books under their arms. She did not disappoint. Reading from *The President's Child*, which had just been published in the States, she seduced her already converted audience to a new level of devotion. Her voice, which continues to be a combination of Grace Kelly and Mother Goose, is the perfect vehicle for her prose because it allows both the humor and the power of her work to come through. Described by one of her sons as "very quiet and terribly English," she nevertheless galvanized her audience. She did not so much read *with* emotion as she read in such a way that her listeners were themselves filled with feeling. She remained dignified and commanding, but also enormously accessible and delighted by the audience response.

Like a conductor before an unrehearsed orchestra, she brought us all into the same key. For example, Weldon would read, in an appropriately resonant voice, a passage from *The President's Child* as follows: "And the valleys shall ring to Thy Praise, O Lord." There would be a momentary pause, during which she might look up over the rim of her glasses before addressing the audience directly and explaining, in more confidential tones, that the cries of passion during lovemaking are the joyful noises we make unto the Lord because "What else could the psalmist have meant? The bleating of sheep on the yellowy Mesopotamian hills? No. I think he too heard the *cries de joie,* which almost, but not quite, blot out the tears of misery and fear which follow them." Dismissing the idea that bleating sheep are the subject of the Lord's attention, Weldon effectively undercut any diversion away from her intended effect. Mixing the profane and the sacred, the familiar and the divine, Weldon was mapping out her usual transgressive territory.

The audience changed from a crowd into a community. We were nodding and laughing and seeing ourselves in what she read. After her reading, dozens and dozens of women and men lined up with their multiple volumes of her work, and I have no doubt that every one of them left feeling as if they had formed a permanent relationship with the author. They told her stories of their marriages and divorces, children and parents, and she listened carefully enough to comment on everyone's remarks. It is a remarkable gift Weldon continues to possess: readings to crowds of several hundred will result in half that number lining up to speak to her, and she never flags in her ability to respond directly to everyone. Perhaps her novels, filled as they are with direct references to the reader and demanding a high level of response, have actually created a sense of dialogue.

I have had the pleasure of hearing Fay Weldon read from many more novels during the last ten years, and I have been able to appreciate, as I did on my receipt of that first letter, her generosity and her ability to fascinate her readers. Weldon's work is worth digging into and, like a healthy garden, yields rich rewards for the efforts made to cultivate its every corner.

Her nineteen full-length works of fiction have been translated into more than a dozen languages; several of these best-selling books have won her critical praise on both sides of the Atlantic. In England she is a familiar figure on television and a much-heard voice on radio. Her nonfiction has appeared everywhere, it seems, from *Allure* to the *New York Times* "Op Ed" page; three works of nonfiction range from discussions of Austen to Rushdie. Most telling, perhaps, is that her wit, erudition, and signature style have already brought the term "Weldonesque" into wide circulation whenever the uncanny, unnerving, wily, or wise comes into view.

A classic "Weldonesque" moment is one in which all the forces in the universe seem to converge in the most unlikely of ways: the day that the cat dies, a new kitten appears stuck in a high branch of the backyard tree; the night that a husband leaves, an old lover telephones for no particular reason, just to say hello; a mother dies young, but her daughter's daughter has the same way of sipping her coffee, or of preferring wool rather than cotton next to the skin; a child fails an exam, but is offered a good job that very afternoon. These moments as often as not tread on one another's heels because, as Weldon writes in the epigram to *Life Force*, "Nothing happens. And nothing happens. And then everything happens." When everything happens, Weldon is there to capture the event. Or we can see it in terms of linkages, unnoticed but nevertheless irrevocable, as she points out in *Remember Me*. "Everything has meaning," cautions the narrator. "Nothing is wasted. Only the young believe that they can stand alone in the world, for good or bad, their own master, independent of the past." As if to convince her readers by offering scientific detail, she goes on to explain that

As we grow older we sense more and more that human beings make connections in much the same manner as the basic materials of matter: that we cluster, in fact, as do those complex molecular structures which we see as models in physical laboratories. The linkages are unexpected; they can be of objects, plants, places, events, anything. It is perhaps why we should take good care to polish furniture, water plants, telephone friends with whom we apparently have nothing in common, pay attention to coincidence, and in general help the linkages along instead of opposing them—as sometimes, in our panic at our very un-aloneness, we are moved to do. [P. 61]

The linkages that Weldon invokes do more than provide a quasi-scientific terminology; the links forged between apparently random people are at once defining a territory and creating a net, thereby keeping safe everything within their protective boundary.

With all these affirming qualities, why choose the word "wicked" for the title? Blame it on alliteration, but "wicked" has been applied to Weldon by critics since reviews of her work began appearing in the late sixties. "Gleefully wreaking havoc," headlined a review in Vogue, "She talks . . . about her wicked, wicked ways." One reviewer dubbed her "a sniper. A sniper for good," implying that Weldon uses her position as an outsider to her advantage. Another declared that "there are demons in the Weldon refrigerator," and endless reviewers wonder if Weldon considers herself the model for female Lucifer Ruth in The Life and Loves of a She-Devil. This linking of Weldon's work to wickedness is not without her approval, it must be said, given that she herself announces that "My moral fiction is slightly amoral because it doesn't toe the party line of moral. It is not ideologically sound, or indeed moral, for an intelligent and competent woman to turn herself into her husband's fancy, pushy, idiotic mistress— now is it? But that is what Ruth does in She-Devil. My idea of morality isn't about women becoming strong and forceful, competent or whatever; it's about having a good time."[1]

So it is obvious that Fay Weldon is not wicked, not really. True, her fiction and her nonfiction alike are filled with images of transgression, subversion, heresy, and hysteria, but her writings are, in the end, humane, compassionate, sympathetic, and merciful. It is equally important to offer a caveat to the second part of the book's title: this collection also deals with Weldon's nonfiction. Clearly, Weldon's nonfiction work is as central to an understanding of her textual territories as is her fiction. The same essential issues are explored: imbalances of power, traced along lines of gender, country, and class, are in the forefront of her essays, articles, and lectures. Robert Sullivan explores Weldon's essays in detail and shows us precisely how her signature narrative voice is as fully present in her nonfiction as in her fiction. Weldon refuses to make distinctions between truth and fiction: "the novel you read and the life you live are not distinguishable," explains a character in Life Force (p. 15).

If you come to any of Weldon's works, fiction or nonfiction, angry, you will be calmed; if you come to them complacent, you will leave outraged.

Women (and men alike) are encouraged to have a good time, it's true, but they also learn to be strong—or, more accurately, to recognize the strengths they have always possessed—and they acquire competence far more easily than they ever imagined possible. Like a good mother or a full-time fairy godmother—both, perhaps, equally fictitious creatures of the imagination—Weldon offers her readers the possibility of recognition and realization in place of a desire for revenge or retribution.

She treats her readers roughly on occasion, expecting a great deal from them and assuming an intimacy that some neophytes find daunting. In *The Shrapnel Academy,* for example, Weldon confronts what can be called "the readerly/writerly battle for responsible literature" by addressing her reader directly and dissecting the relationship: "Now, gentle reader, shall we return . . . Gentle reader! What have I said! You are no more gentle than I am! I apologize for insulting you. You are as ferocious as anyone else. The notion that the reader is gentle is very bad for both readers and writers—and the latter do tend to encourage the former in this belief. We all believe ourselves to be, more or less, well intentioned, nice goodies in fact, whether we're the greengrocer or the Shah of Shahs. But we can't possibly be, or how would the world have got into the state it's in? Who else but ourselves are doing this to ourselves? We simply don't know our own natures" (p. 52).

Accepting responsibility is part of Weldon's regime, for her characters and for herself. Being a woman who lives by her wits, Weldon is the embodiment of the working writer who learned early how to earn her keep by the keen and quick use of her pen. (In an introduction to Louisa May Alcott's thrillers, Weldon presumes that Alcott wrote the gothic tales for three reasons: "She was good at them, they were obviously fun to write (as they are to read) and she needed the money." Much the same can be said of Weldon herself, who always argues that she writes better when she has outstanding bills to pay.) Weldon makes unashamedly declarative judgments, pronouncements on all sorts of topics, and does this verbally as well as on the page. A serious writer, Weldon has no difficulty in staking out an intellectual or conceptual claim and sticking by it. Whether writing about the Anita Hill hearings or why most people are slightly repulsed by scientists, Weldon unhesitatingly takes a position and writes her way into the argument. The daughter of a mother whose fiction was published under the pen name "Pearl Bellairs" and the granddaughter of Edgar Jepson, whose work can often still be found in the less-busy parts of large libraries, Weldon did not glamorize the process of putting one word after the other. Writing is a respectable profession, according to Weldon, nothing to be ashamed of, but one should be careful to avoid the temptation of regarding oneself as too much of an artiste. Writing everything from advertising copy to working for the Foreign Service "writing lies," Weldon continues to be mercurial as a writer. She seems to move effortlessly from dramatist to short-story writer to radio-play author to television scriptwriter, and then back to novelist.

It is more than difficult to document Fay Weldon's life story because she reinvents herself biographically nearly as often as any set of questions can be posed. We would do well to keep in mind remarks concerning the construction of a past that are sprinkled through Weldon's novels, summed up neatly by one paragraph in *Praxis*:

How much is fiction and how much is true? There can be no objective truth about our memories, so perhaps it is idle to even attempt the distinction. We are the sum of our pasts, it is true: we are altogether composed of memories: but a memory is a chancy thing, experience experienced, filtered coarse or fine according to the mood of the day, the pattern of the times, the company we happen to be keeping: the way we shrink from certain events or open our arms to embrace them. [P. 81]

On some matters, the sources of information seem to agree. Born in 1931, Fay Weldon was actually christened Franklin Birkinshaw, a name her mother invented for more or less magical reasons having to do with numerology—this, at least according to Fay-folklorists, has had a number of significant effects. Weldon argues that she was admitted to St. Andrew's University in Scotland because they believed she was a male student, and with a name like Franklin, this is really no surprise. "Otherwise they never would have permitted me to study economics," Weldon offers by way of further proof. The scenario of the female student admitted because of an administrative error appears in various guises in several works, most specifically in *Female Friends*. Growing up "in a house full of women," as she often defines her childhood—which took place first in New Zealand, later in England—she learned to expect a great deal of herself and of women generally.

Her parents divorced when she was five. Weldon lived with her mother, sister, and grandmother until she started college. "I believed the world was essentially feminine," she explains. "It was quite a shock to discover that the world, as other people saw it, was dominated by men. Luckily I had already formed my own opinion."

In her early twenties Weldon was briefly married to a man more than twenty years her senior, from whom she was soon divorced. Raising her eldest son as a single mother, Weldon looks back on her twenties as times fraught with "odd jobs and hard times," and recalls peeling linoleum, cold food straight from the can, defiance, and, finally, success. Eventually she moved from writing for the intelligence service and advertising companies (along the way marrying Ron Weldon, with whom she had three more sons) to writing for television, and then to writing fiction and nonfiction for what would soon become her avid readership. But, thinking of *Letters to Alice*, Weldon's book about Jane Austen, I remember her warning her fictional, novel-writing niece about the needs and desires of literary types, declaring that "I speak as one studied by Literature Departments (a few) and in Women's Studies Courses (more) and I say 'one' advisedly, because it is not just my novels (legitimate prey, as works of what they care to call the creative imagination) but *me* they end up wanting to investigate, and it is not a profitable study" (p. 10).

Unlike many other contemporary writers, Weldon has no problem with her work appearing in women's weekly magazines as well as the *New York Times* or literary journals. The readers of *Cosmopolitan* and the readers of *The New Yorker* finally have something in common. Weldon writes books you can give to your mother, your brother, your students, and your colleagues without risking their wrath or their wariness: students may wonder why readable books are being assigned as course work, perhaps, but that is the worst that will happen.

Giving Weldon's books to colleagues has another advantage; you can telephone and ask them to write essays based on those books they already know by heart. Scholars such as Nancy Walker, Elisabeth Bronfen, John Glavin, and Siân Mile have been addressing Weldon's work in their own writings and lectures for some time; scholars such as Margaret Doody, Rachel Brownstein, Rose Queillo, Lee Jacobus, and Julie Nash are only recently turning their considerable talents toward Weldon's fiction; and working writers such as Bob Sullivan and Pam Katz bring their insight and expertise to Weldon's work in a wholly new way.

Finally, Fay Weldon herself, always and ever generous, has here printed or reprinted some of her most significant, previously uncollected work. This is the first complete book focusing on Fay Weldon's wicked—and kindly—work, but it is surely not the last because, as Weldon observes, "By such discussion and such shared experience, do we understand ourselves and one another, and our pasts and our futures."

Note

1. Interview, "The Life and Loves of Fay Weldon," Eden Ross Lipson, *Lear's* (January 1990): 113–15.

Works Cited

Weldon, Fay. *Letters to Alice: On first reading Jane Austen*. London: Hodder and Stoughton, 1977.

———. *Life Force*. New York: Penguin Books, 1992.

———. *Praxis*. New York: Summit Books, 1978.

———. *The President's Child*. New York: Doubleday, 1983.

———. *Remember Me*. New York: Random House, 1976.

———. *The Shrapnel Academy*. New York: Viking, 1987.

NANCY A. WALKER

Witch Weldon: Fay Weldon's Use of the Fairy Tale Tradition

One story or another, . . . what's the difference? It is all the same. It's the one-way journey we all make from ignorance to knowledge, from innocence to experience. We must all make it; there is no escape.
—Fay Weldon, *Words of Advice*

Lorna Sage, in *Women in the House of Fiction*, comes right to the point: "Fay Weldon's reputation as a 'woman of letters' is itself a measure of . . . how far niceness has fallen out of fashion" (p. 153). Weldon is author-as-good-witch, recovering for fiction a disruptive, irreverent character that recalls the instability and endless revision of the oral tradition. She is a teller of tales whose "truth" lies not in a faithful representation of some objective reality, but rather in the familiar rhythms and tropes of a mythic heritage that wears decidedly twentieth-century dress.

The particular set of myths that Weldon plunders and reworks in her novels and stories is the fairy tales collected by the Brothers Grimm in the early nineteenth century. The Grimms gathered the oral tales from the women who told them, and a century earlier, in France, Charles Perrault represented the teller of the tales he collected as "Mother Goose," an old woman by the fireside. Fairy tales are thus in some senses women's stories: not only were women their traditional transmitters, but the best-known of them narrate the fates of women—Snow White, Sleeping Beauty, Rapunzel, Little Red Riding Hood, Cinderella. And even though some of these heroines end up marrying princes, we must not forget what they endure on the way to those endings: being fed poisoned apples, sleeping for a hundred years, being locked in towers, wearing rags and scrubbing floors. In a post–Walt Disney world, it is easy to lose sight of the brutality and violence of fairy tales. Furthermore, the tales are notably silent on what happens *after* marriage to the Prince. Is he unfaithful, boring, abusive? And if Red Riding Hood escapes from the wolf (as, in some versions, she does), what becomes of her?

These questions and others have intrigued women writers, especially since the 1960s. Two of the most thoroughgoing reworkings of these fairy tales are Anne Sexton's *Transformations* (1971) and Angela Carter's *The Bloody Chamber* (1979). Sexton's alterations of the tales occur primarily in style and context, rather than in the plots of the stories themselves. Her slangy, breezy, crisp style modernizes the tales, while highlighting their horrific elements, and she prefaces and concludes them with analogous stories in order to suggest that they represent just one version of a common human plot. Carter, in contrast, embellishes the tales, making lush and suggestive what was originally formulaic. Other authors, such as Margaret Atwood in "Bluebeard's Egg" (1986) and Jill McCorkle in "Sleeping Beauty, Revised" (1992), tell clearly contemporary stories whose titles compel us to see them as palimpsests for traditional fairy tales.

Fay Weldon uses all of these methods and more. Her characters inhabit contemporary urban centers—primarily London—but also inhabit the tales they have been told, so that life and fiction blur and become indistinguishable, as do past and present. Weldon's female characters and narrators are obsessive storytellers, modern Mother Geese who spin tales compounded of truth and lies, and then revise these stories in much the same way as fairy tales have undergone revision over time. At times, Weldon invokes actual fairy tales, as she does most overtly in *Words of Advice* (1977); at other times, the invocation is more subtle, emerging in a trope or an image, or in the narrator's voice or the structure of the story. Always, though, there is the clear sense that her characters are immersed in a sea of tales—fairy tales, old wives' tales, cultural mythologies, lies they tell themselves and others—in which drowning usually seems a distinct possibility. In short, in an important sense for Witch Weldon, *all* narratives are fairy tales, including those she writes, and because they are fairy tales they are also cautionary tales.

Today's folklorists agree that the fairy tales with which we are familiar did not originate as mere entertainments, but arose in largely preliterate cultures as ways of expressing common people's aspirations, needs, and relations to nature and the social order. They served, in other words, as cultural and sociopolitical oral documents that reflected values, fears, and hopes and that were readily altered as circumstances changed. By the time that Perrault in France in the late seventeenth century and the Grimm Brothers in Germany in the early nineteenth century had gathered folk tales and made them part of written literature as fairy tales, they reflected, as Jack Zipes puts it, "late feudal conditions in their aesthetic composition and symbolic referential system." Because the stories were devised by the "folk" rather than by the ruling classes, Zipes continues, "the initial ontological situations of the tales generally deal with exploitation, hunger and injustice familiar to the lower classes in pre-capitalist societies. And the magic of the tales can be equated to the wish-fulfillment and utopian projections of the people, i.e., of the folk, who guarded and cultivated these tales" (p. 6). In this context, it is easy to see why marrying a prince, turning straw into gold, and having a fairy grant one's wishes assume so much importance in the tales, and also why wolves and other dangers seem to lurk behind every tree in the forest.

There are at least two reasons why fairy tales hold a natural appeal for Weldon. One has to do with class, and the other with gender. The contemporary world of which she writes seems nearly as rigidly class-bound as the postfeudal world of the fairy tale, with the haves and the have-nots separated by a gulf that is both economic and ideological. Thus intones her narrator at the beginning of the story "Pumpkin Pie" (*Moon Over Minneapolis*, 1991):

The rich have got to come to some accommodation with the poor—and by that I don't mean provide housing (though I can see that might help) but "to accommodate" in its old sense: that is to say recognize, come towards, incorporate, compromise. [P. 81]

"Pumpkin Pie" is reminiscent of the Cinderella story—without the fairy godmother or the rescuing prince. Instead of being converted into a coach (à la Disney), the pumpkin is here converted into a pie that similarly becomes an instrument in the class war. The tale is told by a wry, scolding narrator, a contemporary Mother Goose, who warns her listeners to "pay good attention," and later asks, "Are you still listening? Or have you turned the music up?" (p. 81).

The Cinderella figure in "Pumpkin Pie" is Antoinette, the Latino maid at the Marvin household. As "a dumpy 45-year-old Latino with a scar down the side of her face," she "wasn't right for opening doors and smiling" (p. 85), so she is kept in the kitchen to fix Thanksgiving dinner for the Marvins and their guests. The dinner—including the pie—must be strictly non-fat because of Mr. Marvin's heart condition and Mrs. Marvin's ostensible adherence to the Pritikin diet, but when the fat-free pie burns because Antoinette must sneak home to handle a family emergency, she substitutes a traditional pie made with whole eggs. As cholesterol is a slow poison, no one drops dead at dinner, but Weldon's narrator finds the danger sufficient to issue a moral to the story:

The pumpkin pies of the poor taste as good if not better than the pumpkin pies of the rich; so if you can't make your own, do without, and let the hired help stay home for a change. Or you'll find cholesterol in your pie and a knife in your back, and a good thing too. [P. 88]

Yet despite this warning to the rich, Weldon's narrator recognizes that real life is more complex than the fairy tale with its sharp dichotomy between good and evil. Midway through the story, she stops to assess her listener's awareness of this complexity: "Whose side are you on, I wonder? . . . The rich or the poor? Have I loaded the scales? No. You wish I had, but I haven't" (p. 85). The narrator thus signals her position as storyteller, with the power to make choices, revise, and control the reactions of her listeners.

If fairy tales seem to prescribe certain behaviors for women—the passivity of Cinderella and Sleeping Beauty, for example—and to caution against others, such as the gullibility of Snow White and Little Red Riding Hood, this is a legacy of their nineteenth-century versions rather than earlier ones. In some earlier versions of the tales, Cinderella got to the ball because of her own cleverness rather than fairy dust, and "Little Red Riding Hood" was as much a tale of sexual initiation as of girlish innocence, but once the tales became the written property of the literate classes, they could be used to further the goals of gentility and Victorian propriety. Specifically, they could be used to instruct young children in the rules of proper behavior and the dangers of improper behavior. The language as well as the plots of the tales underwent revision in this process, as Angela Carter notes: "Removing 'coarse' expressions was a common nineteenth-century pastime, part of the project of turning the universal entertainment of the poor into the refined pastime of the middle classes, and especially of the middle-class nursery" (*Virago*, p. xvii).

It is these sanitized versions of the tales that permeate the regions "down among the women" in Weldon's fiction. And Gemma testifies to their prescriptive power in *Words of Advice*: "Princes, toads, princesses, beggar girls—we all have to place ourselves as best we can" (p. 20). Weldon's characters not only tell stories, they are surrounded by them, sustained and oppressed by them. "There is more to life than death," says the narrator in *Down Among the Women* (1972): "there is, for one thing, fiction. . . . Give yourself over entirely to fiction, and you could have eternal life" (p. 159). Myths, including fairy tales, allow Weldon's women to dream even while they reveal themselves as false dreams. "Myths," says the narrator in *Down Among the Women*, "are not true. Myths simply answer a need" (p. 158). Nowhere in Weldon's fiction is the need for myths and fantasy more clearly demonstrated than in the character Gwyneth in *Female Friends*, who "retreats from the truth into ignorance, and finds that the false beliefs and half-truths, interweaving, make a fine supportive pillow for a gentle person against whom God has taken an irrational dislike" (p. 45). She raises her daughter, Chloe, on old wives' tales and aphorisms: "Red flannel is warmer than white"; "Marry in haste, repent in leisure" (p. 45). The greatest falsehood that Gwyneth tells herself is that she has only to declare her love to Mr. Leacock, her employer, and her Prince will come to her. "Gwyneth believes she has only to speak the words and Mr. Leacock will be hers; and forever procrastinates, and never quite speaks them. . . . And so [women] grow old in expectation and illusion, and perhaps it is preferable to growing old in the harsh glare of truth" (p. 108).

Living with myths and fairy tales not only insulates women from the truth, it also divides them from one another and makes them competitors for the few available prizes. Indeed, the fairy tales themselves provide the models for such competition, with their endless pattern of beauty contests to determine the "fairest of them all." Louise Bernikow, in *Among Women*, recalls the message of "Cinderella" as one of female hostility:

It is a story about women alone together and they are each other's enemies. This is more powerful as a lesson than the ball, the Prince or the glass slipper. The echoes of "Cinderella" in other fairy tales, in myth and literature, are about how awful women are to each other. The girl onscreen, as I squirm in my seat, needs to be saved. A man will come and save her. Some day my Prince will come. Women will not save her; they will thwart her. [P. 18]

Chloe, as narrator of *Female Friends*, expresses similar sentiments as she reflects on her relationship with her friends Marjorie and Grace. "Fine citizens we make, fine sisters! Our loyalties are to men, not to each other":

Well, morality is for the rich, and always was. We women, we beggars, we scrubbers and dusters, we do the best we can for us and ours. We are divided amongst ourselves. We have to be, for survival's sake. [P. 249]

The most extreme instance of the power of female jealousy in Weldon's fiction is *The Life and Loves of a She-Devil* (1983), a novel saturated with fairy-tale motifs. Mary Fisher is a princess in a tower, both fictional creation and creator of fictions. The popular romances she writes are the modern equivalent of the fairy tale; or, as the narrator, Ruth, puts it, "She tells lies to herself, and to the world" (p. 1). Ruth, in turn, is compounded of Cinderella's jealous stepsisters and the evil fairy who contrives to bring

Mary Fisher down from her tower. The style of the novel is incantatory, the language of spells—"I sing in praise of hate, and all its attendant energy" (p. 3)—and the plot hinges on transformation, that staple element of the fairy tale, by which frogs become princes. Ruth, aided by the modern magic of plastic surgery, transforms herself from a six-foot-two, unattractive woman into the image of the delicate, lovely Mary Fisher and regains her husband, Bobbo, who remains more frog than prince.

One of Weldon's purposes in She-Devil is to deflate the notion of ideality that is the goal of fairy tales and myths, and the perfection of prelapsarian Eden is one of her targets. Ruth and Bobbo live "exactly in the middle of a place called Eden Grove," a suburban development "planned as paradise" (p. 4). The emptiness and artificiality of this "paradise" are immediately evident, not only in the deceit that characterizes their marriage, but also in the social interaction among the neighbors, which is a thin defense against nothingness:

My neighbors and I give dinner parties for one another. We discuss things, rather than ideas; we exchange information, not theories; we keep ourselves steady by thinking about the particular. The general is frightening. Go too far into the past and there is nonexistence, too far into the future and there you find the same. [P. 5]

Bobbo, deep into his affair with Mary Fisher, tells Ruth that "it is a good life," although he is increasingly absent from Eden Grove and therefore "does not say so as often as he did" (p. 5). Ruth, for her part, finds "this centerless place" barely tolerable, and observes wryly that it is "a better place to live than a street in downtown Bombay" (p. 4).

Ruth is thus a dissatisfied Eve in a trumped-up Eden, and it is appropriate that her first major act of rebellion is to burn down the house in Eden Grove, tellingly located at "No. 19 Nightbird Drive" (p. 4). Hers is a willing departure from the Garden, not an expulsion, and it is the beginning of her quest for self-transformation—a quest undertaken out of hate, not love, for love, Ruth remarks, "is a pallid emotion. Fidgety and troublesome, and making for misery" (p. 12). As Ruth undergoes the lengthy process of physical transformation into the image of Mary Fisher, she takes on a succession of false identities, becoming in turn Vesta Rose, Polly Patch, Molly Wishant, and Marlene Hunter as she manages the ruin of Bobbo and Mary Fisher in order to assume her place in the High Tower.

Although The Life and Loves of a She-Devil has been read by many as a triumph of the unattractive, betrayed wife over the forces of idealized romance, a consideration of the fairy-tale elements that inform the novel leads to a much bleaker reading that embodies an even stronger indictment of the romance tradition. Weldon both extends and inverts the Cinderella story to demonstrate the awful power of the ideals of romantic love and physical beauty. As a child, the unlovely Ruth has two lovely stepsisters, and she is early on abandoned by both her stepfather and her mother. Her marriage to Bobbo is occasioned by her accidental pregnancy, and she is as unwanted as a wife as she had been as a child. Her drive to assume the physical image of Mary Fisher requires that her body be mutilated, which recalls that in some versions of the Cinderella story, Cinderella's stepsisters cut off parts of their feet to try to make the glass slipper fit. In the end, Ruth is no longer a woman but an artifice; further, by taking Mary Fisher's place as the author of romances (though she refuses to publish them), she is engaged in perpetuating the same notions of romantic ideality that had caused her, as Ruth, to be shunned. The last lines of the novel invite us to read beneath the wicked comedy of She-Devil: "I am a lady of six foot two, who had tucks taken in her legs. A comic turn, turned serious" (p. 278). Serious, indeed.

Far more triumphant, though no less in thrall to cultural notions of feminine attractiveness, is Gabriella Sumpter in Weldon's The Rules of Life (1987). Having led a thoroughly self-centered life, Gabriella narrates her story from the grave in the year 2004, thanks to the discovery by the priests of the Great New Fictional Religion that the stories of the recently departed can be captured on tape. Gabriella is thus a kind of ultimate Sleeping Beauty, one who cannot be awakened but who can tell her story—a woman who, at the time of her death at the age of sixty-one, was "still capable of inspiring erotic love": "My step did not have time to falter, my spine did not curve; my eyes had wrinkled but barely dimmed: my teeth, with considerable help from my dentist, Edgar Simpson, remained white, firm, even, and above all there" (p. 15). Despite the pleasure that Gabriella has derived from her erotic encounters, she finds death (sleep) preferable to life, for life is painful, and "the briefer the experience the better" (p. 15). In fact, her "great achievement" is that she has not married or borne children, which reverses the fairy-tale trajectory toward marriage to the prince.

Like many a fairy-tale heroine, Gabriella is orphaned and left to find her own way in life. Her mother, a "poor, pretty, inconsequential thing" (p. 36), is killed by a wasp sting, and her father, a largely unsuccessful gambler, dies when their house burns down. Gabriella is rescued—and immediately bedded—by a doctor's assistant, but, in another of Weldon's inversions of fairy-tale plots, this experience neither ruins her nor serves as a cautionary tale for the reader, but instead launches her happily on a life of erotic pleasure. As Gabriella puts it, "One of the great rewards of my life has been the discovery that there is always a better lover than the last" (p. 55).

This portion of *The Rules of Life* engages and subverts some of the earliest versions of "Little Red Riding Hood." In the late-seventeenth-century version as recorded by Charles Perrault, the story of the little girl encountering the wolf in the forest had distinct overtones of sexual initiation and was meant as a warning to trusting, gullible young girls. The color of the girl's red cape has thus been linked by some to the blood of forced sexual encounter. Weldon reverses the moral purpose of the tale and prepares for Gabriella's delight in her first sexual experience with an episode she recalls from her childhood. At a children's mass that she attends, the priest tells a parable about a party at a castle to which only those children were admitted who were dressed in spotless white. A little girl who stains her dress by eating blackberries (like Eve and the forbidden fruit) is excluded from the "endless bliss" of the castle, and the priest warns his young listeners not to "be like the little girl who in her wilfulness stained her purity" (p. 24). At the age of five, Gabriella has already made up her mind on the issue of purity, especially because she senses that the priest, "with his little piggy eyes and his soft mouth," would like to get his "fat white hand" under her dress, and she deliberately spills ink on her white dress. If "purity" leads to the likes of the priest, "I wanted to be stained" (p. 24).

In an even more sweeping way than *Female Friends* or *The Life and Loves of a She-Devil, The Rules of Life* turns on the concept of fiction itself, of which fairy tales are a part. In the futuristic world of this short novel, technology and skepticism hold sway, and the dominant ideology is the "Great New Fictional Religion." The fact that the deity of this religion, the "Great Screenwriter in the Sky," is known to have had "many a bad idea in his time" (p. 13) prevents its adherents from taking much of anything at face value; the priest of this religion who serves as the primary narrator of the novel can foresee the advent of the *Revised* Great New Fictional Religion, which would hold the Great Screenwriter to higher standards than his current B-grade movie tendencies.

The most unvirtuous Gabriella Sumpter has in fact practiced the only virtue possible for one with such a second-rate deity: she has, according to the narrator, followed the script the Screenwriter has written for her. "Virtue," he comments, "lies in consenting to the parts allotted to us, and . . . just as some can't help being victims others can't help being oppressors, and . . . the best we can do is to help the Great Plot of life go forward, with all its myriad, myriad subplots" (p. 21). Life itself is thus a scripted fiction within which, as Gemma says in *Words of Advice*, "we all have to place ourselves as best we can." Gabriella has played the role of mistress to a succession of men; beginning as a potential beggar-girl, she has risen to the role of princess, though never marrying the prince in question.

At the same time, however, Weldon provides ample evidence that Gabriella's story is a tale no more true than any fairy tale. Gabriella herself signals her own unreliability by referring to her story as "fiction" and warning the priest who transcribes her tape that there are no rules in fiction, thus granting herself the freedom of the storyteller. "I have," she remarks, "or had in my life, no particular appetite for truth" (p. 17). Further, the priest several times doubts the accuracy of the tape recording, acknowledging that the "Technology of Truth" is "in its infancy, not its maturity" (p. 16). Finally, the story of the dead is refuted by the living. Timothy Tovey, said by Gabriella to have been the most devoted of her lovers, denies to the priest having seen her in the twenty years before being summoned to her deathbed. "Did she tell you the truth?" Tovey inquires of the priest. "I doubt it" (p. 77). The closest Gabriella has come to royalty is to have lived, as Tovey's mistress, in a house "in the keeping of the Royal Family to dispose of as they want" (p. 17).

Yet unlike Ruth, in *She-Devil,* who ends by inhabiting another woman's story, tower, and even her body, Gabriella is her own creation. In her own tale she is, unlike Red Riding Hood, unafraid of the wolf, and in the end she chooses the role of a Sleeping Beauty who does not wait for the kiss of a prince, but instead captivates the priest who transcribes her story, as if to prove her claim to the part of the irresistible princess.

There may be no rules in fiction, but there are rules in life, Gabriella Sumpter maintains as she distills the "valid rules" from her experience. In a similar spirit of instruction, Gemma passes along "words of advice" in Weldon's novel with that phrase as its title. Like Gwyneth's aphorisms and Gabriella's rules, Gemma's "words" are suspect, arising as they do from the fairy tale that she inhabits as an antidote to reality. *Words of Advice* tells of three women—Gemma, Elsa, and Janice—who must extricate themselves from the mythologies on which they have patterned their behavior and expectations. Instead of palimpsestic images, as they are in *The Rules of Life,* fairy tales are in this novel used overtly as elements of the plot. Elsa tells fairy tales to her brothers and sisters and comes to see herself in terms of the tales, Gemma tells Elsa her own life as a fairy tale in order to save her from ignorance, and Janice awakens from her grim existence as the discarded wife. Transformations abound amid resonances of Rapunzel, Red Riding Hood, Rumpelstiltskin, and Sleeping Beauty.

Young Elsa, secretary to and mistress of Victor, Janice's estranged husband, is compounded of Red Riding Hood, Rapunzel, and the heroine of Rumpelstiltskin, narrowly escaping the fates of all three. Arriving at the home of Hamish and Gemma for the weekend, Elsa finds herself consigned to a high room where she is expected to type inventories of the antiques that the wealthy Hamish will sell to Victor. No more able to type well than she is to spin straw into gold, Elsa is rescued by Hamish-as-Rumpelstiltskin in exchange for sexual favors; here, that is, Rumpelstiltskin not only demands the girl's first-born child, but intends to father it himself. Simultaneously, Elsa as Red Riding Hood is willingly pursued by Victor-as-wolf, a reference that Weldon confirms by several times echoing the language of the tale. Following their predinner lovemaking, for example, Victor prepares to leave Elsa, "the better to change for dinner" (p. 9).

Elsa's youthful innocence is counterpointed to Gemma's cynicism. Whereas nineteen-year-old Elsa is vulnerable to the snares set for fairy-tale heroines, Gemma has willfully constructed her own history to resemble a fairy tale rather than the unglamorous truth that she has married the frog instead of the prince. Gemma recognizes in Elsa the naivete of her own youthful self; what she does not recognize until the end of the novel is that she is just as ensnared in fiction as Elsa is. Early in the novel, Gemma signals their similarity when she says to Elsa, "I have a story to tell. It's a fairy tale. I love fairy tales, don't you?" When Elsa responds that she does, Gemma says, "I thought you would" (p. 20). The tale Gemma then tells concerns the betrothal of Mr. Fox to Lady Mary, who, on the eve of their wedding, discovers Mr. Fox eating human flesh and carries home as evidence a finger with a ring on it. Her brothers kill Mr. Fox to save her from a horrible fate.

The tale is one that Gemma heard on the train on her way to London as a young girl, and she believes that the hearing of it predestined her to fall in love with a Mr. Fox. "Fairy tales," she tells Elsa, "are lived out daily" (p. 21), and the story of her own life that she tells Elsa intermittently during the rest of the novel is as fabricated as the tale of Lady Mary and Mr. Fox that she had heard on the radio—fabricated to explain her missing finger and inability to walk as well as the loss of her prince, Mr. Fox. Only at the end does Hamish tell the truth that frees both Gemma and Elsa: Mr. Fox, his business partner, was a homosexual; rather than being severed by Mr. Fox, Gemma's finger was caught in an elevator door and subsequently amputated; and the paralysis of Gemma's legs is emotional, induced by her realization that she has been betrayed by the prince and has married the frog. Stripped of her fairy tale, Gemma is able to walk, and exhorts Elsa to run away from fairy tales: "Run, Elsa! Run for all you're worth. Don't fall. Please don't fall, the way I did. . . . You must run for me and all of us" (p. 233).

Victor's wife, Janice, is in thrall to the more prosaic cultural mythology of the ideal wife, as defined by Victor. She is to be Snow White, the eternal virgin, "someone as pure and helpful as his own mother" (p. 154). But the mask of wifely respectability she assumes according to his wishes hardens as it obscures her individuality. Finally, she has become a type rather than a person, as Weldon's narrator sarcastically notes:

What we have here, ladies and gentlemen, is no woman, but a housewife. And what a housewife! Note her rigid, mousy curls, kept stiff by spray; her quick eyes, which search for dust and burning toast, and not the appraisal or enquiry of the opposite sex; the sharp voice, growing sharper, louder, year by year: at home in a bus queue or ordering groceries or rebuking the garbage, but hardly in the bed. Does that suit you, Victor?
    No. [Pp. 154–55]

Bored by his own creation, Victor turns to Elsa, but he returns to Janice once she is rejuvenated by an affair with a Polish carpenter and her own daughter's involvement with an American student. The carpenter's wife laments the separation of women required by male fantasies—"I only wish women would stick together a bit" (p. 160)—and Gemma echoes the same sentiment when she says, "If only . . . we women could learn from one another" (p. 183).

Gemma's statement is both plaintive and ironic, reminding us that women in Weldon's fiction *do* learn from each other—sometimes the wrong things, such as Gwyneth's old wives' tales and Mary Fisher's romances, and sometimes the right things, the "words of advice" that cut through the bonds of myths and fairy tales. Weldon's critique of the power of the tale is by no means completely negative. To believe you are a princess when you are actually a beggar-girl may be dangerous, to be sure, and some frogs, when kissed, remain frogs. But Weldon's use of fairy-tale plots and motifs is also a way of honoring that tradition, of honoring women as tellers of tales, and ultimately a way of recognizing the human desire for magic and transformation that created those tales in the first place.

Works Cited ·

Atwood, Margaret. "Bluebeard's Egg." *Bluebeard's Egg and Other Stories.* Boston: Houghton Mifflin, 1986.
Bernikow, Louise. *Among Women.* New York: Harmony Books, 1980.
Carter, Angela. *The Bloody Chamber.* 1979. New York: Penguin, 1993.
Carter, Angela, ed. *The Virago Book of Fairy Tales.* London: Virago Press, 1990.
McCorkle, Jill. "Sleeping Beauty, Revised." *Crash Diet.* Chapel Hill, N.C.: Algonquin Books, 1992.
Sage, Lorna. *Women in the House of Fiction: Post-War Women Novelists.* New York: Routledge, 1992.

Sexton, Anne. *Transformations*. Boston: Houghton Mifflin, 1971.
Weldon, Fay. *Down Among the Women*. 1972. Chicago: Academy Chicago, 1984.
———. *Female Friends*. New York: St. Martin's Press, 1974.
———. *The Life and Loves of a She-Devil*. 1983. New York: Ballantine Books, 1985.
———. *Moon Over Minneapolis*. 1991. New York: Penguin, 1992.
———. *The Rules of Life*. New York: Harper & Row, 1987.
———. *Words of Advice*. 1977. New York: Ballantine Books, 1978.
Zipes, Jack. *Breaking the Magic Spell: Radical Theories of Folk and Fairy Tales*. Austin: University of Texas Press, 1979.

SIÂN MILE

Slam Dancing with Fay Weldon

I am . . . fairly marketable, I don't kick people's ankles or spit into the camera.
—Fay Weldon, *The Guardian*

"You can all stop staring now," [Johnny] Rotten spits after the opening song
deteriorates. "We're ugly and we know it . . ." —Noel E. Monk and Jimmy
Guterman, *Twelve Days on the Road: The Sex Pistols and America*

Fay and Johnny. An odd couple? Perhaps not.

I: The Odd Coupling

What could Fay Weldon and her feminist texts possibly have to do with
punk, a subculture not exactly known for its inclusion of women, let alone
feminists? Punk is the mid-1970s phenomenon which, after all, seems
sexed as male (only men have "sex pistols"), sexualized as heterosexual
(Johnny Rotten is pictured pawing bare-breasted women), and gendered
as masculine (the standard punk leather jackets "prove," says Legs
McNeil, "we aren't wimps"). Given this, how could punk be of any use
to the critic examining a feminism which seems concerned, in Weldon's
case, with unfixing, not bolstering, the identity categories of sex, sexuality,
and gender?

How indeed? My contention is that just as punk can be, and was, used
to explore the "status and meaning of revolution" (Hebdige, p. 2), it can
be used to explore the status and meaning of another revolution of sorts,
feminism, and particularly the feminism of Fay Weldon. What becomes
apparent in such an exploration is the existence of "feminist-punk"; Weldon calls feminist-punk into being as she advances the substance of fem-

inism in the style of punk. Both her persona and her writing style draw, perhaps surprisingly, on the well of punk, even if Weldon herself may "pretend" that they do not.

II: Safety Pinning Down

Feminist

For the purposes of this essay, feminism will become strategically fixed in the constellation of identity politics. The identity of "feminist" may become temporarily less problematic, while remaining, ideally, "permanently unclear" (Butler, p. 14). What I am identifying as "feminist" in Weldon's fictions is her ability to reveal that culturally constructed identity categories (sex, sexuality, gender, and even feminism itself) are, as Judith Butler puts it, "in no way stable." Weldon reveals them as identities "tenuously constituted in time," and "instituted through a stylized repetition of acts" (Butler, p. 270). Weldon is in the business of deinstitutionalization, with one eye, radically enough, on social transformation. This is a feminism of strategic flux, as is my definition of it.

Punk

Punk of the 1970s is primarily a style which articulates on its surface, says Dick Hebdige, both a "breakdown in consensus" (p. 17) and an interruption of the normalized taken-for-grantedness of "anonymous ideology" (p. 9). It is an "intervention" in urban culture. Punk is, particularly, a moment and movement of negation—a negation that calls any and all social facts into question as obnoxiously and optimistically as possible (Marcus, p. 7). Fashioned after the Situationist International of the 1950s and '60s, punk desires, through the creation of a persona and a textual style, to move the audience, the "spectator," from passive to active. The situationist and the punk use "situations" to disrupt a static "spectacle." This spectacle, first outlined by Guy Debord in Society of the Spectacle, is a capitalist stasis characterized by a politics of boredom (interchangeable images, repetition, monologue) and based in an "expert" media culture of abundant commodity and conspicuous consumption. Both the situationist and the punk try to counter the spectacle and the sense of separation from action and from others it induces, by creating "situations"—"constructed encounters and creatively lived moments in urban settings, instances of transformed everyday life" (Wollen, p. 31). Montages, broadsheets, posters, manifestos, and slogans are designed to provoke "scandal and abomination"—the situationist and the punk become, through situations, "a reproach to your happiness" (Genet, p. 22). Now, duly reproached, the spectator should, in Brecht's terms, "take up a position toward the action." In this attempt to "put an end to dead time" and to "get out of the twentieth century" (Gray, p. 5), passive becomes active and the spectacle's thrall is broken. It becomes clear from Greil Marcus' 1989 book, *Lipstick Traces: A Secret History of the Twentieth Century,* and Jon Savage's 1991 book, *England's Dreaming: Sex Pistols and Punk Rock,* that in the breaking of this thrall, the punk persona is centered on a performance of a reinvented identity based on a rejection of expertise, of ideology, and of audience, while the textual style of the punk centers on *détournement* (montage) and on the transitory, revolting gesture.

Feminist-Punk: Collision/Collusion

"Feminist" best articulates, then, the politics of Fay Weldon and her texts; "punk" best articulates the style of her personae and her writing. Weldon both is a feminist-punk and writes feminist-punk—this best describes the manner of her cultural intervention. It is through the creation of a punk persona and through a punk style of language that Fay Weldon attempts, in her novels, to get out of identity categories, particularly those defining sex, sexuality, gender, and feminism.

In many ways, such a coupling seems bound to have happened, sooner or later. Punk has, after all, been used to crack the code of other literary texts. For instance, David E. James uses punk in his analysis of the literary scene in Los Angeles in an article called "Poetry/Punk/Production: Some Recent Writings in LA." Neil Nehring unashamedly collides Graham Greene with the Sex Pistols in a *PMLA* piece called "Revolt into Style." Most recently, Larry McCaffery, in "The Artists of Hell," has defined Kathy Acker's fiction as "fiction to slam dance by" (p. 228). My essay proposes that such slam dancing may be done in the name of feminism and, particularly, in the name of Fay Weldon.

This collision between feminism and punk produces more than a wreck, however. The interaction, however brief, changes the direction and momentum of both feminism and punk, defamiliarizes each, exposes each's inner workings. The collusion becomes apparent as an understanding between the two parties is revealed, and we realize that something can indeed be Johnny Rotten in the state of feminism. The impact reveals a pact. This is a pact that, most recently, the 1990s subcultural phenomenon of the Riot Grrrls has recognized. Erratically organized around punk bands like Bikini Kill, Bratmobile, and the tastily and not-so-tastily named

Cheesecake and Chicken Milk, these grrrls "coopt the values and rhetoric of punk . . . in the name of feminism" (White, *LA Weekly*, p. 34). They realize that the interests of feminism and punk do, in fact, surprisingly enough, coincide. Feminist-punk. Let's dance.

III: A Punk Persona: A Feminist with an Attitude

If cyberpunk is, as Stewart Brand suggests, "technology with attitude," feminist-punk is, most emphatically, "feminism with attitude." Such "attitude" is particularly revealed, as we shall see, in transitory, revolting gestures, but also in the way the feminist-punk fashions her self in relation to the world. In the versions Fay Weldon produces of her self, mostly in interviews, there is feminism, there is punk, and there is the feminist-punk.

To call Fay Weldon a feminist is hardly a radical or an original thing to do. Everyone seems to do it, even though, as Micheline Wandor suggests, "I think it's not particularly useful to spend a long time deciding on whether or not she is or isn't a feminist writer" (*Bookshelf*). Scarcely an article goes by, however, without some discussion of Weldon's feminism and some attempt to pin it down. For instance, David Lodge says categorically that "there is no doubt that she is a feminist writer" (p. 26), while Nancy Walker talks of Weldon's articulation of a "tone of resignation" which seems "antithetical to the necessity for action urged by feminists" (p. 1). Despite this, however, Walker does still see an "overt feminism in much of Weldon's work" (p. 1). In *The Guardian*, Joanna Briscoe says that Weldon writes "deeply undreary feminist novels," while Michiko Kakutani in the *New York Times* complains of a dreary "didactic feminism" on Weldon's part. Weldon herself seems to take no responsibility for the "given" of her feminist identity when she says, "I'm not a feminist because I decided to be a feminist" (Briscoe). She would, rather, seem to resist the category.

Nevertheless, because Weldon's novels center around groups of women (*Female Friends, Down Among the Women*) and typically feminist issues, such as the social construction of beauty (*The Life and Loves of a She-Devil*), reproductive technology (*The Cloning of Joanna May*), and female sexuality and spirituality (*Puffball, Remember Me*), Weldon is assigned the label "feminist." Her work centers around the concerns of feminism, people argue, and so Weldon the writer (the "fictional personality") is perceived, by association, as a feminist. Weldon, I would argue, is, to some degree, as she is perceived. What seems important here is not whether Fay

Weldon is or isn't a feminist, but that she is invariably identified with feminism. She can perhaps be called a feminist writer merely because, if nothing else, both she and her critics consistently raise the issue of, and call attention to, questions of feminist identity and ideology. She is, whether she wants to be or not, fixed in various positions, always within the constellation of feminism. No one, however, (as far as I know) has tried to fix her, and her persona, within the constellation of punk.

What may seem surprising is that this fixing can be done fairly easily. Unintentionally, one would assume, Weldon constructs herself as a literary figure after the fashion of the punk. She emerges with a punk persona in four significant ways: she reinvents her own identity, rejects the value of expertise, rejects the notion of an ideology, and, lastly, refuses her audience the respect they "deserve." It is this punkish fashioning, coupled with her identification with feminism, that makes Weldon, the writer, a feminist-punk.

Reinvention of the Self: "I Am—Until I'm Not"

The identity of Fay Weldon herself seems to be the stuff of fiction. Like Ruth Patchett in *The Life and Loves of a She-Devil*, Weldon's identity is constantly subject to revision—the text of it, therefore, should be used as merely another fiction to inform her novels, not as a means to "master" them. Identity, postmodernly enough, becomes unfixed, unbound, a free signifier, signifying whatever it darn well likes. The antistatic self clings to nothing.

How very punkish. One only has to look at the names of most punks to know that one is in the presence of linguistic reinvention: Siouxsie Sioux, Poly Styrene, Richard Hell, Sid Vicious, and, of course, Johnny Rotten. It is not so obvious that "Fay Weldon" is "one of them" until the *Oxford Companion to English Literature* reveals that Weldon was born "Franklin Birkinshaw." So much for Franklin.

So much too for biographical "facts." The history of punk is shaped by skewed information—as Jon Savage says, "the question of authorship bedevils the whole story of punk" (p. 12). Malcolm McLaren, punk's patriarch, himself performed, Savage suggests, a "shifting, constant parade of mythologizing, selective perception and acute self analysis" (p. 12). History was, it seems, constantly rewritten "according to the demands of [the] current project" (p. 12). The distinction between "fact" and "fiction" collapses for the punk since, says Andrew Loog Oldham, "If you lie enough . . . it becomes a reality" (Savage, p. 12).

In Weldon's performance of her self, there is a similar delight in "skewing." As Giles Gordon, her agent, suggests, the biographical facts "do not add up" (*Bookshelf*). Problems in addition are caused, largely, by Weldon herself, who says, on the one hand, that her "age is printed for all to see on the birthday list," and then, on the other, that "it varies depending on who I talk to" (Briscoe). In a blink, Weldon will shift from one identity to the next—when asked if she is really as calm and confident as she appears, she says, "Well, yes. I am—until I'm not" (Bovey). Perhaps the most strik-ing and biographically-boggling example of Weldon's reshaping comes when she talks about filling up the boxes that constitute her "archives" and which have already been purchased by an American university. "I cheat," she says in "Outing the Dead." In the boxes, she puts "letters to and from the great and possibly famous, and assignations with them— some of them are real and some are forgeries and some of them I just make up to entertain myself." Of course, this information about disinformation may also be "made up"—all that is certain is that nothing is certain. We must, it seems, be like "Mad Doll" in *Female Friends* and simply cease "to trust information" (p. 96).

Expertise: "Be Terrible Too"

Also characteristic of the punk is his/her rejection of "expertise" and the reverence accorded the "expert." For Guy Debord, the expert only serves to guarantee that the spectacle continues unabated—"when individuals lose the ability to see things for themselves," he says, "the expert is there to offer absolute reassurance" (p. 62). In the punk band itself, there is often an absolute and clearly audible antiprofessionalism. After seeing the Sex Pistols in 1975, Bernard Sumner of Joy Division evidently heard the call— he says that he "wanted to get up and be terrible too" (Marcus, p. 7). Punk seems to be a public access identity—as Greil Marcus says, "A nobody like Johnny Rotten could be heard because the voice was available to any-one with the nerve to use it" (p. 2). The "voice" is available because it requires no training—the period between deciding to play an instrument and "having the nerve and confidence to form a group and play in public," is, according to Simon Frith, "remarkably short" (p. 175).

It is Weldon's ability to "play in public" without expertise that, in part, identifies her with the punk. Her rejection of expertise takes several forms. Most obviously, she challenges the monopoly of experts when it comes to stating expert opinions; she takes it upon herself to make "inexpert" pro-nouncements—she realizes that her "opinions are just as good as anyone else's" (*Bookshelf*). One of her delights in writing novels, she claims, is that she can write what she wants "without having to do research" (Mile).

And despite not "doing research," Weldon does not hesitate in giving opinions on science—"Science, in fact, renders us mortal, unimportant, and helpless" (Bookshelf)—the education system—"it teaches us" to merely "reproduce what is in the teacher's mind" (Mile)—linguistics— "the response to language is without gender"—and feminist academics— "they're the only philosophers we have left" (Mile).

As well as promoting a model of "every woman her own expert" and so despecializing "specialized" knowledge, Weldon also refuses, perhaps perversely, to be set up as an "expert" by others. She seems to refuse to be professionalized and fetishized by the academic world. It is true that she courts a somewhat "serious" image—she has spoken at the MLA and has graced the cover of the New York Times Book Review, for example— but, the serious turn, more often than not, turns comic. The Hearts and Lives of Men, for example, was serialized in a "women's" magazine, which Weldon admits is "not the kind of thing one ought to do if one wishes literary respectability" (Thomas). A less-than-"scholarly" image of the writer is conjured up when Weldon describes herself getting up and writing, "wearing whatever I happen to be wearing in bed, which is sometimes nothing at all" (Boylan). In fact, Weldon often appears, starkly enough, to be doing all this, not for some abstract sense of "art," but for money. She admits that writers "market and service" ideas (Briscoe) and that she will dress "nicely" for a book jacket because "better looking equals you earn more" (Davies). She will do the "university and academic thing" because it looks good when put in the blurb on the back of the book. Weldon, like the Sex Pistols, is sure of the benefits of a great rock 'n' roll swindle. In these kinds of moves, she pogos to and fro between the "serious writer" and the "not so serious."

The rejection of expertise on Weldon's part goes as far as her refusal to be constructed as an expert on her own work. As if reinforcing D. H. Lawrence's imperative not to trust the artist, but "trust the tale," Weldon diverts the critic's attention from her. When asked if she feels she can listen to opposing interpretations of Life Force and then declare who is right and who is wrong, she simply, and perhaps dismissively, replies, "I don't have the time" (Mile). When considering if her works fit into modernism or postmodernism, she claims to have once been told by Malcolm Bradbury the definition of these terms, but that she "forgot it at once" (Mile). Put the line between Spark, Eliot, and Weldon "where," she says, "you like" (Barreca, p. 15). She'll only suggest things in novels, she says, that "I don't know myself but I think should be considered" (Barreca, p. 7). Don't look to Weldon for the extended footnote, for the Cliff-Note comment—you're likely to be met with an "I don't know." It is in this shift from "knowing" about things she has no expert knowledge of, to "not knowing" about things that she should have expert knowledge of, that Weldon appears quite the punk.

Ideology: No Headquarters

What seems particularly refreshing, if slightly naive, about the punk is his/her anarchic rejection of dogma, of party politics—there is the avoidance of what George Woodstock calls "systematic theory." The situationists say that "there is no such thing as situationism" and that they have no desire for it, because, as Greil Marcus points out, all ideologies are alienations, "transformations of subjectivity into objectivity" (p. 52). As one gives oneself over to a particular set of beliefs, one becomes an object of them. When Malcolm McLaren bought books on situationism for the pictures, "not the theory" (Savage, p. 30), he was practicing for punk. The Sex Pistols were designed to "make an impression," to make a picture, rather than make a political theory. On (non)principle, the Riot Grrrls advocate a similar rejection of ideology—they claim that they "don't have a doctrine," says Molly Neuman of Bratmobile, or any "10-point program." It seems that style rather than ideological agreement is paramount to the punk and that punk itself seems to operate as a practice rather than a politics. Even though ideological biases can be found in such practices, it is not necessarily because the punk puts them there.

In a similar fashion, Weldon seems to resist ideology and, particularly, a party political, "prepackaged" feminism. Despite the fact that she is invariably called a feminist, she refuses a totalizing notion of feminism and, in fact, ridicules and problematizes feminist identity itself. For instance, Weldon laughs at the fact that the American publishers of The Life and Loves of a She-Devil cut out Ruth's less-than-joyous trip to a feminist commune—"no ideological unsoundness" for them, she chuckles. When asked to define feminism, she dismissively says she can't remember what she said the last time, but that there is, for her, "no party headquarters," "nobody to issue an ideological card" (Mile). Clearly for Weldon, feminist identity is as slippery as all the other kinds. Sometimes, in fact, she seems highly critical of the movement's single-mindedness—"In recent years," she argues, "feminism and the preoccupation with domestic justice has blinded us to the wider issues" (Bovey). Feminism cannot offer decrees for Weldon, that much seems certain.

The Audience: No Respect

Weldon may take responsibility for her own identity and its invention, its knowledge, and its affiliations, but she clearly takes no responsibility for her audience. This refusal is essentially punk in nature. For the punk, the audience is often, as Siouxsie Sioux puts it, "a miserable bunch of twisted people" and a legitimate object of abuse. The punk is not interested in idolatry of, or even respect for, the audience, and is "sick," as Mary Haron puts it, "of people being so nice" (Savage, p. 133). According to Greil Marcus, the "passive neologisms of the 1970s" like "thank you for sharing your anger with me" are translated by the punk into "active English": "Fuck off and die" (p. 89). Not in so many words, but in effect, Fay Weldon constructs a persona who also tells her audience to "fuck off," to find validation elsewhere.

Weldon doesn't expect her "friends to behave well and they don't" and says that she has "no illusions about people." Such disillusionment is not expressed by Weldon by the grabbing of ankles or spitting in cameras. It is, rather, expressed by a refusal to nurture her readers—Molly Hite says that "she is hardly a nurturing feminist, unless you count nurture a reading experience rather like being suckled on lemons." Weldon refuses to respectfully guide her reader through the text and tells you to "think what you like" (Mile) and to "work." Reading a Weldon novel should, she says, "be exhausting" (Barreca, p. 7), because she is not willing to "come to conclusions for you" (Mile). That, she says, would be "immoral" (Mile). If we want to find her books "disgusting," like her son's English teacher does, then so be it—the Sex Pistols were accused of "disgusting" behavior too. When I interviewed Weldon in July 1992, looking for validation for my literary critical analysis, she quite merrily refused to give it. "How could" literary criticism "matter, possibly?" she asked. It's better than making armaments, it seems, but not much else. Happily invalidated, I left.

IV: Writing Style: As the Word Turns

The quintessence of punk textual style—of situations—is the transitory, revolting gesture, rooted in the everyday and "saved" by what Larry McCaffery calls a "perverse optimism" (p. 221), a desire to change the world. The punk gesture is often violent (Rimbaud's "paradise of violence, of grimace and madness"), and often repulsively humorous, quite ridiculous. It is also, invariably, noisy—has what Marcus calls a "blinding intransigence" (p. 12). It also leaves a lot to be desired: it offers no coherent or formalized ideology but instead operates as a warning, Hebdige says, of difference—a difference that raises suspicions, elicits rage, but gives no answers (p. 2).

A safety pin through the Queen's mouth; the Sex Pistols say "fuck" on live television; Sid Vicious wears a swastika in downtown Paris. These verbal and nonverbal grand slams are designed to generate shock as the ordinary becomes extraordinary. More than anything, they do not bear repetition. They aim to move in the moment; almost like Gertrude Stein's continuous present, these gestures define a discrete moment, a "space of time filled with moving" (p. 457). Once the moment has passed, it should remain in the past; once safety pins become high fashion, they pin together the parts of the integrated spectacle.

It is perhaps easy to see how Roseanne Arnold's 1990 crotch grabbing is a feminist-punk gesture—an "abominable" moment which resexes "woman" as "man" and regenders her as "masculine" in one fell squeeze. It is perhaps also easy to see how Sinéad O'Connor's tearing of the Pope's picture on "Saturday Night Live" in 1992 revoltingly unfixes the gender and ethnic category of "good Irish Catholic girl." It seems clear, too, when Stevie Smith says, "If I'd been the Virgin Mary, I'd have said: 'No'" (Whitemore, p. 54), that the "no" negates all expectations of female subservience. This all seems to be feminist-punk—the style is punk, the nature of the negation, feminist. Fay Weldon's linguistic gestures are a little less melodramatic, but they are there nonetheless. Particular moments of negation in Female Friends and The Life and Loves of a She-Devil fit the category of transitory, revolting gesture precisely because they are so unfit— they suggest, abominably, that, in certain cases, feminist and gender identity might not be as they seem.

Well

In 1974's Female Friends, Weldon has both Chloe and an omniscient narrator tell the tale of three female friends, Chloe, Grace, and Marjorie. At the novel's beginning, we hear from Chloe as she contemplates the "feminine" model of morality passed on to her by her mother: "Understand and forgive. It is what my mother taught me to do. . . . Understand, and forgive, my mother said, and the effort has quite exhausted me. I could do with some anger to energize me, to bring me back to life again" (p. 5).

Anger, energy, and resuscitation are not long in coming. Within thirty pages, in fact, our omniscient narrator seems to renounce such feminine compliance in a transitory, revolting word. The gesture is, as we shall see, rooted in the everyday, humorous, noisy, nondogmatic, and thoroughly optimistic. It is, in addition, a gesture carefully prepared for. We have learned first that Chloe is, in fact, neither understanding nor forgiving. Her friends, who are "as much duty as pleasure" (p. 8) are objects of her pity—"poor little Marjorie, obliged by fate to live like a man" (p. 11)—and her piety—

"Chloe feels herself morally superior to Grace" (p. 15). She neither understands their predicaments nor forgives them their lapses. And, therefore,
when the narrator speaks of Chloe's attachment to Grace's family at The
Poplars, we understand what is really meant:

And perhaps it was not cupboard love which drove Chloe to choose The
Poplars as her second home, and Esther as a second mother, and Grace and
Marjorie as her friends, but her recognition of their grief, and their inner homelessness. It was not that she used them, or that they used each other, but simply
that they all clung together for comfort.
    Well. [Pp. 32–33]

"Well." A single verbal gesture, a single word, which, for a moment, revolts
against the previous sixty-three. "Well" means "I doubt it," "I don't think
so," in short, "Not." Chloe has no fine feelings. Said and gone. The reader
gets rooted in the everyday, mundane clichés of "cupboard love," "second
home," and "they all clung together for comfort" and then reaches "Well,"
and, probably, laughs. We chuckle as we hit the ridiculous, bathetic bottom
of real human motives, after being taken in by the possibility of ideal ones.
As the incongruity between what is "true" and "untrue" is established,
the "perhaps" of the first line, which merely qualifies there, becomes
unequivocal.

    Not only is the moment cynical and funny, but it is also noisy—the
space that follows is filled with the noise of Weldon's intransigence
("Well" period), but also with the sound of the response demanded from
the reader. In an interview in Belles Lettres, Weldon discusses her fondness
for "little one-line throwaways," which she "could explain" but chooses
not to. "Somehow," she says, "the reader has to work out a response before
carrying on" (Barreca, p. 7). The reader is asked to reject accept-ability in
favor of response-ability. Even though only a space follows this gesture,
the space is "filled with moving," and the period, it seems, is only a temporary definitive. One may conclude that the gesture revolts against and
unfixes gender roles, but nothing about the moment itself reveals a coherent ideology. We are merely offered the optimistic and punkish possibility
of some kind of revolt.

    Of course, this kind of amorphous blob of an ideology may infuriate a
radical feminist sensibility. Where here is a plan for social transformation?
Where is the sociopolitical, economic strategy? Where is the "running beyond" to go with the "questioning of existing relations" (p. 72) that Richard Johnson speaks of? This seems, rather, to be a Nike kind of feminism—
the feminism, in fact, of Toni Cade Bambara, who, when asked if fiction
is the best way to unite the wrath, vision, and power of women of color,
replies, "No. The most effective way to do it, is to do it!" In a single four-

letter gesture, Weldon both forces the reader to "just" reconsider feminist strategies and unfixes existing notions of what radical feminism should and can be. Is her kind of feminism, she forces us to ask, really enough?

This "well" also forces a reconsideration of the "feminine" gender and, in particular, its relation to morality. Weldon questions the "femininity" of both the narrator and Chloe at this moment. Indeed, the narrator herself displays none of the "feminine' acquiescence (understanding and forgiving) required by the gender police. The "well" "understands" Chloe's motives all too well and offers no redemption for them. This lapsed narrator also reveals Chloe's "good girl" image as a sham—she is not acquiescent either, it appears, only cupboard loving. Weldon is, here and elsewhere, much more interested in "immorality" than "morality," in the "disadvantages of being good" rather than the advantages; she says that she "refuses to preach a false morality which states that it is advantageous for a woman to be good, or grow old gracefully, or any of this absolute nonsense we have been fed for so long" (Bovey). In a transitory "well," the "absolute nonsense" of gendered morality is revolted against.

I Do

A little language goes a long way in Weldon. She tells us this directly in *Female Friends*, when she remarks that once the word "cancer" is said, "the disease, dormant until the moment of recognition, proliferates and spreads" (p. 19). At the end of the novel, Chloe's last word shows just how much a "disease" has spread through the system of gender classification— the "wife" falls ill, becomes invalid-ated. Chloe, faced with her husband Oliver's petulant, "But you can't leave me with Françoise" (his mistress), replies, "I can, I can, and I do" (p. 237). Space. The novel ends.

The ordinary marriage vow becomes extraordinarily ironic here. "I do" now undoes the marriage; a dis-a-vow frees the "good wife." The space after is filled with the sounds of Chloe's leaving and with, it is said, real women taking leave of their husbands. "Words" really may, as Weldon suggests elsewhere, "turn probabilities into facts" (*The Fat Woman's Joke*, p. 32). Again, the nature of the "fact" is left up to the reader—Weldon gives us no twelve-step program, only an "I do." We are left to our own devices. So just as Chloe's morning seems "ordinary enough," but is, in fact, the morning of "the day Chloe's life is to change" (p. 6), "Well" and "I do" seem like "ordinary enough" words, but perhaps are words that may change the world, or at least the perception of feminism and gender. Feminist-punk—both of revolt, and into revolt.

I Can

In 1983's *The Life and Loves of a She-Devil,* Weldon declares that "All our sentences are immortal" (p. 51). And, at various moments in the text, words do seem to act with this kind of arrogance. In what must come as a horrible shock to the French feminists, in one verbal sweep, Weldon manages to relieve both Ruth Patchett and "woman" herself from motherhood.

The magic moment in this novel comes about a third of the way through. Again, the reader is more than ready for it—Ruth has already begun to unfix her gender. As one of the "dogs" of the world, Ruth finds pleasure in acting unfittingly for a woman. Not only does she make pastry cut-outs of her husband's pretty mistress, Mary Fisher, and burn them to a crisp, she also decides to burn down the house (wouldn't anybody?)—"At that moment," we are told, quite matter-of-factly, "the kitchen exploded" (p. 69). Ruth is clearly set up as someone willing to un-become her self (or at least the "good wife") in a series of unbecoming behaviors (Mary burning, house burning). As she embraces she-devildom, she decides that there is only "in the end, what you want" (p. 48), and she realizes that she doesn't want her children. She takes them, therefore, to Bobbo and Mary Fisher. Bobbo and Ruth chat:

> "But where are you going?" he demanded. "To friends?"
> "What friends?" she inquired. "But I'll stay here, if you want."
> "You know that's out of the question."
> "Then I'll go."
> "But you'll leave an address?"
> "No," said Ruth, "I don't have one."
> "But you can't just desert your own children!"
> "I can," said Ruth. [Pp. 84–85]

She does.

In two ordinary, matter-of-fact words, "I can," Ruth makes a feminist-punk gesture of great wit. This is the humor of the possible. It is generated from the jar between what Bobbo says is absolutely impossible ("you can't") and what Ruth sees as paramountly possible ("I can"). The two don't go together and the laugh is at their incongruous expense. This optimistic "can" releases Ruth from the condition of motherhood and into a series of other 'cans": she can now reinvent herself, she can now have revenge, power, money, and "be loved and not love in return" (p. 49). As the state of "mother" is transcended, Ruth brings hope of salvation to others—as "Jesus did in his day for men" (p. 192), so she will do for women.

On behalf of women, Ruth and Weldon do, in fact, challenge the kind of valorization of motherhood propagated by the French feminists. So

much now for Cixous's insistence that women harness their milky maternity and write (Ruth has "dry dugs"); so much also for Kristeva's vision
of motherhood as the bedrock of a unified being (Jones, p. 86) as a means
to break down the opposition between "self and other"—Ruth isn't interested in others. So much for the stability of any feminist position.

So much too for systematic ideology. "I can" offers no plans, no strategies, but is a moment of enormous catalytic power. Its beauty lies in its
capriciousness. For many readers, it may be nothing more than a "horrible
abuse" and may not be remotely funny. But, for this reader, at least, it
provides real entertainment. This is, for a second, the feminist-punk can-
can.

V: No Future?

This essay complete, I am, whether I like it or not, left with Fay Weldon's
question, "how could it matter, possibly?" How could it matter that I have
managed to "upgrade" Weldon from "feminist" to "feminist-punk," that
I have disgraced her with a new title?

For me, at least, coupling Weldon with punk presents me with a way
to describe what it is like to read her and read about her. It describes just
how Weldon calls me into being: I hear the call to slam dance, to pogo.
Off we go, pogoing from place to place, gesturing mildly, landing in
different spots, always in motion, always unstable. No wonder this is
exhausting.

"Feminist-punk," however, doesn't just articulate what the experience
of reading Weldon is like. It also, I think, poses a challenge to the feminist
academic. Is there a way, I wonder, that we might be a little more inventive
in our identities, a little more inept, a little more "ideologically unsound"
and, perhaps, a little more disrespectful toward our audience? Might we
be a little less "nice," and a little more capricious, a little more revolting?
Is there a way, in short, that we might produce a feminist literary criticism
to slam dance by? Maybe. Maybe not. Maybe such a plan has no future,
no chance of success. And even if it did, well, I ask you, "how could it
matter . . . possibly?"

Works Cited

Bambara, Toni Cade. "In Search of the Mother Tongue: An Interview with Toni
    Cade Bambara." *First World Journal* (Fall 1980).
Barreca, Regina. "Fay Weldon Speaks with Regina Barreca." *Belles Lettres*
    (September/October 1987).

Bookshelf. Produced by Abigail Appleton. 14 Feb. 1992.

Bovey, Shelley. "Does a Woman Really Need a Man These Days?" *She* (Spring 1988).

Boylan, Clare. "Out of Crumpled Sheets." *The Guardian* (Spring 1992).

Briscoe, Joanna. "Sweet Anarchy, Poisoned Utopia." *The Guardian.* 19 Sept. 1990.

Butler, Judith. "Performative Acts and Gender Constitution: An Essay in Phenomenology and Feminist Theory."

———. "Imitation and Gender Insubordination." *Inside Out,* ed. Diana Fuss. New York: Routledge, 1991.

Cixous, Hélène with Annie Leclerc and Madeleine Gagnon. *La Venue à l'écriture.* Paris: Union General d'Éditions 10/18, 1977.

Davies, Hunter. "Life Is an Open Fridge." *Daily Mail.* 16 Feb. 1993.

Debord, Guy. *Society of the Spectacle.* London: Black and Red, 1973.

Drabble, Margaret, ed. *The Oxford Companion to English Literature.* Oxford: Oxford University Press, 1985.

Frith, Simon. "The Cultural Study of Popular Music." *Cultural Studies,* ed. Cary Nelson, Paula A. Treichler, and Lawrence Grossberg. 1992.

Genet, Jean. *The Thief's Journal.* New York: Penguin, 1967.

Gray, Christopher, ed. and trans. *Leaving the Twentieth Century: The Incomplete Work of the Situationist International.* UK: Free Fall, 1974.

Hebdige, Dick. *Subculture: The Meaning of Style.* New York: Methuen, 1979.

Hite, Molly. "Gentle Readers and Lemon Suckers." *Belles Lettres* (September/October 1987).

James, David E. "Poetry/Punk/Production: Some Recent Writings in LA." *Postmodernism and Its Discontents,* ed. E. Ann Kaplan. New York: Norton, 1988.

Johnson, Richard. "What Is Cultural Studies Anyway?" *Social Text* 16 (1986–87).

Jones, Rosalind. "Inscribing Femininity: French Theories of the Feminine." *Making a Difference: Feminist Literary Criticism,* ed. Gayle Greene and Coppelia Kahn. New York: Methuen, 1985.

Kakutani, Michiko. "Fallout From a Multitude of Liaisons." *New York Times.* 7 Feb. 1992.

Lodge, David. *After Bakhtin: Essays on Fiction and Criticism.* New York: Routledge, 1990.

Marcus, Greil. *Lipstick Traces: A Secret History of the Twentieth Century.* Cambridge: Harvard University Press, 1989.

McCaffery, Larry. "The Artists of Hell: Kathy Acker and 'Punk' Aesthetics." *Breaking the Code.* New York: Routledge, 1992.

Mile, Siân. Personal interview with Fay Weldon. 20 July 1992.

Monk, Noel E., and Jimmy Guterman. *Twelve Days on the Road: The Sex Pistols and America.* New York: Quill, 1990.

Nehring, Neil. "Revolt into Style: Graham Greene Meets the Sex Pistols." *PMLA* (March 1991).

Savage, Jon. *England's Dreaming: Sex Pistols and Punk Rock.* London: Faber and Faber, 1991.

Stein, Gertrude. "Composition as Explanation." *The Selected Writings of Gertrude Stein,* ed. Carl Van Vechten. New York: Random House, 1946.

Thomas, Jo. "Writing While the Messenger Awaits." *New York Times Book Review.* 13 Mar. 1988.

Walker, Nancy. "Truth or Lie? Irony and Fantasy in the Fiction of Fay Weldon." *PMLA* (Dec. 1989).

Weldon, Fay. *Life Force.* London: Harper/Collins, 1992.

———. "Outing the Dead." *Daily Mail.* 8 Aug. 1991.

———. *The Cloning of Joanna May.* London: Collins, 1989.

———. *The Hearts and Lives of Men.* New York: Viking, 1988.

———. *The Life and Loves of a She-Devil.* London: Hodder and Stoughton, 1983.

———. *Puffball.* New York: Pocket Books, 1980.

———. *Remember Me.* New York: Ballantine, 1977.

———. *Female Friends.* Chicago: Academy Chicago, 1988.

———. *Down Among the Women.* Chicago: Academy Chicago, 1984.

———. *The Fat Woman's Joke.* London: Coronet, 1982.

White, Emily. *LA Weekly.* 10 July 1992.

Whitemore, Hugh. *Stevie.* Oxford: Amber Lane Press, 1984.

Wollen, Peter. "Bitter Victory."

Woodcock, George. *Anarchism—A History of Libertarian Ideas and Movements.* London: Penguin, 1975.

Classic Weldon

It would sound very odd to refer to Fay Weldon as "classic." A classic is a book written a long time ago. Booksellers sometimes use the heading "Classics"—but what writer would not prefer to be in that other and bigger section labeled simply "Fiction"; or even "Popular Reading"? This is certainly preferable to the author—not least because the author of "classics" is, or is assumed to be, long dead. Fay Weldon is very much alive, and kicking. We depend on her to give us reports from our own world, and the contemporary is not classic, usually, save in disaster or misfortune (as in "a classic case of pneumonia" or "the classic symptoms of recession").

It would be probably even odder to refer to her as a *classical* writer, or a writer in a classical style. Weldon is not elegant—elegance is not what she is trying to achieve. She is certainly not controlled and balanced in the Jane Austen manner. "It is a truth universally acknowledged, that a single man in possession of a good fortune, must be in want of a wife." This is precisely not the kind of sentence that Weldon would ever write. Weldonesque sentences find it their duty most of the time to parody and trounce such elegance by bursting through the restraints of style and taste. Take, for example, the opening three sentences of *Little Sisters* (1978):

We all have friends who are richer than ourselves and they, you may be sure, have richer friends of their own. We are most of us within spitting distance of millionaires.
Spit away—if that's what you feel like. [P. 5]

That's what happens in Weldonstyle when elegance is acknowledged; the parodic elegance works on a simple level, customarily through formulae of repetition, until it is just big and visible enough (like a balloon being blown up) to be effectively punctured, when it explodes with a little bang. We are not to be puzzled or teased by subtle meanings; the sentences do not shimmer in midair, demanding our sustained attention. Austen's sentences are more like icicles or prisms; they do not balloon and bang.

The demotion of elegance in Weldon, the eschewal of certain kinds of subtlety, the delight in violence—these qualities are very far from what we think of as Austen's, and make Weldon a surprising choice as the dramatizer of *Pride and Prejudice* for the 1980s television production. Surprising, but not boring—Weldon's product was memorable, unlike some of the dusty and pulverized versions of novels offered on British telly. Her product was in some ways refreshing—just as it would be refreshing to have Mark Twain dramatize Nathaniel Hawthorne. Or what about getting François Rabelais to dramatize Chrétien de Troyes?

Rabelais, once he has come to mind, offers some happy comparisons. Weldon's physical comedy, and her sentences that turn on—or turn to— the physical—have much in common with the manner and meanings of Rabelais. Here is a typical passage of Rabelaisian description:

Panurge estoit de stature moyenne, ny trop grand, ny trop petit, et avoit le nez un peu aquilin, faict à manche de rasouer; et pour lors estoit de l'eage de trente et cinq ans ou environ, fin à dorer comme une dague de plomb, bien galand homme de sa personne, sinon qu'il estoit quelque peu paillard, et subject de nature à une maladie qu'on appelloit en ce temps-la "Faulte d'argent, c'est douleur non pareille"—toutesfoys, il avoit soixante et troys manières d'en trouver tousjours à son besoing, dont la plus honnorable et la plus commune estoit par façon de larrecin furtivement faict . . . [*Pantagruel*, ch. xvi, p. 280]

Panurge was of middling height, neither too large nor too small, and his nose was a little aquiline, shaped like the handle of a razor. And at that time he was thirty-five years old or thereabouts, a youth as gilded as a leaden dagger, a very gallant man in his person, save that he was somewhat horny, and subject by nature to a malady which folks in those days called "Lack of money, a pain without equal." But he always had sixty-three ways to find what he needed, of which the most honorable and the most common was by act of larceny furtively carried out . . .

Here is a passage of description from (early) Weldon:

Victor is six foot two and weighs fourteen stone. He is a powerful man with a high domed head, and a smooth bald patch, flanked by downy hair, running up and over it, like some spiritual landing strip (Elsa's fancy) for flights of mature imagination. His soft brown eyes are deep set; his nose is long and hooked; his penis is long and sturdy, easily moved to stand erect. No trouble there. No trouble anywhere, except for the occasional cold in the nose or a white-capped pimple erupting on his chin, the better to display his inner juiciness. (*Little Sisters*, p. 8)

Rabelais at the beginning of the modern age of Realism uses realism perpetually and perpetually discards it in a buoyant play of classical and medieval literary techniques. The scrupulous exactness about detail, the modest reality of Panurge's middlingness, is counteracted by the gay contradictions: to be as gilded as a leaded dagger is not to be gilded at all, and a leaden dagger is a cheap and fairly useless article. The statement matches Chaucer's "she was as digne as water in a ditch." Rabelais's pretended-scruples create comic qualifiers, modest vaguenesses that confuse: we see how somebody can be "*about* thirty-five years old" but how can a nose be "*a little* aquiline"? The combined notions of realism, modesty, masculinity, and good looks are overthrown in the slang phrase "un peu paillard." Again, the qualifier is useless—how can one be a little horny, somewhat raunchy? Clichés of style are exploded. This passage of Rabelais is atypical only in that it does not move as forcefully as usual into the physical, for references to penises and physical eruption are found almost everywhere in his works.

Weldon exhibits the penis and the erupting pustule in a description which becomes more mocking as it proceeds. Victor is done in by his author, as the ostensible narrative realism is done in by her procedures. Factual description becomes troubled by the "spiritual landing strip" of Victor's head. The next sentence gives us the nice clichés again: "His soft brown eyes are deep set"—the sort of phrasing one might find in a description of a romantic hero. But this sweet image is crossed by "his nose is long and hooked," a description resembling that of the aquiline nose of Panurge. Weldon too connects nose and penis—a connection she makes overt in the next phrase. The reader is surprised, for descriptions of a character's penis are not common in literature, certainly not part of the modified realistic blazon describing a novelistic "character," at least as we have come to understand that entity through the guidance of the nineteenth century. The "white-capped pimple" is another confusing item, for the modifying adjective is rather pleasant, standing as it usually does for the sea. Pimples, if mentioned in literature, indicate the diseased or adolescent state of a person, and are overt, emblematic negative signs—yet this one is used as if it were a positive sign, becoming associated with "inner juiciness," a term feminizing Victor into a fruit. This "juiciness" relates to Rabelais's medlars, "ce beau et gros fruict" eaten with such gusto by mankind at the beginning of *Pantagruel*, with such various physical effects, including swellings of belly, virile member, and the nose:

Et l'autres tant croissoit le nez qu'il sembloit la fleute d'un alembic, tout diapré, tout estincelé de bubeletes, pullulant, purpuré, à pompettes, tout esmaillé, tout boutonné et brodé de gueules . . . (*Pantagruel*, ch. 1, p. 219)

And others grew in the nose so much that it resembled the spout of an alembic, and was all multicolored, all spangled with little buboes, proliferating, empurpled, pom-pommed, all enamelled, all buttoned and broidered with gules . . .

Weldon's armory of stylistic devices includes the Rabelaisian catalogue, the comic technique that involves dazing the reader with a seemingly unstoppable list. The list is most often a recitation of objects, or the attributes of objects, in their unignorable physicality, which is itself a reflection of the profusion of Nature. At times the list may be mockingly organized under a teasing scheme of pseudo-coherence, as in a recipe:

"Take ½ pt of vinegar," she said, "2 oz Fuller's earth, 1 oz of dried fowl dung, ½ oz of soap and the juice of two large onions. . . ." [*The Rules of Life*, p. 40]

It is an aspect of Rabelaisian humor that such objects in a list need not by any means be attractive—at least according to the official view of the attractive, though they are always sensuous:

Elsa, stopping to do up her zip, stumbles over her own yellow and crimson platform heels and drops her shoulder bag. Its contents roll down the steps: hair rollers, pay slips, brush, old underground tickets, deodorants, contraceptive pills, her change of clothes—pink satin shirt, yellow cheesecloth blouse, clean red bikini pants—and so on. [*Little Sisters*, p. 7]

Every item reminds us of the physicality of Elsa, untameable, though she may try to tame her hair with curlers, her power to conceive with pills, her odor with deodorant, and her red crotch with red pants. The list most often implies body contact with inanimate objects, the possibility of carnally caused dirt and disorder. The more a list spreads, the more it spreads the possibility of contamination, the miscellany hinting at a miscegenation, the union of things that ought to be kept separate—like dung and onions, or dung and drapery:

Puis je me torchay aux linceaux, à la couverture, aux rideaulx, d'un coisson, d'un tapiz, d'un verd, d'une mappe, d'une serviette, d'un mouschenez, d'un peignouoir. [*Gargantua*, ch. xiii, p. 78]

Then I wiped myself on cloth hangings, on the coverlet, on the curtains, on a cushion, on a carpet, on a green rug, on a wiper, on a napkin, on a handkerchief, on a dressing-gown.

The effect of unstoppability, of excess reflecting nature's thoughtless excess, is never more pronounced than in the employment of lists involving food.

Grandgousier estoit bon raillard en son temps, aymant à boyre net autant que homme qui pour lors fust au monde, et mangeoit volontiers salé. A ceste fin, avoit ordinairement bonne munition de jambons de Magence et de Baionne, force langues de beuf fumées, abondance de andouilles en la saison et beuf sallé à la moustarde, renfort de boutargues, provision de saulcisses . . . [*Gargantua*, ch. iii, p. 46]

Grandgousier was a boon companion in his day, loving unwatered drink as much as any man in the world, and by choice he ate salt food. To this end, he ordinarily had a good supply of hams of Mayence and Bayonne, many smoked tongues of beef, an abundance of tripes in season and beef salted with mustard, reinforcements of caviar, provision of sausages . . .

Women writers of recent times, including Margaret Atwood, have made an effective use of the listing technique, especially in enumerating food items to create huge surplus, but Weldon is a superb and constant player of this game of disconcerting abundance:

"I dream of strange and marvellous things. I dream of fish and chips and bread and butter and cups of sweet tea. I dream of ship-loads of boiling jam cleaving their way through the polar ice-caps." [*The Fat Woman's Joke*, p. 63]

So says the dieting Alan, discovering the important agony of deprived orality in the Weldonesque world of oral cravings and experience. The chief mediator between Rabelais and Weldon—if any is wanting—must be James Joyce. Yet Joyce is sentimental and romantic by comparison with Weldon, as with Rabelais. If Weldon resembles Rabelais who is a "classic" author (in sense of distinction), she may become a "classic" too.

Also, Weldon is "classical" (in another sense), then, for if we divide the world (or at least Literature) between Classical and Romantic, well, Weldon can certainly never be termed *romantic*. We don't usually think of Rabelais as "classical" in the way that we use the word when we say that Austen is "classical." But the work of Rabelais has predecessors in the "classical" period or, rather, periods, from Aristophanes to Lucian. These, however, are writers who disturb our sense of the regularity, the desire for high-minded order that the Renaissance and the Enlightenment taught us to associate with the "classical." Rabelais is as classical as any other modern European writer in bearing a strong relationship to Greek and Roman literary forebears. And Fay Weldon's novels likewise have a strong relation to certain Greek and Roman antecedents. It does not matter that she herself is not a "classical scholar" in the sense that we might use such a phrase in speaking of Rabelais, or, say, Thomas Love Peacock, for an author gets the message most often and most effectively perhaps through diverse mediators. Keats did not know Greek and did not have to know Greek to make a contact that mattered with styles, manners, and concepts flowing from the Greeks.

Our own concept of "the classical" has been confused by the emphasis on realism in the nineteenth and early twentieth centuries. Classical satirists such as Aristophanes, Apuleius, Petronius, and Lucian use enormous amounts of realistic detail—so far, so good. But then they puzzle us by employing what we term the "fantastic." We have been reluctant to come to terms with the multiple kinds of nonrealistic styles and manners. As the novel, above all, has been considered the special abode of realism, we have found It hard to describe our reading experience when works of very animated prose fiction do not take what we might call the George Eliot line. Here Joyce is not problematic (save in *Finnegans Wake*), for the Joyce of *Portrait of the Artist* and *Ulysses* keeps to strict realism in event and situation; the nonreal, including the mythical and the obscene, resides in the language and in the multitudinous references. But some writers in various periods are not content to rest there. You cannot enjoy Apuleius' *The Golden Ass* unless you are willing, playfully at least, to entertain while you are reading the possibility that a man can—and does—turn into an ass. Similarly, you cannot quite enjoy *The Cloning of Joanna May* unless you are willing playfully to entertain (at least for the length of time it takes to read the book) the idea that a woman's egg might be cloned so that she arrives at middle age to discover that she has four other selves, all versions of her young self.

Of course, Fay Weldon uses realism. The realism—sometimes even perhaps naturalism—comes in the form of the details, inescapable physical details, grossly and inexorably moving in upon the reader.

Chloe is shown to a table between the kitchen door and the toilets. She asks for a Campari while she waits, and is given a Dubonnet.
... They order *antipasto*. He brings dried-up beans, hard-boiled eggs in bottled mayonnaise, tinned sardines and flabby radishes prettily arranged in bright green plastic lettuce leaves. [*Female Friends*, pp. 35, 42]

In this description of lunch at a sullen restaurant, one sees that the author is aware of history, of fashion, of the names of products. She also knows that even an unpleasant physical experience is a sensual experience. Weldon is as good at the mildly disgusting, the merely displeasing or off-putting, as she is at the extreme edge of the revolting (broken houses, dead bodies). She orders her world. But we realize that the thick realities, such realities as a dingy salad on bright plastic lettuce leaves, are only an outer layer. She is interested in situations, imaginative situations in which the characters can reveal—oh, not themselves, for Weldon's interest in selves has conscious limits. Characters can reveal the animal impulses of the human, and the deeper irrationalities of the ways in which human beings interpret their lives, and use themselves and each other. Such revelation is subversive, for it involves testing and rejecting most conventional interpretations of character and almost all moral exhortations. It would be quite wrong to say that Weldon reveals "the worst" beneath a smiling veneer of gentility or civilization. The *veneer* often really is "the worst"; what lies behind it is often very cruel, but often potentially fine and lively. Unorthodoxies and secrets may sometimes be the sources of consolation and the symptoms of a struggling vitality. Characters must be given situations in which the multiplex nature of humankind can reveal itself, and the reader too needs to be startled out of orthodoxy by being made to accept some nonrational surprising story-concepts—like the existence of Joanna's four clones, or the power of a Mab and Mrs. Tree in witchcraft.

That the insights of morality and the insights of fiction can be at odds is itself the subject of *The Rules of Life* (1987), which postulates the overthrow and replacement of conventional religion by "the GNFR, or Great New Fictional Religion" (p. 7). In *Letters to Alice*, Weldon complains of the duty attributed to the writer of coming up with answers, moral solutions, guidance, and consolation:

It puts, of course, quite a burden on the writer, who is expected to direct all this mental theatre, to be seen as an Agony Aunt as well as the translator of the Infinite, and the handmaiden to the Muse . . . [P. 74]

But Weldon herself, it might be retorted, has invited such treatment by the authoritive—even authoritarian—voice by which the narrator or one of the characters trumpets opinions. It is one of the attractions of novels, ancient and modern, that they are gnomic, that they offer wisdom in various observations. Weldon sometimes overdoes the gnomic, the didactic; *Darcy's Utopia* seems nothing but opinion, and surprisingly boring. Weldon is at her best when attending inventively to the situation and not overdoing her (or her characters') commentary. A little of the gnomic goes a long, long way. The ironic distance sustained in both *She-Devil* and *The Hearts and Lives of Men* makes for their success.

Weldon's "characters" interest her only in a limited way, one feels—they are the practical means to the end which is the whole novel, the action. This makes her in some respects an Aristotelian. Aristotle stressed that tragedy is "the imitation of an action" and made character (*ethos*) secondary. Of course, tragedy is not what Weldon is after—and we have lost Aristotle's lectures on comedy, so we don't know what he would have said. (He might even have been as dull and regular on the subject as some reconstructors have made him out to be.) Aristotle's *Poetics* is in any case a sleight of mind, a brilliant trick. At one stroke he got the West for over two thousand years to discuss tragedy and drama as humanistic matters alone, subject to the rational criteria of *belles lettres*. Aristotle ignored (astonishingly) the nature and purpose of the *dionysia*, the religious ceremonies at which Athenian plays were presented. The religious, celebratory, and sacrificial nature of the Greek plays, and the drumbeat of blood, flesh, and need behind them were superbly snubbed by Aristotle, whose own act of *hubris*, when one comes to think of it, has few equals. It took Nietzsche to restore the balance and put Dionysius (his Dionysius, at all events) in the picture. Fay Weldon does not believe in regularized Aristotelian tragedy, and all her works might be called Dionysian. She dislikes religion, almost as much as Nietzsche, disapproving both Jewish and Christian, her references to Christianity being more caustic and detailed in the aggregate than those to Judaism. Yet she is often at her best, her most witty, when pondering or playing with some piece of Scripture: "If thine eye offend me take a good look at yourself. If thine I offend thee, change it" (*Cloning*, p. 324).

At times Weldon seems to be trying to invent or interpret a religion of Darwinism; although she speaks negatively of Hardy's *Tess* in *Letters to Alice*, there are moments of approximation of a Hardyesque cosmology, but without any tragedies or Presidents of the Immortals. Weldon is not trying to do without religion altogether; the religion summoned up in the novels is less rational Epicurean than a mythical or mythological relative of Wicca, even though one can sense the author trying to keep the lid on this.

At one point in *Puffball* (1980), the narrative voice remonstrates against personifying blind forces:

Not that "nature" can reasonably be personified in this way—for what is nature, after all, for living creatures, but the sum of the chance genetic events which have led us down one evolutionary path or another. And although what seem to be its intentions may, in a bungled and muddled way, work well enough to keep this species or that propagating, they cannot be said always to be desirable for the individual. [P. 14]

No, perhaps nature cannot *reasonably* be personified, but what excites Weldon is not reason but the great Life Force, the biological drive which generates life.

Having repudiated personification, Weldon brings it back:

We no longer see Nature as blind, although she is. Her name is imbued with a sense of purpose, as the name of God used to be. . . . if we can not in all conscience speak of God we must speak of Nature. Wide-eyed, clear-eyed, purposeful Nature. Too late to abandon her. Let us seize the word, seize the day; lay the N on its side and call our blind mistress ƨature. [*Puffball*, p. 118]

At one level, this is prosy nonsense. Of course, some of us, another "we," can in "conscience" speak of God and have more difficulty speaking of "Nature." And why is it "too late" to abandon "her" rather than perhaps merely too early? Weldon's rather labored and hectoring narrative statement is refreshed by the invention at the end, the expression of desire for another word that would call for another typography. The word beginning with an N-on-its-side *looks* like "Sature" and creates interesting resonances with "Saturn," "satire," and "suture." A new word is needed for the mental suture or stitching together of a gap or rent, though this reconciliation can be performed only satirically. And yet there is need for recognition of a feminine force in things, "our mistress" who is, however,' to be recognized as old, slow, determined, inconsiderate, somewhat baleful—a female counterpart of Saturn. This is the female Life Force.

Women are interesting to Weldon because they have a close and unreasonable relation to the female Life Force, to generative power, a matter which men don't understand. When women try to intercede with the Life Force, begging it to obey their personal wishes by taking contraceptive pills or undergoing abortion, they are meddling in a masculine way, and Weldon enjoys the comeuppance administered by pregnancy. The generative religion is Weldon's religion, which makes her a dangerous companion at times, admittedly. She is best when she can project and laugh at her own tendencies to fascistic control through nature-ism. Comedy customarily intervenes to save her from Lawrentian solemnities. Yet conceptually her novels sometimes wobble a little on their axes.

Puffball itself presents an interesting internal conceptual conflict—never resolved—between the philosophical vision of ultimate Meaninglessness and a Wicca or Goddess-shaped vision of Meaningful Rhythms. Liffey, the heroine, is one of the yuppies who try to order the world according to their wishes, symbolized by her willful repudiation of conception. It is not only biology (rationally considered) that intervenes but the power of Glastonbury Tor, the old gods and forces that refuse to be thwarted. Mabs Tucker, the jealous witch who tries to curse Liffey's pregnancy, is herself a representative of that older world of blood-knowledge, the forces that must be respected. In *Puffball* Weldon carries to its most extreme degree the interest in the great drama of egg and sperm. (At times, one could wish her drama were more Shandyesque in the treatment.) Weldon characters often have sex, and the encounters are wittily described, usually in terms of comic disappointment or some other form of inappropriate behavior and reaction. It is not the fuck that interests Weldon, but conception and generation. Her comedies are comic formally in the way that they support generation, the rhythm of life moving from the mature adults (woefully immature as they all are) to the fetus and child.

There is thus always some hope for the future. Liffey's pregnancy is ultimately redemptive—there is no greater believer of the power of pregnancy in all of English literature than Weldon. For an equivalent, one must turn—where? Not in general to women writers or to the modern male sex-writers (though Lawrence's *Rainbow* might be cited, and the beginning of *Sons and Lovers*). I think in this aspect of Weldon she finds her closest relative in the Shakespeare of the last plays. Not that she has anything of Shakespeare's *tone*—but one can imagine the story of *The Winter's Tale* retold by Weldon, who would lay even more stress than Shakespeare does on the progress of Hermione's pregnancy. *The Cloning of Joanna May*, a story of jealousy, revenge, and redemption, has some of the resonance of *The Winter's Tale*.

Weldon always seems to try to give cosmic rationalism a place: the cosmos is a set of accidents describable by Science, but in need of no explanation; human life is a fragile accident of random evolution—human beings behave brutally and irrationally and then they die. But such a tough negative sense is always counteracted by a more optimistic view—in part a progressive Darwinian or even Lamarckian vision. The knowledge as well as the sins of the parents may be taken on board, there are patterns in life—and there is a moral order. That moral order, however, is not the order we are most usually taught about by the Church or State. Weldon would undoubtedly argue against Aeschylus and his Athena, who sold women down the river to support a stiff masculine order. She is much more on the side of the Furies, the female powers of knowledge and retribution that can stagger even a Victor, an Oliver, a Clifford Wexford, a Carl May.

The drumbeat of flesh and blood is always heard in Weldon's novels—she is a supporter of the flesh, of woman's flesh, of fat women and of the carnal in a manner that would give Aristotle the heebie-jeebies. She is still, however, I insist, an Aristotelian in some degree in her interest in situation above character. She says in *Letters to Alice*, "Plots, I assure you, are nothing but pegs. They stand in a row in the writer's mind. You can use one or another for your purposes, it makes some difference, but not much, which one it is" (pp. 95–96). Although she speaks of them as pegs on which the story hangs, her plots, or story lines, are much more like the interior scaffolding of a house. Without them the novel is nothing, just a set of commentaries and description; related to the plot (peg or scaffolding) the story becomes an entity, gathers its meaning—and the characters have something to do. It is not fashionable in England to put plot above character, not since the Victorians came and conquered the novel, so it's no wonder that Weldon in *Letters to Alice* becomes almost tiresomely Forsteresque. Her real strength is that she can imagine not the character, but characters *in situations*. The bizarre circumstance is not there for its own sake, but to keep us alert to the true situation which invites us to pursue essential matters, considering the variations, the wildness, and yet the predictability of human behavior. What might be called "expressive situational narrative"—in which the *situation* is the chief image and object for which the characters exist—differs from the "situation" in "situation" comedy only in that the latter is more watered-down and subjected to both mimetic realism and rapid neat closure. As a descendant of the drama of Menander (whose plots are closely related to the plots of ancient novels), television's situation comedy inherits its situational interest. Weldon's situations—rather than her characters—are capable of development and are richly meaningful. Just as it isn't Oedipus the personality who interests us, but the man who doesn't know he killed his father and is living with his mother, so it is not the "She-Devil" or her rival Mary Fisher who can interest us, but the way in which the "She-Devil" takes her revenge and works out her relationship to the ladylike mistress of her husband. That interests us a lot.

The morality that informs Weldon's situations is a morality that urges us to reconsider moral life, especially the assumptions we have been bred on, or have bred in ourselves. Most particularly is that necessary for women, who have been fed so many cultural lies about their own wellbeing. It is thus inevitable that a woman character—any woman character—once she comes to act for herself will make mistakes and even commit brutalities, but that process seems necessary for her to reach any point of independent action. All of Weldon's novels illustrate the dictum so cogently put in *Letters to Alice*: "It has come to my notice, Alice, that in the real world the worse women behave, the better they get on" (p. 135). As what the world calls "good" behavior in a woman is the most self-suppressing, timid, doormatlike abjectness, and what the world calls "bad" includes manifestations of sexuality, self-esteem, and energy, it is (or becomes) easy to see why Weldon comically champions the "worse" behavior and persuades us that giving virtue the go-by may have its own rich rewards.

We are so accustomed to thinking of Weldon in a context of late-twentieth-century feminism that it is difficult to offer her full context, the

long and large literary background out of which she emerges. Yet I want
to spend the rest of this essay pointing out that in the realm of the Novel
she has predecessors in late antiquity, that she is more classical than may
be quite easy or comfortable for most readers (including Fay Weldon herself) to believe. The Novel in the West comes to us from the late Roman
Empire, from a place (a very widespread place) and a time (a longish time)
in which members of different cultures around the Mediterranean had to
deal with one another and were thus able to recognize, with a certain
degree of relativism, that there are different modes of behavior and different ways of going about things. The lack of a pure and perfect orthodoxy,
applicable internationally, was one of the factors that made the novel possible. There is in these old works an ability to accept the existence of different nationalities and language groups and to set up one standard of
manners beside another. One of the most surprising things about the ancient novels, particularly those in Greek, is the emphasis on female life
and experience. The surviving "Greek" novels were written in the Greek
language, but not by Athenians or others from the Greek mainland. The
principal novelists whom we know about were by and large from the areas
now called Turkey and Syria. As Asia Minor and parts of western Asia
were regions supporting the goddess-cults, and had been the home of the
Great Mother,[1] they were perhaps more hospitable to the representation of
female experience as meaningful.

Probably the earliest surviving of all the antique novels is one called
Chaireas and Kallirrhoe by one Chariton. He was secretary to a *rhetor*, that
is, a sort of big-time lawyer and public speaker in the world of the Roman
Empire, and he came from a beautiful town in Asia Minor called Aphrodisias, dedicated to the goddess Aphrodite. In his novel (which has been
dated anywhere from 50 B.C. to 150 A.D.) the man from Aphrodisias celebrates the work of Aphrodite—that is, the work of generation and the
pulse of life. In the story, beautiful young Kallirrhoe and handsome young
Chaireas of Sicily fall in love and marry. But jealous former suitors of Kallirrhoe soon cheat Chaireas out of his happiness by "proving" his wife
unfaithful, using a trick very like that in *Much Ado about Nothing*. He
comes home in a rage and kicks his wife in the stomach. She falls lifeless.
Her family have her buried in a beautiful tomb, and Chaireas is almost
beside himself with grief and self-accusation.

Kallirrhoe, however, is not dead. She comes to in the tomb (a very frightening experience) but is inadvertently rescued by grave robbers. They take
her away from Sicily and sell her as a slave in Ionia. The heroine's new
owner, Dionysius, recently widowed, to his own embarrassment falls violently in love with the beautiful girl. She rejects his advances—but then,

her fellow slave Plangon, the steward's wife, tells the girl what ignorance kept from her—she is pregnant! Kallirrhoe is miserable. She knows the child is the product of her and Chaireas' love, but people will say she got pregnant while with the bandits—and in any case, what point is there in bearing a child who must be born a slave? Kallirrhoe believes she should have an abortion. She addresses the baby in her womb:

"It will not be agreeable to you, Child, to be born into a life of suffering; having come to be, you ought to flee it. Die free, ignorant of misery." [Apithi eleutheros, apathēs kakōn.] [Chariton, Chaireas and Kallirrhoe, pp. 87–88][2]

Although she believes it is her duty to spare her child the wretched life of slavery, Kallirrhoe has many pangs, accusing herself of being a Medea (who killed her sons). Plangon the fellow slave offers to help her with an abortion if she wants, but Plangon has a better idea. Dionysius is so madly in love with Kallirrhoe—why not marry him?—and then she can father her unborn child on him. It is early enough, Plangon calculates, for Dionysius to be none the wiser. Plangon does not, of course, tell Kallirrhoe that she sees rewards in this arrangement for her husband and herself; Dionysius has urged her to work on the beautiful slave girl for him.

Kallirrhoe has some doubt as to whether she ought to consent to this arrangement. She goes to her own room and closes the door—the first instance of a Room of One's Own for a woman in Western literature, I think. (Penelope, always surrounded by maid-servants in the Odyssey, can scarcely count.) Then she holds a kind of council:

She put the picture of Chaireas on her stomach and "Now then," she said, "here are the three of us together, man and wife and child. Let us hold a council about our common concerns." [P. 90]

The result of the "council" is very satisfactory. Kallirrhoe, ventriloquizing all parties, finds that they agree that it is best for her to give Chaireas' son (she is sure it will be a son) a rich new father.

Thus we watch Kallirrhoe, a model of virtue and wifely chastity, decide her own and her child's life. Of course, the reader, ancient or modern, must root for her to do what she does—and what she does do is decidedly subversive. She is in the wrong by very social (male) law and by the laws of all male religions. According to the Greek and Roman law that pertained in Chariton's world, a mother, even if she were not a slave, had no rights over her own child. Roman law had become increasingly anxious about property and under Augustus was clamping down on (female) adultery, so anxious were the upper-class citizens of the Roman Empire to preserve purity of bloodline and property. A slave, of course, could have no rights

over a child, which as soon as born became the property of the master and
part of the wealth of the estate. A slave also had no right to abort, destroying the master's property. In Chariton's novel we are made to forget all
that, or to hold it of no account. The novelists of antiquity take more liberties with the social and moral order than Menander, who must soon
compromise his interesting situations with prevailing moral norms—a
perennial weakness of situation comedy, as not of the situational novel.
Kallirrhoe, the heroine of virtue, of sōphrosynē, takes a second "husband,"
commits bigamy or, rather, seduces (in some lights) a man who must really
(if unwittingly) take the position of an adulterer (moichos) instead of a
true husband. She also puts a large cuckoo in his nest. Kallirrhoe well and
truly disturbs the bloodline and the flow of property, the orderly masculine "civilized" order of inheritance.

Chariton's Kallirrhoe acts as if she were the real parent of her child and
is never concerned by Roman law regarding marriage or childbirth or slavery. She learns how to grow out of mere dutiful virtue into a wiser self-
preservation. In the terms of the world around her, she is a-moral or even
immoral. Her rebirth from the tomb means she is no longer purely daughter or wife, but a moral being. She is a magnificent illustration of the Weldon dictum "the worse women behave, the better they get on." Kallirrhoe,
instead of having to mope about the back kitchens as a slave, gets a fine
new husband, a house and clothing, and access to money, as well as a
father for her child. Aphrodite approves of Kallirrhoe, and supports her;
Kallirrhoe always looks like Aphrodite herself.

One sees how much better off Chariton is than Weldon; he does not
have to re-invent Nature or fumble for new terms for "our mistress." The
Goddess can be appealed to, represented, generalized about, and comically used in the narrative which supports the work of Aphrodite, the
generative and redemptive creation, as Weldon is later to do. As in Weldon,
males who try to meddle with or undo Aphrodite's operations are going
to have to pay for it, whether or not they recognize retribution for what it
is. The Goddess sees to it that Chaireas is punished for his violence to the
wife Aphrodite gave him. On the track of Kallirrhoe, Chaireas is able to
punish the bandits who abducted her, but when he gets warm in his
search, Dionysius sees to it that Chaireas is spirited away and sold into
slavery himself. He is nearly crucified before he starts recovering his fortunes again; at last he obtains a position by which he can hope to recover
his lost wife. He does, of course, recover her, although during the law case
in Persia where he appears against Dionysius, some of Kallirrhoe's female
supporters are unromantically critical of him and sardonically warn her
against returning to her childhood sweetheart:

"And what if Chaireas reverts to temper tantrums? Back to the tomb?" [P. 151]

Dionysius, a hopelessly un-"Dionysian" man proud of his own rectitude, a slow, self-righteous, and self-pitying person, is treated so tactfully by Kallirrhoe, even as she leaves him, that he never knows his son is not his, and can even persuade himself that Kallirrhoe goes back to Sicily with her first husband only because she must. Kallirrhoe's last letter to him is a model of intelligence and heartfelt deceit through suggestion. She has evidently learned not only how to survive, but how to ensure that her son survives in prosperity, and even that Dionysius' self-love should survive.

I tend to think of Chariton's *Chaireas and Kallirrhoe* as "the first Fay Weldon novel." Chariton's novel didn't get into print until 1750, and its eighteenth-century English translations are not widely known. It is not and cannot be a direct influence on Weldon's work; I'm not here dealing with direct influences but with patterns of resemblance. The kind of novel that Chariton's book represents is a kind of novel that hasn't been dealt with very well by criticism informed merely by ideas of the realistic and moral novel trumpeted by F. R. Leavis. To oppose to that novel we have only the often crude concept of the "romance," which is frowned upon in English criticism and used as a dungeon into which we pile the Brontës and some of Dickens only when we wish to be unkind. Chariton's witty novel shows us the charm of the situational novel, its power to question received cultural assumptions—about marriage, for instance, and about property and choice. Situational works can use realistic materials and touches, as Chariton does all the time. Consider, for instance, his description of Kallirrhoe coming to in her tomb:

As she began to arise, with difficulty, she encountered the crowns and fillets. She made a noise of gold and silver. There was a strong smell of spices. [P. 62]

How nicely Chariton has calculated what it would be like to come to in a tomb *in the dark*. His narrative here follows the heroine's senses—the tinkling noise of the gold and silver objects as she brushes against them, the confusing smell of heavy spices—all puzzling, sensuous experiences to a person who can make no use of her eyes. Such realistic detail does not bind Chariton to the realistic or naturalistic in his story. What he looks to—and what we look for—is a strong situational pattern. Novelists who do not employ nineteenth-century realism, or the romantic patterns as we have understood them, have been imperfectly visible to us; in modern times such writers are labeled "experimental." Much fiction of both past and present is situationally devised and, while not primarily concerned with pure realism or development of organic character, it is at the same

time not particularly romantic and does not need either dragons or
haunted castles to achieve its ends. (Though in defence of Radcliffe and
Co. one might remark that an imprisoning castle offers a strong situation
from which a good deal of moral, sexual, and social observation can be
expected.)

In some of her novels Fay Weldon has very visibly employed the techniques and references of a more ancient fiction—and done it so well that
puzzled readers have not been able to call her "romantic." My own favorite
among all her novels so far, *The Hearts and Lives of Men* (1987), appears
to be a deliberate adaptation of the plot patterns and tropes of ancient fiction. The heroine of the story, "little Nell" (an overt reminiscence of Dickens) is the child of the beautiful Helen, a woman whom we may think will
be the heroine. But Nell is that favorite of ancient fiction, the rescued girl.
These magical females traditionally survive shipwreck, and even burial
alive, in order to pursue their rescuing vocation. When she is snatched by
a bandit, Mr. Blotton (who is trying to snatch her for her father), Nell is in
a plane that crashes—but she is wonderfully saved:

But what happened to the tail was this. It floated down, quite gracefully,
the air billowing through it and sustaining it by some phenomena of aero-
dynamics, tilting first a little to the right, then a little to the left, as if it were
a parachute, and in it were two seats, and sitting side by side were Nell and
Mr. Blotton . . . [P. 11]

Nell is carrying a talisman, her mother's emerald pendant—and emeralds
have been a favorite associate of heroines from time immemorial. The emerald is a stone of chastity and high aspiration; in Heliodorus' *Aithiopika*
the heroine's treasures, given her as a baby by her unknown mother, include emeralds. Armed with her emerald maternal pendant, and her fate,
Nell escapes (a pleasant) imprisonment in a château through a fire which
spares her and no other. She is always looked after, for she has a meaning
and purpose different from her parents' limited and selfish objectives
(their affairs, jobs, and remarriages). And she is always busy:

But, reader, the fact is that Nell was simply not destined for a quiet life. It was
always to be like this. Fate would allow her some small pleasant respite, then
whirl her up and set her down on an altogether different and not necessarily
pleasant path. Good fortune and bad were always, for Nell, to follow close upon
each other's heels, and snapping at hers. [P. 161]

Fate is a favorite figure of the ancient novelists—Fate (*Tychē*) being a
feminine deity who takes part in the action. As Chariton has it, leading
into Kallirrhoe's pregnancy and her marriage with Dionysius, "Fate (*Hē
Tychē*) was plotting against the chastity (or virtue: *sōphrosynē*) of the

young woman." Fate is always up to something—and, as the ancient novelists (like the moderns) know, novel characters are there for nothing if not to have fates, although those fates are really handed them by their authors. Woman's anatomy, her fate to be a reproducer, is always in large part her "Fate"—a notion that Weldon celebrates. That sexual "Fate" always plots against virtue, niceness, nice-mindedness, sōphrosynē. The Fate of many novels is felt to be in Eros-Amor, Love, which, as Chariton says in the beginning of his novel, loves to stir things up and take control: "Eros loves conflicts." So it does in *Hearts and Lives*—which begins with "Love at first sight—that old thing!" (p. 1). Nell is, of course, to be restored to her parents, recognized through the classic token, her emerald, although by this point she has had a life and has embarked herself on the course of love and sexuality. Her parents, however, can rejoice in their renewal: "But how lucky they were, to be given this second chance—and how little, you might think, they deserved it" (p. 373).

The parents in this kind of novel, ancient or modern, often do *not* deserve to have the children restored to them—the very children whom their own carelessness or cruelty, greed or frailty have put at risk. Nell is restored, like the heroine Charikleia of Heliodorus, or like the heroine in *Evelina* by Frances Burney (another situational writer). But the process of restoration portrays the independent agency of the child and the weakness of the parents. The weakness of the parents is most strikingly seen in *The History of Apollonius King of Tyre,* one of the ancient novels best known to us because of Shakespeare's adaptation of it in *Pericles, Prince of Tyre.* In the novel, which is the basis of the play and which bears some odd ancestral relation to Weldon's *Hearts and Lives,* the heroine grown up is not rescued by the parent, but must herself perform the rescuing of a parent gone astray spiritually and emotionally.

Secrets of human behavior, of human meanings, of the possible ways we can relate ourselves to the cruel but fascinating physical world in which we find ourselves—these are "secrets" that the novel as a form of literature can deal with, partly by setting us upon a quest for meanings, an increased attentiveness to what we are and what we do. Attentiveness may sometimes be increased by a jolt, a sudden shove, a journey away from what we find comfortable and ordinary. Jean Marsh introducing the dramatized *Cloning of Joanna May* to the Arts and Entertainment Network in the United States calls it "surreal," and suggests that the story relates to science fiction. This is true enough, but the terms don't get us very far. We don't think of *Cloning* as science fiction much more than we think of the ring of Gyges as science. What we see in this situation is certainly an image of the world our society has used science to produce, the world in which men are trying to control the business of generation. The author's production of an expressive central comic situation works by giving us (as well as the characters) extra bursts of energy combined with astonishment. The situation is a comic emblem with possibilities that the author as narrator can then set out and read or interpret with hermeneutical gusto.

Fay Weldon's kind of novel is sometimes treated as if it were altogether new. While such a view may be flattering to the author, it can also be disturbing. Credit for originality is given only in exchange for an admission of shallowness. It is not doing the author out of her true originality to claim that her kind of novel is the more powerful because it has long roots and is securely grounded in a classical tradition. Weldon doesn't have to write like Jane Austen in order to be "classical." But Jane Austen herself in her *early* works is all expressive comic situation—all game and play. G. K. Chesterton, looking at the early works in *Volume the Second*, asserts that Austen's inspiration "was the inspiration of Gargantua and of Pickwick; it was the gigantic inspiration of laughter."³ That Austen herself is Rabelaisian (or has her Rabelaisian aspects) can be seen in reading her earlier or less official works, now freshly collected in *Catherine and Other Writings*. The elegant restrained realism of the six Austen novels, like the apparent modesty of the narratives, was something the author had to consent to acquire in order to get published.

Austen's early writings have the high comic energy, the sudden audacious push as if the reader has been sent on a rush in a swing, losing footing while gaining altitude. Her works exhibit the robust sense of the absurd and an insistent sense of the import of the physical. They break through reserves of feminine modesty on marriage, as of feminine respect of men:

He is quite an old Man, about two and thirty, very plain *so* plain that I cannot bear to look at him. He is extremely disagreeable and I hate him more than any body else in the world. He has a large fortune and will make great Settlements on me; but then he is very healthy. In short I do not know what to do. ["The Three Sisters," in *Catharine*, p. 55]

Such a blowing of the gaff, such overt deriding of the love story—possible for the early Austen, as not for the Austen who had tamed herself for her publishers—resembles the frequent gaff-blowings in Weldon:

Look around you. All the women nicely groomed and attractive and good-looking, and the men no better than fat slugs, for the most part, or skinny runts. Unshaved and smelly as often as not. They get away with everything, men. [*The Fat Woman's Joke*, p. 102]

So says Brenda's mother after "cutting through a *mille feuille* with a silver cake fork in the tea-rooms at the top of Dickens and Jones" (p. 101). Weldon women in discontent very often find refuge in food. Depression or pregnancy, both important states, make the female characters all the more interested in ingestion. It is no wonder that the witchy Mabs Tucker in *Puffball* is able to poison Liffey, poison being administered (as it customarily is) in food and drink. Mabs is a bad-fairy Queen Mab, but her last name Tucker means "food" in Australian and New Zealand English. Esther Sussman, in *The Fat Woman's Joke*, is the most food-abandoned of Weldon's characters, abandoning even the slow pleasure of cookery:

She picked out a tin of curry and a tin of savoury rice from the shelf.
"It's not real curry, this, of course. Real curry is very tricky to make. You use spices, added at precise intervals, and coconut milk. It's not just a matter of making a stew and adding curry powder and raisins and bananas. You have to devote a whole day to making a true curry." [P. 53]

Esther, gaping ever for more food, is knowledgeable about the time-wasting cookery she has given up, and would be understood by one of Austen's most self-referential characters, the manic cook Charlotte Luttrell in "Lesley Castle" who is so disappointed when her sister's fiancé is killed as her wedding preparations have been in vain: "I had the mortification of finding that I had been Roasting, Boiling and Stewing both the Meat and Myself to no purpose" ("Lesley Castle," in *Catharine*, p. 110). Madly active and overproductive cooks are likely to turn up in Jane Austen's early fiction, as in "A beautiful description of the different effects of Sensibility on different Minds" in *Volume the First*, in which the narrator consoles an invalid friend:

I am usually at the fire cooking some little delicacy for the unhappy invalid— Perhaps hashing up the remains of an old Duck, toasting some cheese or making a Curry which are the favorite Dishes of our poor friend. [*Catharine*, p. 68]

Delicate attentions turn into indelicate attentions—strong, gamey, and spicy. Austen—the early, less-inhibited Austen—has her own enjoyment of comic lists and oral parades. Behind Austen and Weldon, behind even Rabelais, there is the carnal ass of Apuleius, jauntily eating with an appetite to equal Gargantua's or Esther Sussman's. The ass enjoys himself in the home of the cook and the pastry-cook:

In the evenings, after their most luxurious dinners most splendidly served, my masters used to bring back to their apartment great portions of the excess: the one pork, fowl, fish and all sorts of tasty things, enormous leftovers; the other, breads, cookies, doughnuts, hook-shaped cakes and lizard-shaped cakes and more honey-sweet delicacies. As soon as they closed the room and sought the

baths to refresh themselves, I would cram myself to the full with these di-
vinely-offered feasts (*oblatis ego divinitus dapibus affatim saginabar*) [Apu-
leius, *Metamorphoses* or *Asinus Aureus*, Bk X, c.13][4]

Not only satire but all rumination on human behavior and human fate
demands attention to the ignoble, unignorable physical home of desire—
the body with its open mouth, chomping jaws, and almost-interminable
digestive tract.

Weldon's power lies partly in her ability to unite the satiric-fantastic,
in which she is a descendant of Apuleius and Rabelais, with the ironic
expressive situational story of human love and fate, in which she is a descendant of Chariton. She is thus a descendant of at least two strands of
"classical" tradition and a relative (as each novelist is) of numerous other
writers of fiction. She has her Austenian aspects. Austen has her Weldonesque side. Perhaps any strict barriers between narrative kinds of writing—or between narrative writings—must at some point break down.
Chrétien de Troyes is after all very fond of teasing expressive situations,
and if Rabelais had dramatized Chrétien, the result would have been interesting at the very least. All of these authors have a relation to an older
and bigger narrative tradition which includes many more models than we
have previously liked to acknowledge. Narrative tradition is a big affair.
In her own ways of wedding satire and domestic crisis, sex and expressive
nonnaturalistic situation, Weldon is truly in the classical vein. She is the
stronger as she has her roots in the true Great Tradition.

Notes

1. Some will demur at this reference to the *Magna Mater*. At present, in
reaction against a strong current in contemporary feminism, there is a determined scholastic endeavor to repudiate ideas of female power in any form as
being associated with antiquity in any period. Mary Beard, in *The London
Review of Books* (13 May 1993), refers scornfully to the "lunacy" which imagines "primitive mother goddesses ruling the roost in the never-never land of
Stone Age matriarchy," along with other "arguments about women and religion that would be promptly—and rightly—laughed into the dustbin in almost every other field" (p. 19). She follows Mary Lefkowitz, whose *Women and
Greek Myth* (1986) seems chiefly designed to tell us that the Goddess is dead
because there never were any real goddesses. Stone Age matriarchy has been
attacked by Stella Georgoudi in "Creating a Myth of Matriarchy" in *A History
of Women,* ed. Georges Duby and Michelle Perot (1990); see English translation
by A. Goldhammer (Cambridge, Mass.: Harvard University Press, 1992),
pp. 449–63.

Certainly, feminists should and must search into the evidences of history,
and it is true that some enthusiasts have leaped into premature assertions

about the Goddess Religion. Nevertheless, the chorus of negative Marys is not without ideological objectives, and may be treated as an academic backlash. Traditional classical departments (or leading members of these) often have a strong vested interest in sustaining a traditional view of the classical era—a nineteenth-century view, very largely. Any woman who visits Asia Minor today is likely soon to be struck by the insistent presence of images of female divinities and the remaining evidences of worship of a being or beings describable as female. If there never "really" were a Cybele or Aphrodite, it would only be in the same sense that there never "really" was an Apollo or Dionysius. Contemplation of the history of the novel in the West has given me a considerable respect for the possibility of goddess-centered religion(s).

2. Page references to Chariton's novel are to Budé edition (see Works Cited); the translations offered here are my own. The reader may wish to turn to the English version in *Collected Ancient Greek Novels* (see Works Cited).

3. G. K. Chesterton, "Preface" to *Love and Freindship* [sic] *and Other Early Works . . . by Jane Austen* (New York: Frederick A. Stokes Co., 1922), pp. xiv–xv.

4. The Latin is taken from the Loeb edition of Apuleius' *Metamorphoses*, translated by J. Arthur Hanson (Vol. 2, pp. 238–41); my translation is slightly different.

Works Cited

Apuleius. *The Metamorphoses of Apuleius*. Ed. and trans. J. Arthur Hanson. Cambridge, Mass., and London: Harvard University Press, 1989. Translations in essay are not Hanson's but my own.

Austen, Jane. *Catharine and Other Writings*. Ed. Margaret Anne Doody and Douglas Murray. Oxford and New York: Oxford University Press, 1993.

Chariton. *Chaireas and Kallirrhoe*, as *Le roman de Chaireas et Callirhoé*. Ed. Georges Molinié and Alain Billault (French-Greek dual language Budé edition). Paris: Les Belles Lettres, 1979. For another translation see B. P. Reardon, *Chaereas and Callirhoe*, in *Collected Ancient Greek Novels*. Berkeley, Los Angeles, and London: University of California Press, 1989, pp. 17–124.

Chesterton, G. K. Preface to *Love and Freindship* [sic] *and Other Early Works . . . by Jane Austen*. New York: Frederick A. Stokes Co., 1922.

Rabelais, Francois. *Oeuvres Complètes*. Ed. Guy Demerson. Paris: Editions du Seuil, 1973.

Weldon, Fay. (Works are in chronological order; list includes only books quoted.)

———. *The Fat Woman's Joke*. 1967. London: Coronet Books, Hodder and Stoughton, 1990.

———. *Female Friends*. 1975. London: Pan Books in association with William Heinemann Ltd., 1983.

———. *Little Sisters*. 1978. London: Coronet Books, Hodder and Stoughton, 1987.

———. *Puffball*. 1980. Harmondsworth, Middlesex: Penguin Books, 1990.

———. *Letters to Alice on first reading Jane Austen*. 1984. New York: Carroll & Graf Publishers, Inc., 1991.

————. *The Rules of Life*. 1987. London: Arrow Books, Century Hutchinson Ltd., 1988.

————. *The Hearts and Lives of Men*. 1987. New York: Bantam Doubleday Dell Publishing Group, Inc., 1989.

————. *The Cloning of Joanna May*. 1989. London: Fontana, An Imprint of HarperCollins, 1990.

RACHEL BROWNSTEIN

The Importance of Aunts

Fay Weldon has been compared to Jane Austen—but then so have Anita Brookner, Georgette Heyer (the author of Regency Romances), Alexandra Ripley (who wrote the sequel to *Gone with the Wind*), and even Doris Lessing, whose novel *The Fifth Child* reminded *Partisan Review*'s reviewer of "a bit of Jane Austen but with a Mary Shelley twist." *The New Yorker* invoked "Jane Austen's description of her novels as fine brushwork on a 'little bit (two Inches wide) of Ivory'" in a piece on a nonfiction book about poor Americans by the writer Melissa Fay Greene.[1] Flattering on the face of it, the pervasive comparison verges on the odious, having come to mean mostly that the writer at hand is a woman.

To praise every writing woman as a species of Jane Austen is, of course, to diminish significant differences (and Jane Austen, and women generally). One way to arrest the lamentable tendency is to read Austen's books and savor their particularity. This is what Fay Weldon urges us to do in *Letters to Alice on first reading Jane Austen* (1984). Weldon is a writer who likes to buttonhole a reader ("Reader, I am going to tell you the story of Clifford, Helen, and little Nell," *The Hearts and Lives of Men* begins); direct address is a mode that suits her. But Alice, to whom these letters signed "Aunt Fay" are directed, is not a surrogate for the rest of us. The implied reader of this epistolary novel is older and wiser than Alice, and has read Jane Austen already. She is meant to look indulgently down on "Aunt Fay's" correspondent (whose own letters we never see) while savoring her delightful naivete—to see her as one sees, say, Austen's Emma.

Modern Alice dyes her hair green and black, has quarreled with her parents, and lives with her boyfriend. Required to read Jane Austen's novels for a college course, she thinks them "boring, petty and irrelevant"—

and has written to ask advice of her literary aunt, who is in Australia on a book tour. (Alice's name must be meant to suggest the girl who went to Wonderland; "Fay" coyly promises a peek at the well-known novelist behind the scenes.) Raised on television, Alice doesn't read much, but this doesn't stop her from trying to write a novel, predictably about her own eventful love life. Its tentative title is *The Well of Loneliness*. In the single letter she writes to Alice's mother, Fay recalls her own mother's discovering a copy of Radclyffe Hall's book under her pillow and "ceremoniously burning it, as indecent and likely to corrupt"; she will persuade her niece to change the title of her novel and the plot as well, and effectively change her life, in the course of writing letters to Alice about Jane Austen. For discussing Jane Austen and the reasons why Alice should read her leads Weldon to consider from several angles the blurry and fascinating line between real lives and fiction. In the process, she places her own good sense and wit, her own ideas about women and novels, her own distinctly feminine tone of authority right beside Jane Austen's. She dares the daunting comparison with her great precursor mostly by setting up as an aunt.

Motherhood and daughterhood and sisterhood, real and metaphorical, have interested contemporary feminists to the exclusion of aunthood. This dismissiveness is by no means eccentric: one consequence of the nuclear family's psychosocial effects is that everyone thinks in terms of it. Furthermore, while uncles have important and well-defined roles, in some cultures, aunts are most acknowledged in ours when they are not really aunts—when the word is used as an honorific, "endearingly of any benevolent practical woman who exercises these qualities to the benefit of her circle of acquaintance," as the Oxford English Dictionary pithily puts it. (The OED describes that usage as American, but one edition of the American College Dictionary [1951] calls it "chiefly British.") Two further meanings of *aunt*, "an old woman; a gossip" and "a bawd or procuress; a prostitute," are listed in the OED as obsolete; also obsolete is the slang "Aunt Nancy men," used of male supporters of the movement for women's rights in nineteenth-century America. Nevertheless, the derogatory aura lingers. Auntie Mame and Charlie's Aunt and My Aunt Tillie are not to be taken very seriously. This is perhaps about to change, at least among feminists. Kate Millett suggested at a recent academic conference that Simone de Beauvoir should not be called the mother of us all, but the aunt; and Catharine R. Stimpson's neat chiasmus, that "mothers and aunts give the [Nancy Drew] books to their nieces and daughters," was quoted on the first page of the *New York Times*.[2] Having thought long enough about mothering and its discontents, feminists may be about ready to move on. And

Fay Weldon might have been prophetic as well as wise in understanding, as early as 1984, that the feminist Jane Austen is Aunt Jane.

The insight is on the face of it perverse: isn't *that* Austen the decorous prim spinster in the parsonage, working away at her novels with her very fine brush, hiding the pages under the blotter when the parlor door squeaked—a good woman who (therefore) never took herself too seriously as an author? It was her nephew J. E. Austen-Leigh who fixed this image, in an 1870 memoir. (Its mock-humble or mock-heroic epigraph is taken from a biography of Columbus: "He knew of no one but himself who was inclined to the work.") Austen-Leigh had been the youngest person at Jane Austen's funeral; he wrote as an old man. Like most eulogists of dead women, he focuses on his subject's piety, humility, cheerfulness in the face of adversity, etc. His authority is bolstered by his status as a man of the family (his sister Caroline also wrote a memoir, *My Aunt Jane Austen*) and by the pervasive stereotype of the maiden aunt, not to mention those memorable aunts of fiction—often not spinsters but widows—who, however personally outrageous, are stiff-necked sticklers for propriety: Tom Sawyer's Aunt Sally, Wilde's Lady Bracknell, Austen's own Lady Catherine de Bourgh. Nevertheless, the best things in his book work to subvert that too-familiar image of an aunt. They are quotations from Jane Austen's lively letters to him and her nieces, in which she elaborately plays the aunt, playing against the popular conception. The American novelist Mary E. Wilkins Freeman, assigned to write a chapter of a group novel, *The Whole Family*, from the point of view of a maiden aunt, threw a monkey wrench in the works by having her character run off with the heroine's husband-to-be: Austen's letters overturn preconceptions about tone rather than plot. But of course the real issue is character—the fun of working against the social pressure to see individuals, when they are women, as representative and emblematic.

Jane Austen preempted the unattractive portrait of herself as a spinster aunt before it was quite dry—took it on for herself in order to send it up. She writes, for example, to her novel-writing niece Anna Austen Lefroy, "I have been very far from finding your book an evil, I assure you. I read it immediately, and with great pleasure. Indeed, I do think you get on very fast. I wish other people of my acquaintance could compose as rapidly." The compliment is arch and a bit smug: Anna, after all, is trying to equal her aunt's accomplishment as well as to please her. Austen gleefully points to Anna's amateurishness: "St. Julian's History was quite a surprise to me; You had not very long known it yourself, I suspect—but I have no objection to make to the circumstance—it is very well told—& his having been in love with the aunt gives Cecilia an additional Interest with him.

I like the Idea: a very proper compliment to an Aunt!—I rather imagine indeed that Neices are seldom chosen but in compliment to some Aunt or other. I dare say [your husband] was in love with me once, & wd never have thought of you if he had not supposed me dead of a scarlet fever" (*Letters*, pp. 420–21). This aunt's advice is tempered by a sense of her own potentially comical position—and other people's.

A quick survey of Austen's novels yields an aunt's-eye view of the variety of aunts: in *Pride and Prejudice*, Lady Catherine stands corrected by Elizabeth's aunts Gardiner and Philips, who balance one another; Mrs. Norris and Lady Bertram are opposite kinds of aunts in *Mansfield Park*; the middle-aged aunt mentioned in *The Watsons* surprises her niece's family by still being a scandalously sexual creature; and *Emma*, of course, is among other things a novel about auntship, with its heroine who draws hasty chalk portraits of her sister's children (all looking more or less the same) and claims she will never marry partly because she "will always have a niece with me" as an object of affection. Miss Bates, whom Emma insults, is Jane Fairfax's doting aunt; like Frank Churchill's tyrannical aunt she is crucial to the plot. "I have always maintained the importance of Aunts as much as possible," Austen wrote to her niece Caroline, who had just become an aunt herself, "& I am sure of your doing the same now" (*Letters*, p. 428).

Austen's liveliest letters are to her brother's daughters, marriageable or recently married young women—would-be heroines and novelists, like Weldon's Alice. How is the girlish wish to live a romance related to the desire to write one? How influential, in this connection, are the words of a novelist-aunt? Aunt Fay, like Austen before her, is aware of the muddled ambitions of her niece, who wants mostly to distinguish herself from other people. She is a briskly professional critic of her niece's plans for her novel (modern Alice evidently doesn't mail text), who advises against self-indulgence and first drafts: "Novels are not meant to be diaries, you know" (p. 110). She encourages Alice to notice the fine points of literary craft, and to look at her own story from another person's point of view—for example, her lover's wife's. (The final title of her novel will be *The Wife's Revenge*.) And mostly she encourages her to read—Jane Austen and the other great literary works that make up what she reverently calls—with a nod to Bunyan—The City of Invention, "the nearest we poor mortals can get to the Celestial City" (pp. 15–16). The very thought of the City heightens Weldon's rhetoric: "You must *read*, Alice, before it's too late. You must fill your mind with the invented images of the past: the more the better. . . . These images, apart from anything else, will help you put the two and twos of life together, and the more images your mind retains, the more wonderful will be the star-studded canopy of experience beneath which you, poor primitive creature that you are, will shelter: the nearer you will creep to the great blazing beacon of the Idea which animates us all" (p. 15). The aunt's passion for literature is nearly religious, but this is also simple good advice. J. E. Austen-Leigh's precocious sister Caroline recalled her aunt's telling her "that if I would take her advice I should cease writing till I was sixteen; that she had herself often wished she had read more, and written less in the corresponding years of her own life" (Memoir, p. 304).

Older and wiser than their nieces, Aunt Jane and Aunt Fay understand the vital connection between living and writing love stories; otherwise, a niece would hardly turn to her aunt. But the connections novelists relish are not the easy ones that most people see. A novelist thinks in terms of craft. To her niece Fanny's account of a romantic encounter, Aunt Jane writes, "Your trying to excite your own feelings by a visit to his room amused me excessively. The dirty Shaving Rag was exquisite!—Such a circumstance ought to be in print. Much too good to be lost" (Letters, p. 412). Pay attention to salient details and differences, is the auntly message; keep on your toes and look sharp, and keep your distance from the swamp of sentiment. That way your feelings will be sharper, and your judgment—and your prose as well. Now here is Aunt Fay, who loathes academic critics, working at training her budding novelist: "You write complaining of the dreadful feeling of dry despair which your course in English Literature induces in you: you feel you are suffocating; as if your mouth was being stuffed with dry leaves; as if your brain was slowly dying of some mental poison. It makes you want to scream. How well you put it. I really have hopes for your novel: how is it going?" (p. 130) Ironized affection and shifts in tone calculated to startle are keys to auntly camaraderie. Writing as an aunt, to Fanny or Alice or about Emma, one keeps one's little distance.

By virtue of her own status in the world and the family, by virtue of her own self-confidence, by virtue of her distance and experience and clear standards, a writer aunt can teach important lessons. Before Jane Austen was born, Mrs. Chapone addressed her conduct book, Letters on the Improvement of the Mind, Addressed to a Lady (1773), to a niece. It begins, "Though you are so happy as to have parents, who are both capable and desirous of giving you all proper instruction, yet I, who love you so tenderly, cannot help fondly wishing to contribute something, if possible, to your improvement and welfare: As I am so far separated from you, . . . it is only by pen and ink I can offer you my sentiments. . . . And if you pay me the compliment of preserving my letters, you may possibly reperuse them at some future period, when concurring circumstances may give them additional weight:—and thus they may prove more effectual than the same things spoken in conversation" (p. 1). The little distance between an aunt and her niece's immediate family (Australia!), the regard her writing enjoys in the world, her difference from a nearer, more domestic and docile mother can be invaluable to an ambitious niece. An aunt is in a position to be an example to a young woman with dreams and ideas. And the writing aunt herself is gratified by the chance to have an immediate influence—to contribute to her niece's improvement and welfare, as Mrs. Chapone puts it. Austen goes so far as to hint that an intimacy with a niece is a nearly romantic thing, as fleeting as romance is: "Oh! what a loss it will be when you are married," Aunt Jane writes Fanny, sentiment neatly balancing irony. "You are too agreable in your single state, too agreable as a Neice. I shall hate you when your delicious play of Mind is all settled down into conjugal & maternal affections" (*Letters*, pp. 478–79). (Austen's most recent biographer, Park Honan, conjectures that Fanny was a lot duller than her aunt chose to think she was.)

Weldon's Fay, who is divorced, gads about the world alone; Alice's mother bakes breakfast rolls for her husband every morning (and suspects her sister Fay made fun of her in a novel for doing so). The rebel who read Radclyffe Hall as a girl has much in common with her green-and-black-haired niece: her irreverence is a kind of sustained youth. Of Jane Austen, Honan reminds us that "at just the period of her greatest creativity, Jane Austen was happiest and most fully herself among children." Her niece Caroline remembered that of her two sister aunts "Aunt Jane was by far my favourite," although she "did not *dislike* Aunt Cassandra" (Honan, pp. 270–71). Austen was in her thirties when she wrote her lively letters to Edward and Caroline and Anna and Fanny, then in their late teens and early twenties.

It seems to me significant that Jane Austen's well-known comments on the practice of writing novels exist largely in her teasing critiques of her young relations' fiction. "By the bye, my dear Edward," she writes, "I am quite concerned for the loss your Mother mentions in her Letter; two Chapters & a half to be missing is monstrous! It is well that I have not been at Steventon lately, & therefore cannot be suspected of purloining them;—two strong twigs & a half towards a Nest of my own, would have been something.—I do not think however that any theft of that sort would be really very useful to me. What should I do with your strong, manly, spirited Sketches, full of Variety and Glow?—How could I possibly join them on to the little bit (two Inches wide) of Ivory on which I work with so fine a Brush, as produces little effect after much labour?" (*Letters*, pp. 468–

69). And to Anna, "You are now collecting your People delightfully, getting them exactly into such a spot as is the delight of my life;—3 or 4 Families in a country Village is the very thing to work on—& I hope you will write a good deal more, and make full use of them while they are so very favourably arranged. You are but *now* coming to the heart & beauty of your book; till the heroine grows up, the fun must be imperfect—but I expect a great deal of entertainment from the next 3 or 4 books, & I hope you will not resent these remarks by sending me no more" (*Letters*, p. 401). The famous maxims of the novelist seem drenched in irony when put back in context, at the heart of the friendly effusions of a vastly entertained, drily encouraging, playfully teacherly aunt.

Letters to Alice begins by observing, quite as Alice does, that the world of Jane Austen's novels was nothing like our own. It is, accordingly, full of information about the worth of money and the age of menarche and the way people cooked cabbage and the percentage of servants in the population of England and the risks of childbirth in Austen's day—facts that shed valuable light on the novels. But a larger point about difference is made as well: arguing for literature against trash and television, Weldon stresses the great divide between a serious novel and a simple and simplifying transcription of fantasy, "real life" mediated by clichés rather than observation and wisdom. In this she echoes Austen. Behind Austen's youthful fiction in letters—and all the rest of her work—glimmers the wicked, benevolent intent to parody and thus improve on popular romantic fiction. It shows itself most openly as narrative self-consciousness and consciousness of the reader. Toward the end of *Northanger Abbey*, for example, the narrator observes "the tell-tale compression of the pages" that makes us conclude that we and our hero and heroine are "all hastening together to perfect felicity," then challenges the reader to decide "whether the tendency of this work be altogether to recommend parental tyranny, or reward filial disobedience." Aunt Fay quotes that passage to her niece, and takes it very seriously: "What do you think, Alice, since it does concern you? She is still talking to you, and she knows you are there. You, the reader, are involved in this literary truth, as much as the writer." You must know the City of Invention, she insists, if you plan to build there. You must learn from example to think of your reader—and also to think more, demand more, of both literature and life. When writing, the important thing to remember is "that, in generosity, forgetting your individual self, you must use your craft to pass on energy and animation and involvement; and if you do it properly, then the craft is understood to be art. You must *aspire*, in order that your readers can do the same" (p. 124). The aunt preaches aspiration not only to good writing but to "moral refinement," lessons which are taught by *Emma*, which Weldon therefore terms "subversive reading" (p. 70). Subversiveness of a banal culture (ours) is not a matter of dyeing your hair or indulging in adultery with your English teacher; one would do better to observe the complex texture of human relations, as Austen did, and keep true, as she did, to standards of fairness and honesty. This is the ultimate lesson of *Letters to Alice*, Weldon's reason for revering Jane Austen and her claim to being connected with her.

Weldon, I said, comes on as an aunt; she comes on even more strongly as a novelist. *Letters to Alice* insists it is a novel even before it begins, in a dedication: "To my mother (who is not, I may say, the one in this book, this epistolary novel; *she* is an entirely invented character, along with Alice, Enid and so forth. . . ." Why then does Weldon sign the letters "Fay"—especially as she is honoring the least unzipped of novelists, who never even put her name on her novels? The answer, I think, is implicit in Weldon's amused view—she shares it with Jane Austen—that the reader's expectations and the writer's self-awareness are equally involved in the production of what she calls "literary truth."

Weldon would probably shudder to be classed among proponents of "personal criticism," which is a term some critics—largely feminist—use to characterize the kind of writing about literature and culture in which the writer's strong emotion, personal history, physical being, or other undignified aspects are revealed, confessed, exhibited, or performed. But she might fairly be accused of writing it, in *Letters to Alice*. Nancy K. Miller, tracing the history of such criticism, describes it as a reaction to the academic criticism that takes for granted a strict separation between the intellectual and the personal life, and puts the first first; she locates the strength and specificity of personal criticism in its commitment to overturning the (gendered) hierarchy.[3] Fay Weldon might not invoke this (American) practice (defined since 1984) to describe *Letters to Alice*, but she enthusiastically embraces a more venerable tradition of criticism (Jane Austen's own) which seems to me to be distantly but palpably related to it—one might say, reaching out for a metaphor, as an aunt and a niece are related. Self-revelation is eschewed by Weldon as it is by Austen; dignity and decorum are maintained; but the partisanship for a devalued "feminine" genre is personal and passionate.

Declaring solidarity with her fellow novelists, the narrator of *Northanger Abbey* protests, "Let us not desert one another; we are an injured body. Although our productions have afforded more extensive and unaffected pleasure than those of any other literary corporation in the world, no species of composition has been so much decried. From pride, ignorance, or fashion, our foes are almost as many as our readers. And while the abilities of the nine-hundredth abridger of the History of England, or of the man who collects and publishes in a volume some dozen lines of Milton, Pope, and Prior, with a paper from the *Spectator*, and a chapter from Sterne, are eulogized by a thousand pens,—there seems almost a general wish of decrying the capacity and undervaluing the labour of the novelist, and of slighting the performances which have only genius, wit, and taste to recommend them." What writers speak of as "only a novel," she concludes, is, "in short, only some work in which the greatest powers of the mind are displayed, in which the most thorough knowledge of human nature, the happiest delineation of its varieties, the liveliest effusions of wit and humour are conveyed to the world in the best chosen language" (pp. 37–38). The rival sides are clearly and unsurprisingly marked: there are essayists and novelists; they are men and women; and Austen, overturning the usual ranking, proudly embraces the second group. Fay Weldon is proud to follow her.

At the end of *Letters to Alice*—which is, after all, only a novel—order is reestablished as in Austenian comedy. The young heroine has not married but published; she has reconciled with her family, and let her hair grow in brown; and maverick Aunt Fay is planning to dine with her sister and even her brother-in-law (of whom we can trust her to continue to take a dim view). Has Alice—as the English teachers ask, about Emma—*learned* anything? Well, her novel is an enormous success—possibly because Fay has instructed her to rewrite and to think of her audience, but possibly because it is a novel simple and silly enough to please a reading public that lacks discrimination and taste. "You have sold more copies of *The Wife's Revenge* in three months than I have of all my novels put together (well, in this country at least. Let me not go too far)," Fay writes in her last letter—keeping a rein on her auntly enthusiasm, and keeping her dignity and distance, and edging her happy romantic ending with irony, as Austen does. A niece, however lucky and happy, does well to keep mindful of the importance of aunts.

Notes

1. See, e.g., Michael Malone, review of Fay Weldon's *Life Force*, *New York Times Book Review*, April 26, 1992, p. 11; William Phillips, review of Doris Lessing's *The Fifth Child*, *Partisan Review* 1 (Winter 1989): 143; James Lardner, "Books," *The New Yorker*, April 13, 1992, p. 104.

2. "Nancy Drew: 30's Sleuth, 90's Role Model," *New York Times*, April 19, 1993.

3. Nancy K. Miller, *Getting Personal: Feminist Occasions and Other Autobiographical Acts* (New York and London: Routledge, 1991), pp. 1–30.

Works Cited

Austen, Jane. *Northanger Abbey and Persuasion*. Ed. R. W. Chapman. London: Oxford, 1954.

Austen, Jane. *Jane Austen's Letters*. Ed. R. W. Chapman. London: Oxford, 1952.

Austen, Jane. *Persuasion*, with *A Memoir of Jane Austen* by J. E. Austen-Leigh. Ed. D. W. Harding. Harmondsworth: Penguin, 1965.

Chapone, Mrs. *Letters on the Improvement of the Mind, Addressed to a Lady*. London, 1773; A New Edition. Printed by C. Whittingham, 1806.

Honan, Park. *Jane Austen: Her Life*. New York: St. Martin's Press, 1987.

Weldon, Fay. *Letters to Alice on first reading Jane Austen*. 1984. New York: Carroll & Graf Publishers, Inc., 1991.

Weldon, Fay. *The Hearts and Lives of Men*. New York: Dell, 1987.

ELISABETH BRONFEN

"Say Your Goodbyes and Go": Death and Women's Power in Fay Weldon's Fiction

In her seminal article "Metaphor-into-Narrative: Being Very Careful with Words," Regina Barreca argues that one of the strategies contemporary women writers have developed, in order to critique the cultural image repertoire within which and against which they write, could be defined as a translation of traditional tropes into tellingly critical stories. "By attaching a buried literal meaning to what is intended to be inert and meaningless," she argues, "women subvert the paradigmatic gesture of relief that is seen to characterize comedy" (p. 244). Reliterализing what has become merely symbolic, this strategy serves to uncover some of the presuppositions tacitly accepted in an act of "feminine transsubstantiation that makes a word the thing itself as well as the representation of the thing." Where the joke depends on the mistake of taking something figuratively when it turns out to have been meant literally, Barreca adds, comedy is more apocalyptic than reassuring.

Giving somatic materiality to what seems safely symbolic in a sense, however, becomes a fascinating and dangerous game with fatality as well. Not only because the resubstantiation turns a living body into a dead sign, but also because it seems to be endowed with an "ability to bring the 'dead' back to life." The duplicity this narrative strategy unfolds is the following. Even as it reduplicates cultural conventions of femininity—by figuratively deadening the stories of real women into clichés—it also revives the dead metaphor in a twofold manner. The cliché as "dead met-

aphor" is shown to be alive after all. At the same time, this resubstantiation also serves to articulate another meaning, namely feminine power,
buried beneath woman's social deformation by cultural representations.
In the following discussion I will offer a reading of two novels by Fay Weldon—*Remember Me* and *Life and Loves of a She-Devil*—so as to delineate
how taking the figurative literally, how giving somatic, bodily quality to
what seems to be safely symbolic can involve fatality as well. The ensuing
"comic turn, turned serious" (*She-Devil*, p. 278) may be seen as a specific
feminist confrontation between comedy and death.

To do so, however, I must add another rhetorical device to my discussion. For in his semiotic analysis of contemporary myths, Roland Barthes
has given a definition of tautology that is apt for an analysis of the feminist
strategy of plot-revision that Weldon employs. "One takes refuge in tautology," he argues, "as one does in fear, or anger, or sadness, when one is
at a loss for an explanation: the accidental failure of language is magically
identified with what one decides is a natural resistance of the object"
(p. 142). The narrative use of tautology involves taking recourse to a rhetoric where like is defined by like, because the reality one seeks to describe
has led one into a discursive impasse. However, rather than attributing
this impasse directly to the condition one seeks to describe, one faults
language instead. In so doing, one shifts the problem of descriptive failure
from one level of signification to another, from the phenomenological or
material to the rhetorical. "In tautology," Barthes continues, "there is a
double murder: one kills rationality because it resists one, one kills language because it betrays one. Tautology is a faint at the right moment, a
saving aphasia, it is a death, or perhaps a comedy, the indignant 'representation' of the rights of reality over and above language. . . . Now any
refusal of language is a death. Tautology creates a dead, motionless world."

I want to highlight the conjunction of death and comedy. Tautology may
testify to a profound distrust of language, which is rejected because it has
failed. At the same time, tautology may also be used to deconstruct why
a certain type of language—certain established plots and metaphors—
ought if not to be rejected, then at least to be mistrusted. If one turns
Barthes's argument inside out, one could argue that narrative instances,
where the comic and the fatal come together, in some way also necessarily
employ the rhetoric strategy of excess as redundancy. For another definition of tautology is that this rhetorical figure produces an emphasis or
precision in definition through the admission of superfluity. Given that in
patriarchal society both the dead and women have, at least in their cultural
constructions, repeatedly been defined as superfluous, the conjunction of
these two concepts—Weldon's repeated use of a dead woman returned to

the living—once again points us into the direction of tautology. This ghostly aspect of the rhetoric of tautology will allow me, a little further on, to discuss two aspects of the uncanniness of the double. For the uncanny double can refer to a dead body returned in the diegetic world of the narrative, but it can also refer to the rhetorical strategy of duplicating a figurative with a literal meaning on the extradiegetic level, the text's structure.

When one is concerned with feminist revisions of cultural representations, it seems necessary to highlight both the axis of continuity and the axis of disruption. That is to say, we need to ask what elements of Western patriarchal culture continue to inhabit our image repertoire as we rethink the stories that are useful for women to write today. I have chosen these two novels by Fay Weldon because their theme is a common one in our culture—ghost stories that delineate the power dead women have over the living. I want to argue that these two novels serve as particularly salient examples for a feminist strategy of writing that undermines the clichés of patriarchal culture by making dead language excessively and thus self-consciously dead, because in these two texts the ghost theme supports a ghostly rhetoric. For the notion both novels address is that feminine characters acquire their power only once they are dead—as angels or demons, as phantoms or ancestors, as monuments or mummys—all of which ultimately point back to the maternal body lost with birth. Or, as Sigmund Freud (1913) formulates the mythopoetic conjunction between femininity and death, there are "three inevitable relations that a man has with a woman—the woman who bears him, the woman who is his mate and the woman who destroys him." The three forms taken by the figure of the mother in the course of a man's life are "the mother herself, the beloved one who is chosen after her pattern, and lastly the Mother Earth who receives him once more" (p. 301). Weldon's comic tautology, her feminine resubstantiation, seems to ask, what does this tripartite feminine death figure look like from the position of the woman, rather than the man? Is it still reassuring, is it so inevitable?

Her narrative strategy of feminine resubstantiation deconstructs this common patriarchal mythopoetics, however, not only by thematically addressing the issue of the powerful feminine ghost, but also by rhetorically constructing a textual revenant. What is significant about these two novels by Fay Weldon, I want to argue, is not only the fact that they disrupt a conventional cultural plot motive in order to offer a feminist deconstruction of presuppositions about femininity, power, and death. Rather, they do so by virtue of the rhetorical strategy of hyperbolic tautology, that is to say by virtue of excess, of exaggeration. The genre these texts can be subsumed under is that of the humorous, which, when in conjunction with a thematic concern with death and when taken to an excessive degree, becomes the macabre. My concern is thus Weldon's use of excessive humor, with her notion of a rhetoric of overturning or redundant doubling that moves back into the literal, to the real, to the serious, even as it remains within the semiotic space of the text and never entirely abandons a comic tone.

The plot common to both novels is that the heroine is placed in a liminal period between life and death, and that she gains authority from this position. Each novel addresses the issue of mourning as a dialectic between remembering and forgetting. In each the dead woman continues to have power over the living, to influence their lives. These revenants are doubled because they appear to be both present and absent, alive and dead. Death places the survivors in a liminal position as well, destabilizes their sense of self and of their position in the world. These dead but returned heroines, these feminine corpses that won't lie still in their graves, pose what Margaret Higonnet has called a "hermeneutic task." They force the survivors to read their death. In order to reestablish peace and sever themselves from the dead woman, the survivors must produce an explanatory text. They must settle on a satisfying interpretation of the death they are suddenly faced with, even as the double body of the deceased woman must be restabilized in the form of a clear separation between her body and her soul. Her grave must be closed, concomitant with a closing of her case. All duplicity and ambivalence that were initially engendered by her ghostly presence and the uncanny power connected with this liminal position must be eliminated.

These two novels by Weldon thus serve as superlative examples for the narrative technique of tautological resubstantiation of clichés, for here the rhetoric of reliteralizing is doubled by the theme of revivification. A safe, figurative meaning loses its reassuring quality by turning literal in narratives where the protagonist either dies to return as a revenant or where she kills her body so as to return as the living embodiment of a cliché of feminine beauty. However, as a dead woman is literally unburied and revived, two forms of rhetorical unburying occur. The socially dead feminine body has its analogy in the supposedly inert and meaningless figurative phrase used to characterize it: in *Remember Me*, the discarded first wife is accused of being a parasitic, burdensome vampire; in *Life and Loves of a She-Devil*, the protagonist realizes that the world wants women to "look up to men." These dead tropes, i.e., cultural conventions, can be materialized only in the advent of death—Madeleine's ghost returns to restructure the lives of those she left behind, and Ruth literally cuts her body up so as to comply with her culture's feminine beauty myth. The sad paradox Weldon deconstructs is that actual death endows her heroines with a power they never had in life.

Yet what radically irritates us, is that these heroines gain power by confirming to excess the cultural formations that were shown to turn them prematurely into inert and meaningless beings. Weldon thus deconstructs clichés of femininity so as to uncover an array of tacitly accepted presuppositions, by showing that curtailing language can conceivably produce real suffering. Yet she does so by having her protagonists perform these cultural formations to excess, in a ghostly representation with their body that reliteralizes the contradiction—Madeleine and Ruth have power, but they are dead or bodily transformed. In her texts, the enactment of a non-coincidence of the story of real women and the cliché "Woman" is such that each female character self-consciously turns her historical self into a figure, resisting an identification with these curtailing images precisely by complying with them, but to excess; "a comic turn, turned serious." They enact what it looks like if the language that performs tropes of femininity becomes reality, so that the figuratively dead feminine body is literally killed, only to become alive and socially powerful for the first time.

In order to illustrate more precisely in what sense each of these texts makes use of a feminist strategy of turning the comic into the serious or turning the serious, on the face of things, into the comic, so that it is this doubled turning that makes up the real tautological excess of these narratives, it will be necessary to digress briefly by turning to a psychoanalytic discussion of the theme and rhetorical function of the ghost as an uncanny double. In his discussion of the concept of the uncanny, Sigmund Freud (1919) turns the lack of a clear definition into the crux of this concept's rhetorical strategy—namely as a semantic subversion based on the blurring of stable concepts. In order to explain the fundamental instability at the core of the uncanny, Freud focuses on two central features. Because in German the word uncanny (unheimlich) refers both to the familiar and the agreeable (one could add the culturally accepted figural meaning) and to something concealed, kept out of sight (the buried, literal meaning) it comes to signify any moment where meaning develops in the direction of ambivalence until it coincides with its opposite. Semantic oppositions collapse and a moment of ambivalence emerges, which induces intellectual hesitation (unsicherheit). As a situation of undecidability, where fixed frames or margins are set in motion, the uncanny also refers to moments where the question whether something is animate (alive) or inanimate (dead), whether something is real (literal) or imagined (figural), a unique original or a repetition, a copy, can not be decided. Again, I would add, the uncanny also marks such moments where serious and comic can not be differentiated. One could extend Freud's definition to include instances that involve the ambivalent distinction between a material animate, immediate and literally self-present body and its representation, as immaterial, inanimate, belated figural body signifying through the interplay of absence and presence. Because the uncanny in some sense always involves the question of visibility/invisibility, presence to/absence from sight, and the fear of losing one's sight serves as a substitute in Western cultural myth and image repertoire for castration anxiety, the uncanny always entails anxieties about fragmentation, about the disruption or destruction of any narcissistically informed sense of personal stability, body integrity, immortal individuality.

Freud locates the main source for an experience of the uncanny in the compulsion to repeat, to re-present, double, supplement; in the recurrence or re-establishment of similarity; in a return to the familiar that has been repressed. This doubling, dividing, and exchanging can, furthermore, involve the subject in his relation to others as she or he either identifies with another, as she or he substitutes the other, external self for her or his own, or as she or he finds her or himself incapable of deciding which of the two her or his self really is. Since the most important boundary blurring inhabited by the uncanny is that between the real and fantasy, Freud finds analogies to the animistic belief in an omnipotence of thought in primitive cultures. He also draws a parallel between the uncanny omnipotence of thought and the developing infant's unrestricted narcissistic valorization of psychic processes over material reality. This gesture of potency is repeated in adult neurosis whenever the ego needs to defend itself against the manifest constraints and prohibitions of the symbolic and the real. An effacement of the boundary distinction between fantasy and reality occurs when something is experienced as real which up to that point was conceived as imagined; when a symbol takes over the full functions and meanings of the object it symbolizes; when a symbol enacts a sublation of signifier and signified or an effacement of the distinction between literal and figural.

One could also extend Freud's definition to say the uncanny marks a moment where desire for something, along with an unbroken belief in the omnipotence of one's ideas, sublates into anxiety about something, into a disbelief in one's own self-construction. When Freud says that the most common images of the uncanny are *doppelgänger* and revenants, the dead returned, he points to a fundamental instability in our attitude toward death. In the figure of the double, death returns as something known but defamiliarized by virtue of a substitution. Instances of the uncanny mark psychic moments where that which returns points to the castration of human existence, more globally understood as its fragmentary, imperfect, and mortal aspect. The double is an ambivalent figure of death since it signifies an insurance that one will continue to live, that the soul is eternal even as the body decomposes, and as such signifies a defense against death. The ghost, and ghostly representations, serve as a triumph over and against material decomposition in the realm or system of real bodily materiality. However, the double is by definition also a figure for a split or gap, a figure signifying that something that was whole and unique has been split into more than one part, and as such a figure for castration or fragmentation. The double simultaneously denies and affirms mortality.

Turning to the two novels by Fay Weldon that I want to focus on, one can ask, how is the excessive rhetorical turn, or the rhetorical turn of excess, that causes a sublation of comic and serious, of figural and literal, or animate and inanimate and produces the ghostly double brought into play? In *Remember Me*, Madeleine, the deserted first wife of the architect Jarvis Katkin, dies in a car accident at exactly the moment that her ex-husband drinks a toast, "death and damnation to all ex-wives," only to add, "Madeleine, I hate you . . . die" (p. 83). While she was alive, she was figuratively compared by her husband and his new wife, Lily, to an ogre, a vampire, a leech, to succubi and to old women "who suck men's blood, destroy their life forces" (p. 80). As her dead body lies more or less uncovered on the road, in the hospital, in the morgue before its final interment, she literally becomes a revenant. In accordance with vampire legends, she splits in two. Though the state of her body is such that life cannot possibly be present, her face is that of a person in deep sleep. In the course of her uncanny presence beyond death, she repeatedly opens and closes her eyes, and to her spectators her face, drained of blood, smoothed out, is "as beautiful as it has ever been" (p. 91).

At the moment of death, uncanny disturbances occur; the window bangs and rattles, clocks stop, and Lily's son gets a fever, only to remain ill until the corpse is safely buried. More importantly, at the moment of death, Madeleine takes possession of Margot Bailey, her friend and ex-mistress of Jarvis, so as to turn her into her body double. At first Margot merely symptomizes the pains Madeleine would have felt had she not died, notably her severed leg and her crushed chest, and these pains remain with her for the period of the deceased woman's presence beyond death. In the course of her revenant visitations, however, Madeleine uses Margot's body to proclaim her own subversive statements on the subjugation of women, to which her peers would not listen during her lifetime. With the dead woman inside her, "warming her up to unspeakable deeds"

(p. 212), Margot is herself endowed with an uncanny power to articulate her own grievances to her husband in a way she never could before. Significantly, her husband responds to this doubling of roles by saying, "Margot . . . you are not Madeleine. You are my wife. Madeleine is dead. This is some kind of hysteria" (p. 224).

Furthermore, Madeleine uses her body double to regulate the future of her daughter Hilary. For at the moment of death she significantly forgets her anger at her husband and remembers her responsibility as mother. She thus returns from the dead, in accordance with vampire lore, not only to articulate her grievances but also because her child needs her to find her a more suitable home with the Baileys, away from a stepmother and a stepbrother. Madeleine's death comes, in Hilary's words, to be "the best thing she could do for me: this was her best and final gift" (p. 230).

The cultural commonplace Weldon thus resubstantiates so as to disclose its tacit assumptions is that a woman who alive, it seems, was nothing, once dead at least "proves a point and becomes the focus of womanly discontent" (p. 100). More effective in death than in life, the dispossessed Madeleine comes to assert her power as she haunts and takes possession of her survivors. Because the freezing unit at the morgue is full, her body remains among the living, lying sheeted and seemingly harmless on a trolley. In fact, as though Weldon wanted to show death to excess, Madeleine remains unburied for an exaggerated period of time because, as the undertaker drives her away, a second road accident occurs, and her corpse is returned to the morticians. Yet, far from lying still, forgetting the wrongs done to her, saying her good-byes and going, she visits her friends and family to proclaim precisely these wrongs.

Once she haunts Jarvis, he consciously acknowledges her interests in a way he didn't while she was alive, and for the period of her revenant return she causes strife and difference in his marriage. In a sense, her haunting presence unburies a hidden truth in the romantic and social exchanges among her survivors which, under normal circumstances, lie tacitly submerged. Only once she has been properly identified, inquested, taken to the undertaker's, and safely buried can a semblance of domestic order be recuperated. If during her life she used to bother her husband with her vengeful presence to no avail, her visitations as a dead woman have such an effect that Jarvis sides with her against his second wife (though ironically the issue is the cost of Madeleine's funeral). He accuses Lily of callous and monstrous selfishness in much the same way that Madeleine did, though unheard, while she was still alive. Furthermore, once Madeleine is dead, Jarvis desires her again precisely because her uncanny death undoes a firm division between the present and the past. One of Weldon's points, of course, is to show that in love the concrete woman is inter-changeable, insofar as she, reduced to being an object of desire, corre-sponds to a mental image of the beloved. Yet Weldon's critique is such that, in the midst of Jarvis's erotic bliss, the body double speaks the de-ceased woman's accusations: "You took away my life, my home, and gave them to Lily" (p. 205). Jarvis in turn comes to recognize "I was unfair to her." When in Weldon's text the dead beloved returns, she does so with a voice of her own that can now be heard for the first time.

Indeed, Madeleine's uncanny presence after death creates social bonds that stand diametrically opposed to her uncanny absence in life. The par-adox Weldon enacts is that her body "so little regarded in life, has in death become the focal point of some kind of group energy . . . which sends our communities lurching in one direction or another towards their gradual betterment" (p. 147). At the same time, her uncanny corpse also serves as the site for a general accusation of the mortification of women in culture. In her presence, the two mortuary attendants, Clarence and Goliath, seem to hear a chorus of voices asking "Why is she dead? Who killed her? Who drove her to it?" Yet hearing these voices merely serves to confront them with the insinuation of their own guilt—"some man . . . who? You?" (pp. 100, 135).

Juliet Mitchell has suggested that the woman writer might well be a hysteric. Hysteria, understood as the simultaneous acceptance and refusal of the fictions of femininity culture offers, is, she suggests "what a woman can do both to be feminine and to refuse femininity, within patriarchal discourse." Rejecting the notion of female writing, of an authentic wom-an's voice, she argues instead for "the hysteric's voice, which is *the wom-an's masculine language* . . . talking about feminine experience. It's both simultaneously the woman novelist's refusal of a woman's world—she is, after all, a novelist—and her construction from within a masculine world of that woman's world" (p. 290). Or, to fit the theme of my discussion, it is the woman writer's comic refusal of the metaphorical death or non-existence culture ascribes to her—for, after all, she writes and signs her text—and her hyperbolic performance from within the masculine discur-sive formations of precisely that death which is woman's terrain.

Linda Hutcheon in turn suggests that postmodern parodic strategies are often used by woman writers "to point to the history and historical power of those cultural representations, while ironically contextualizing both in such a way as to deconstruct them" (p. 102). She adds that such a strategy may make for an ambivalent political stance, since its double encoding means the simultaneous complicity with and contestation of the cultural dominants within which it operates. Yet I want to argue that though comic hyperbole, understood as a hysterical rereading against the grain, may be complicitous with the values it inscribes even as it subverts them, subversion does remain. I would thus like to call this comic hyperbole, this ghostly feminine transubstantiation, a hysterical strategy, so as to link parody explicitly with the feminine position.

What Jarvis says about the body double Margot/Madeleine he is erotically attracted to is equally applicable to Weldon's text as a whole: this is some kind of hysteria. There is no dialectic resolution or recuperative evasion of contradiction even as there is also complicity. The problem is that if the mastering gaze that separates the subject from the object of gaze is inherently masculine, can there be a feminine gaze? In response to this impasse, hysterical writing responds with a tautology. It installs conventions such as the masculinity of the gaze, the deadness of the feminine body, only to subvert and disturb the security of these stakes in cultural self-representation. Though such a critique is inscribed by complicity, such complicity may also be the most effective critique. As Hutcheon notes, "complicity inevitably conditions the radicality of the critique and the possibility of suggesting change, but it may also be one of the only ways for feminist art to exist" (p. 102).

The comic turn, turned serious in Weldon's narrative hinges on precisely such a ghostly hysterical duplicity of critique and complicity. For although Jarvis's joke turns literal and endows the revenant Madeleine with a power she never had in life, the seriousness is such that it takes the resubstantiated joke one turn further to the impasse that her heroine can also have this power only once she is dead. At the same time, though the last sentence of the novel implies that with Madeleine's burial, trouble was dispersed and peace has been restored, Weldon suggests that a moment of difference, of the woman's self-articulation in death, is preserved precisely at the site of her body double. It is not clear whether Margot speaks in her own voice or with the resonance that came with Madeleine's death. In fact, she says "I am Margot and Madeleine in one, and always was. She was my sister, after all, and she was right: her child was mine, and mine was hers" (p. 232).

In the other novel I want to discuss, Life and Loves of a She-Devil, the big, clumsy, and sulky Ruth enacts her social death as the first step in an intricate plan of revenge against her husband, Bobbo, who has deserted her to live with the graceful, delicate, and elegant romance writer, Mary Fisher. She burns down her house, sends her children to their father, and disappears, taking on the duplicitously ghostly position between presence and absence. As a result, Bobbo can't marry Mary Fisher because he can not get divorced from a woman he can't produce in court; though she might very well be dead, the law will not declare her so without specular proof of her corpse. In the liminality between a social and a biological death, with no distinct identity, the revenant Ruth, a double of herself, assumes different names to perform a variety of professions as part of a brilliant design meant to destroy her rival and get her husband back, "but on my own terms" (p. 85).

She works as a nurse in an insane asylum, learns accounting and book-keeping, opens an agency that places secretaries with firms, and finds a position as housekeeper to a judge, and then a priest. In the course of her monstrous plan, she breaks into Bobbo's office, alters his files to assure that he will be put on trial for embezzlement, convinces the judge to give him a seven-year sentence with no bail, and transfers two million dollars from his personal account to their joint account in Switzerland. Mary Fisher, in turn, loses all her money in the lawsuit, is forced to watch the slow deterioration of her beautiful home in a tower by the sea, and loses her gift for writing successful romance novels. Tired, impoverished, with Bobbo in prison and refusing to see her, she wants to be dead in the ro-mantic image of being "at one with the stars and the foaming sea" (p. 243). Yet she dies in a hospital, forlorn and deserted by all, deprived even of her beauty as a result of medical treatment.

In this text also the excessive rhetorical turn, or the rhetorical turn of excess, engenders a sublation of the comic into the serious, a disturbingly uncanny enmeshment of the figural with the literal. The brilliant twist Weldon gives to the resolution of Ruth's vengeance against her husband and her rival is a critical rereading of the theme of the dead first wife re-turned at the body of her double, for which one could see Poe's romantic horror story "Ligeia" as the model. The exchange between social death and rebirth Ruth enacts with each new profession becomes concrete, or rather is enacted at her body, when in the course of surgery, this body is literally killed and reborn. And this desubstantiation and return is, fur-thermore, mirrored by the trajectory of her double, Mary Fisher's life. The more Mary Fisher's beautiful body deteriorates physically, the more Ruth changes her ugly body into a beautiful one; gets new teeth, loses weight. Indeed, the body she convinces her surgeons to change her into, with the money she has transferred to Switzerland, is precisely the pretty, delicate body of Mary Fisher, as Ruth finds it on the dust jacket of one of her novels. Recreating herself in the image of the woman her husband preferred to her, she recreates herself as a repetition of the publicity image of that fantasy.

The trope Weldon thus installs so as to critique it is first the cliché that woman needs to kill herself into a beautiful ideal to have power over her husband. At the same time, she deconstructs the definition of love, which poses woman as man's phantom, as the symptom of his fantasies. Her story of a woman of six foot two, "who had tucks taken in her legs," literalizes the cliché of the perfect beloved serving as the site where an earlier love object or mental image is refound by the masculine lover, yet she does so to such an excess that the result is literally a comic turn, turned serious. Due to her exaggeration, Ruth exceeds, even as she performs the cultural dictate that if woman needs man's gaze to assure her being alive, she is as good as dead once she has lost this eye, so she can just as well literally kill her body. She fulfills the social death her husband performed by leaving her, and which she embellished by literally disappearing when, about to enter surgery, she says good-bye to her body "that had so little to do with her nature, and knew she'd be glad to be rid of it" (p. 242). Her social resurrection can only occur when she takes on the body of the woman who displaced her in her husband's gaze, when she returns as a copy of the body of Mary Fisher.

Furthermore, her recreation is seen in analogy to the conventions of fairy-tale and gothic imagery, as though her reshaped body were not only resurrecting her dead predecessor but also revitalizing these clichés. Of one surgeon, she says "he was her Pygmalion," only to add "but she would not depend upon him, or admire him, or be grateful" (p. 249). When she finally leaves the hospital, she evokes Anderson's Little Mermaid, for the final dance with her doctor is such that "with every step it was as if she trod on knives" (p. 275). Another surgeon refers to her "as Frankenstein's monster, something that needed lightning to animate it and get it moving" (p. 271), and indeed, what is being reanimated are doubly dead body parts—her killed body and the imitation of the dead Mary Fisher. Rhetorically, one could thus add, Ruth seems to resubstantiate these cultural texts in the same gesture that she revitalizes Mary Fisher's conventional beauty. Yet the feminine transsubstantiation is here, too, duplicitous. In the monstrous act of totally refashioning her body, she both is and isn't the first Mary Fisher. She both confirms and critiques the textual models of Pygmalion's and Frankenstein's creations.

In that she reemerges in the guise of the second beloved, who herself has died for loss of Bobbo's supporting gaze, Weldon's narrative ends with the first wife returned at the site of the second beloved's body, but as the ghost of the second woman. At Mary Fisher's funeral, Ruth makes her first appearance and is duly recognized by her rival's mother as the deceased sending "her own ghost to her funeral!" Bobbo, to whom she says she is his wife, answers, "My wife died . . . long ago . . . but there was someone called Mary Fisher. Aren't you her?" (p. 272). What Weldon implies, with the resubstantiation of a trope over the resurrected body of a dead woman, is that when the beloved is literally a refound mental image, she proves to be monstrous and duplicitous—the angel and the she-devil in one, both alive and dead. Ruth's self-creation out of death permanently installs an uncanny double—she is Mary Fisher in body and the vindictive Ruth in spirit, the dead body of her rival returned and her own body destroyed. She triumphs over her social death by confirming this social death, since the body she returns in is that of her rival. She says of Bobbo, "he has us both in the one flesh: the one he discarded, the one he never needed at all. Two Mary Fishers" (p. 277). As an uncanny double, she simultaneously affirms and denies both her and Bobbo's mortality.

In this pose of the uncanny double, Ruth is so monstrous because external bodily perfection shelters the aggressive desire to reek destruction. As she explains, "I cause Bobbo as much misery as he ever caused me, and more." Yet, the act of realizing her deep-seated desire for destruction is a sword that cuts both ways. Ruth has gained power by having resubstantiated an image. But this acquisition of power required that she deform herself into the image of perfect feminine beauty. Taking the desire of her husband too seriously, Ruth exaggerates her attempt to comply to such a degree that she discloses the underlying cruelty. The impasse her excessive performance enacts is that in order to castrate her husband, and with him the cultural formations he represents, she has to castrate herself, to die socially and then somatically. Therein lies the monstrosity of tautology, of which Barthes says, it is an ugly word, but so is the thing.

In both novels, then, Weldon uncannily returns to her heritage, to the image repertoire of patriarchal culture, so as to repeat, invert, and reinvent in the duplicitous gesture of miming and disclosing. In both texts, she demonstrates a hysteric's voice, oscillating between complicity and resistance. She accepts the validity of masculine narrative formations and tropes only to show that these may be a necessary truth, but not the only truth there is. She plays with these narrative plots, takes them seriously by representing what it looks like if conventions are taken to their hyperbolic extreme, or purposely misunderstood so as to move from the figural into the literal. By using distance and comedy she takes conventions to excess only to transform them into the macabre and the grotesque. Even as this excess, this hyperbolic overturning of the trope, engenders a comic mode, it makes the resulting clichés true, and in this tautology unbearable because obvious, unavoidable, irrevocable. By reliteralizing tropes, and thus disclosing the presuppositions hidden beneath cultural commonplaces, Weldon's parody or excess of the hysteric voice stages the impasse women find themselves in. Her rhetoric of tautology self-consciously engages with the deadness of the tropes and plots which continually fashion women's stories by compulsively repeating this mortification. Showing heroines who take on the guise of the revenant so as to refuse the metaphorical death culture ascribes to them even as they perform that death which is the prescribed woman's terrain, she ultimately discloses the tautology beyond which a woman writing as yet can't move.

Bibliography

Barreca, Regina. "Metaphor-into-Narrative: Being Very Careful with Words." *Last Laughs. Perspectives on Women and Comedy*, ed. R. Barreca. New York: Gordon and Breach, 1988.

Barthes, Roland. "Myth Today." In *A Barthes Reader*, ed. Susan Sontag. New York: Hill and Wang, 1982.

Berger, John. *Ways of Seeing*. Harmondsworth: Penguin, 1972.

Bronfen, Elisabeth. *Over Her Dead Body. Death, Femininity and the Aesthetic.* Manchester/New York: Manchester University Press/Routledge, 1992.

Freud, Sigmund. "The Theme of the Three Caskets." London: Hogarth Press. *The Standard Edition XII*. London: Hogarth Press, 1913.

———. "The Uncanny." *The Standard Edition XVII*. London: Hogarth Press, 1919.

Higonnet, Margaret. "Speaking Silences: Women's Suicide." *The Female Body in Western Culture*, ed. Susan Suleiman. Cambridge: Harvard University Press, 1986.

Homans, Margaret. *Bearing the World. Language and Female Experience in Nineteenth-Century Women's Writing*. Chicago: University of Chicago Press, 1986.

Hutcheon, Linda. *The Politics of Postmodernism*. London: Routledge, 1989.

Kofman, Sarah. *Quatres romans analytiques*. Paris: Galilée, 1973.

Lacan, Jacques. *Feminine Sexuality*, eds. Juliet Mitchell and Jacqueline Rose. New York: Norton, 1985.

Mitchell, Juliet. *Women: The Longest Revolution. Essays in Feminism, Literature and Psychoanalysis*. London: Virago, 1984.

Weldon, Fay. *Remember Me*. New York: Random House, 1976.

———. *The Life and Loves of a She-Devil*. New York: Random House, 1983.

Zizek, Slavoj. *Enjoy your Symptom! Jacques Lacan in Hollywood and out*. New York: Routledge, 1992.

ROSE QUIELLO

Going to Extremes: The Foreign Legion of Women in Fay Weldon's *The Cloning of Joanna May*

No man should marry until he has studied anatomy and dissected at least one woman.—Honoré de Balzac

You're a piece of drifting slime in a murky female pool. You're all alike, you women.—Carl May, from *The Cloning of Joanna May*

You "skirts" are all alike.—Philip Scarpellino, my grandfather

Recombinant DNA is the process of "unzippering" elements of the DNA molecule and recombining them in different ways. Through recombinant DNA we now have the potential to create organisms that nature never dreamed of, and by doing so, challenge the whole idea of what is natural or normal. New organisms created by genetic intervention can be cloned indefinitely. We simply need to look at the uniformity and the flawlessness of the red delicious apples at the supermarket to realize that we now have the reproductive technology, should we choose to implement that knowledge, to nail down the color, sex, and IQ, as well as a host of other characteristics of our children, in utero. In *The Cloning of Joanna May*, Fay Weldon takes the scientific theories of "parthenogenesis" (that is, the reproduction arising from a fertilized egg that has *not* been fertilized by the male, or what is more commonly known as "unisex" reproduction) and recombinant DNA[1] (which is composed of spiral threads that encode and perpetuate genetic history in every cell), and she plays with them on an imaginative level: "Not cloning in the modern sense," says Carl May, the stern-daddy husband of Joanna in Weldon's novel, "but parthenogenesis plus implantation, and a good time had by all" (p. 34). Science never answers the question of "why" we do the things we do; it only answers the question of "how" we do them. But Weldon explains *why* as she explores the problematic subject between the patriarchal power that accompanies scientific knowledge and women's rights. *The Cloning of Joanna May* is unabashedly a book about women's rights and the violation of those rights: particularly, women's reproductive rights. Ultimately, Weldon moves women centrally into the political process as she wrests the power from men and assigns her women the right to determine their own fate. *The Cloning of Joanna May* is not a love story.

Carl May would like us to think that he is entrapped and beguiled in a hellish marriage to Joanna (and perhaps he is)—one in which Joanna violates all his expectations of fidelity by committing the ultimate transgression of adultery. After all, Carl *was* willing to give Joanna a home, if she only would agree to stay in it. But Weldon, who is unusually affectionate and never malicious in her treatment of Carl, reminds us that it is Carl's sense of a scarred and troublesome past which now informs his misogynistic view of women. Like the very structure of the DNA that Carl and his colleague Dr. Holly manipulate, threads of Carl May's past get tangled and tighten inside him like a string inside a cat's stomach. As the first few chapters of the book unfold, Carl is stuck in the mud of his own childhood horrors and has nothing left to do now but spin his intellectual wheels.

When Carl no longer gets sexual and emotional satisfaction from unzippering his fly, he (in collaboration with Dr. Holly) decides to "unzip" the DNA molecule and clone his wife, Joanna, in the hope of capitalizing on the multiplier effect: "When he multiplied Joanna, he had not so much tried to multiply perfection—that was a tale for Holly—he had done it to multiply her love for him, multiply it fourfold: to make up for what he never had" (p. 241). It is important to note that Joanna's eggs were removed by Carl and Dr. Holly while she was under anesthesia for a "mock abortion," for her "hysterical pregnancy," which was replete with all the symptoms of a visibly swollen belly and morning sickness. Weldon conjoins the nexus of power and sex with the metaphor of Joanna's vacant, pseudo-pregnant womb, the symbolic repudiation of women's subjugation in which legitimate sex is harnessed to its reproductive consequences. Joanna's body speaks boldly as a spontaneous form of women's anger because, for Weldon, female sexuality need not find its sanction in procreation and marriage.

Weldon attacks the medical profession's tendency to diagnose women's illness as psychosomatic; performing an abortion on a "non-baby," so to speak, was Carl's and Dr. Holly's clever way of promoting the idea that Joanna was "sick" while at once denigrating her. It is because Carl does not have the capacity to provide "Love and Kisses" (p. 33), the alternative treatment that Dr. Holly suggested in lieu of a "mock abortion," that Carl opts for the surgical removal of Joanna's "non-baby" (p. 33).[2] Carl explains his manhandling of Joanna's body to his new, young lover, Bethany: "So that's what we did. Told her she was to have a termination, anaesthetized her, and whee-e-ee, like a balloon going down, went Joanna's belly. When she woke up she was cured. My lovely wife, slim and fresh and all for me again" (p. 33). While under anesthesia and consequently unconscious of what was happening to her, tentacles of the patriarchy now reached literally into Joanna's womb to remove her eggs as Carl reminisces on his Frankensteinesque omnipotence: "While she was opened up we took away a nice ripe egg; whisked it down to the lab: shook it up and irritated it in amniotic fluid till the nucleus split, and split again, and then there were four. . . . We kept the embryos in culture for four whole weeks, had four nice healthy wombs waiting at hand and on tap for implantation" (p. 34). *The Cloning of Joanna May* is replete with examples of medical atrocities performed in the interest of male power, in which women's bodies are violated: "'Bloody men,' said Mavis, Dr. Holly's secretary, 'so competitive, always muscling in on women's wombs'" (p. 183). And Annette, the surrogate-mother of one of the clones, underscores the antiwoman bias of the medical community when she says: "They told a friend of mine she had cancer and they'd got the slides mixed. She got the radium treatment and the worry while the other stayed home happy and died. They'll tell you anything that suits them, these doctors" (p. 212). Weldon contextualizes women's vulnerability as the policing of women's bodies becomes more and more intrusive and fundamentally antidemocratic. Annette goes on to say: "No such thing as rights. . . . A girlfriend of mine was raped under anaesthetic, but would anyone believe her? No" (pp. 212–13). One need not delve far into the annals of medical history to locate the inestimable damage done to women's bodies by male doctors. Weldon sees the horror of the medical profession's abuse of women and, in response, we see the horror.

Weldon, however, delights in fouling up male expectations by presenting us with women who are legitimate spoils of power. She constructs a kind of inverted pyramid of unlikeliness, the whole thing balanced precariously on the idea (or *absurdity*, if one is already familiar with Weldon's work) that in cloning Joanna May, his unfaithful wife, Carl "might create the perfect woman, one who looked, listened, understood and was faithful" (p. 78). Selective breeding; gene splicing: "I can make a thousand thousand of you," Carl tells Joanna, "fragment all living things and recreate them. I can splice a gene or two" (p. 109). If genes determine human behavior, Carl wonders why *women's* behavior shouldn't be genetically determined. And once Carl had Joanna cloned, he "thought if he had Bethany [his present young lover] cloned, he could undo the effects of her upbringing" (p. 78). Nevertheless, Weldon reminds us that breeding can't be done along benign lines, and that women cannot be culled as plants.

Carl May's self-serving notion that cloning Joanna would produce genetically-linked, submissive paper-dolls ultimately backfires: "How much easier theory was than practice. . . . He had thought to breed passivity, and had manufactured its opposite" (p. 231). What were intended to be fetishized, uniformed personifications of subjectivity, all under the tutelage of Carl, turn out to be unsubdued, uncensored, and unfaithful heroines who come in all shapes and sizes and who are only related by their unfaithfulness. In the spirit of Joanna, their "mother," the clones had no intention of remaining monogamous: "Like their master copy, Jane, Julie, Gina, and Alice, for good or for bad, were of a nature which preferred to have the itch of desire soothed and out of the way rather than seeing in its gratification a source of energy and renewal. Here comes sex, they said in their hearts, here comes trouble" (p. 81). Taken out of the context of their own oppression, the clones can only be seen by Carl as monstrous. Hélène Cixous's eloquently argued essay "The Laugh of the Medusa," which is an invocation to all "monstrous" women to acquiesce to their desires, addresses society's inability to accommodate women who refuse to capitulate to convention: "Who feeling a funny desire stirring inside her (to sing, to write, to dare to speak, in short to bring out something new) hasn't thought she was sick? Well, her shameful sickness is that she resists death, that she makes trouble" (p. 876). Despite Carl's wish for Joanna that "she must die, [because] she'll go on to ruin other men" (p. 209), Weldon's heroines don't die. As Weldon trenchantly dismantles the old double standard, unrepressed female sexuality does not lead to death. Weldon knows better. Her protagonists "resist" death because truth-telling for Weldon does not consist of the nihilism of women. Instead, her protagonists flaunt convention and law as they go on to commit a kind of cultural genocide.

Weldon provides a satiric commentary on the stifling institution of motherhood, which she cites as oppressive to both mothers and those who are not mothers. She presages an endangered future in presenting us with heroines who refuse to reproduce or who are unable to. In terms of progeny, the May nest is empty. And Alice "discovered the power of active nonpleasing . . . looked at herself in the mirror one day and decided not to have children, not to get married" (p. 92); Gina, in which the "double helix of DNA became blurred," had "one stillborn baby, Down's Syndrome, and four abortions" (p. 88); Julie, who was born with "one tooth already cut" and who had bitten her surrogate-mother on the way out (p. 87), "would have loved to have children, but Alec couldn't have them" (p. 86); and even proper mothering creates problems for Jane who, by the way, is also childless: "It was my mother made me what I am, and what I am is what I'm not. So thought Jane, as she looked for forks clean enough to lay the table with" (p. 221).[3] Here Weldon provides us with the ultimate breakdown of the tradition of woman-as-mother, and subverts cultural expectations by presenting us with heroines who refuse to conform to the gendered roles of wifehood and motherhood.

In Freudian terms, cloning might imply a return to the womb. In Christian terms, a cloning symbolizes a return to a particular God that Joanna's English teacher, Miss Watson, drummed into her impressionable young head: "I would define God as the source of all identity," thinks Joanna to herself at the outset of the novel, "the only 'I' from which flow the myriad, myriad 'you's'" (p. 45). It is interesting to note that later on in the novel Joanna dismisses her earlier "concept of a single God" which she now considered to be a "narrowing of [her] perception, not an expansion" (p. 98). The following passage is worth quoting at length:

God flew off in three stages, if you ask me. . . . God the Father flew off on the day mankind first interfered with his plans for the procreation of the species: that was the day the first woman made a connection between semen and pregnancy, and took pains to stop the passage by shoving some pounded, mud-steeped, leaf inside her. He flew off in a pet. "But this is *contraception*," he cried, "this is not what I meant. . . ." God the Son flew off the day the first pregnant woman made the next connection and shoved a sharpened stick up inside her to put an end to morning sickness and whatever else was happening inside. "But this is *abortion*," he cried, "it's revolting, and no place for a pro-lifer like me to be. . . ." And God the Holy Ghost flew off the day Dr. Holly of the Bulstrode Clinic, back in the fifties, took one of my ripe eggs out and warmed it, and jiggled it, and irritated it in an amniotic brew until the nucleus split, and split again, and split again, and then started growing, each with matching chromosomes, with identical DNA, that is to say faults and propensities, physical and social, all included, blueprint for four more individuals, and only one soul between them. [P. 155]

In this passage, Weldon cogently demonstrates how the ideologies of womanhood and motherhood are historically, ecclesiastically, and scientifically constructed. She shows how institutional religion, which devalues women and practices censorship of opposing voices, provides no comfort as she invites all women to redefine for themselves what is sacred.

Sherry Ortner's well-known article "Is Female to Male as Nature is to Culture?" is relevant in helping us to understand that the issue of women's reproduction is directly linked to the valuation of women and the location of their cultural, economic, and political power in society. The thrust of Ortner's elegantly argued essay is that cultural notions of women center on their biological functions as women, which universally get allied with what is natural, primitive, and untamed. Men, in contrast, are associated with "culture": they decide essentially what is valuable or worthwhile or weighty in this world—they make the rules. Patricia Meyer Spacks underscores Ortner's thesis when she writes that "Culture is a male concept. The woman dismisses talk about it as mere 'babble,' her own orientation personal. Its personal quality, however, implies her capacity—contradicting Freud's generalization—to accept 'the great exigencies of life' not by explaining them, but by enduring them" (p. 46). It should come as no surprise that when Mavis revisits the locus of her own psychic pain after her abortion, she reflects on it with hardly suppressed outrage: "They knocked you unconscious and did what they wanted: you couldn't object, what you were doing was wrong, illegal. She was sorry to have to speak like this, it sounded unhinged, but she'd never recover from the experience, for it was thirty-five years ago" (p. 215). The intimidatory tactics of the medical and legal system leave very little room for moral diversity and speak to women's lack of legislative power. Weldon drives home the point that still to be heard are the voices of women, like Mavis, who have chosen abortion, and their complicated and legitimate reasons for opting to terminate pregnancies. Adrienne Rich touches the philosophical essence of Weldon when she writes: "The repossession by women of our bodies will bring far more essential change to human society than the seizing of the means of production by workers. . . . We need to imagine a world in which every woman is the presiding genius of her own body. . . . Sexuality, politics and intelligence, position, motherhood, work, community, intimacy will develop new meanings; thinking itself will be transformed. This is where we have to begin" (p. 292).

Also in keeping with Ortner's argument, the text invites another reading: cloning Joanna symbolically embodies Carl's masculine fantasy of giving birth as a way of compensating for his inability to reproduce biologically, as he attempts to transcend nature and by extension women who, because of their reproductive capacities, get allied with nature and all that is natural. Carl tells Joanna: "I, man, want to teach nature a thing or two, in particular the difference between good and bad" (p. 111). The ideological implications of Carl's thinking are readily apparent to us as Carl realizes that "the shuffling of DNA, the improvement of physique and personality, could now be done at will. . . . What could you do to them? Require the skill, refine the spirit, make *good* (Weldon's italics) not bad" (p. 240). In *Women Under the Knife: A History of Surgery*, Dr. Ann Daly writes that "Science tends to grow from the established ideas and institutions of its age. . . . The strongest powers of science were invoked to keep women in their place. . . ." (p. 69) Of importance is the implication we can garner from the scientific framework for understanding genetic reproduction, which then takes on the significance of superior/inferior or masculine/feminine or active/passive within the framework of values that are culturally developed and defined.

Yet to focus on the cloning of Joanna by Carl as a masculine and therefore artificial substitute for the creative process would be to miss the wider and more dangerous significance of Carl's action. We are talking about much more than womb-envy here. We need to put Carl's ambitious effort into a political context as we take into consideration what Carl means when he talks about "shuffling" the DNA molecule and making "good not bad." We know that what constitutes good and bad is all relative to the person who is doing the identifying. It is also crucial to note that a "good" gene, in biological terms, is that which is capable of differential reproduction success; that is, that which reproduces at the greatest rate. Here Weldon explores what happens when scientific theories, which are primarily male constructs, are applied to social thought in which women occupy a fringe, political position. Carl's and Dr. Holly's misogyny comes under the guise of scientific authority, as well as their desire to better "mankind" (and I use "mankind" here purposefully):

Dr. Holly felt, and Carl felt with him, that an evolutionary process which caused so much grief could surely be improved upon by man: genetic engineering would hardly add to the sum of human misery, so a great sum that was, and might just possibly make matters a good deal better. . . . No doubt in time techniques of artificial reproduction would be further advanced and manipulation of DNA itself made possible so that improved and disease-resistant human beings could in the end be produced. [P. 89]

But those in power decide what is genetically desirable, both inside and outside the laboratory and inside and outside the womb. After all, for Hitler, the Holocaust was a side effect. Hitler's quasi-honorable aim, like Carl's and Dr. Holly's, was to improve mankind. But the concomitant of Carl's argument is that artificially reproducing women—manufacturing them as assemblages of parts without rights, which, by the way, is at the very core of the outrageous violence toward women—gives Carl the illusion that he will be able to control them.

To be sure, Weldon can see through Carl May's and Dr. Holly's actions, and can see clearly where their machinations will end. She has her heroines plot a punishment for Carl and Dr. Holly which is far more appropriate (and funnier) than the one that they had planned for them. The downhill slide begins to Carl May and Dr. Holly when Joanna's clones—Julie, Jane, Gina, and Alice—set out to find each other and eventually unite. The results are disastrous for the men. At one point, Dr. Holly, who "suffers from gigantitism of the head" (p. 243) wonders: "Supposing they felt as entitled to end him as he has to begin them? What would happen to his research? Has he remembered to put away his own dehydrated DNA?" (p. 235) And by the end of the novel, nuclear-devotee Carl May abandons his own nefarious scheme as he slides inexorably toward his own extinction. He ridiculously "jumped into the cooling pond [of a nuclear reactor] to prove low-level waste was no threat to anyone, and the future of nuclear power, clean, efficient, safe, would be assured" (p. 258). "Fate was unkind," writes Weldon, "but just" (p. 262).

Carl and Dr. Holly—with the physician's arrogance that historically comes from knowing that patients will hang on his every word and then accept unquestioningly what he tells them—are not prepared for the reaction of the clones. Using Carl's idea, Weldon transforms the masculinity of his fantasized omnipotence into a subversive critique of patriarchy: "You should carry on," Joanna tells Carl, "you might end up doing more good than harm" (p. 109). Weldon inaugurates a counterstrategy as she subverts Carl's notion of cloning as a loss of individuality. Joanna offers the cloning of women as a creed against the prevailing ideology which manhandles and regulates women's bodies. She tells Carl: "I see a different world. . . . I see one which is perfectible without tampering" (p. 109).

Nevertheless, Weldon's heroines forge a pact and fight back, and the collective sisterhood of Joanna and her clones, Julie, Gina, Jane, and Alice, provides Joanna with an emotional network in which her power is quadrupled rather than divided: "When I acknowledged my sisters, my twins, my clones, my children, I stood out against Carl May. . . . Joanna May is now Alice, Julie, Gina and Jane" (p. 247). In Weldon's matrilineal line of descent, only the malignant guilt is divided: "They felt the inherent guilt of the female, but not all powerfully; being four that guilt was quartered. The soul was multiplied, the guilt divided. That was a great advance" (p. 236). Weldon's works configure into a tradition of novels by women writers in her illustration of the ways that society psychologically and sexually ravages women: "We've had so many oughts and shoulds, all of us, we're all but given up being critical of one another. Good for her, say we" (p. 265). With astonishing psychological acumen, Weldon understands women who have been bamboozled into creatures of someone else's making as she openly acknowledges what women have been forced to fight.

In *The Cloning of Joanna May*, Weldon hopes to flash a warning signal about dead-end values which imply that intellectual excellence requires depersonalization as Dr. Holly laments the condition of his office: "The room was male, male; straight lines, hard-edged: he now saw what was wrong with it. No pot plants, no family photographs, no cushions—not an ashtray, not a coffee cup—nothing to bear witness to human frailty, everything to further unimpassioned thought, that divine inspiration, that necessary trigger if Utopia was ever to be achieved" (p. 232). To be sure, Weldon, whose stories are like pieces of a jigsaw puzzle, not strings of beads, disestablishes scientific authority as she exposes the narrowness of antihuman behavior which does not include potted plants, family photos, and coffee cups and all that they come to represent. She is asking us to rename the affective lives of women.

Weldon's women throw open the curtains of the bay windows and take a penetrating look at the outside world: "Nail me and alter me, fix me and distort me," Joanna tells Carl, "I'll still have windows" (p. 110). Joanna's rebuttal to Carl articulates Weldon's plurality of vision—a kaleidoscopic view—an interplay of infinite possibilities for women. And after her heroines have looked outside, they know enough to look inside themselves as well, and they often like what they see. Not the kind of pabulum which makes us feel good, Weldon's stories nevertheless offer us an inspirational message and convince us that things will get better: "We are not denatured remnants of the human race," Weldon once said in an interview. "On the contrary we are more sensitive, more humane, more culturally aware than our forefathers. We understand better what it feels like to be someone else." Weldon also offers us women a future as she makes us feel the risky joy of venturing beyond our circumscribed, narrow plots. For her optimism, as well as her wry skepticism, her readers—including this one—are grateful.

Notes

1. For an in-depth discussion of DNA, see Sam Singer's *Human Genetics: An Introduction to the Principles of Heredity* (San Francisco: W. H. Freeman & Co., 1978).

2. In her discussion of the thematics of birth in Mary Shelley's *Frankenstein*, Susan Winnett provides a theoretical grid for understanding Carl's be-

havior: "Frankenstein is a *male* mother; unlike the women in the novel, he is entirely unwilling to nurture the creature(s) dependent on him." Winnett goes on to write that: "In other words, his indulgence in the retrospective mode of 'male' sense making keeps him from acknowledging his ongoing responsibility to the birth he clones as well as from seeing that henceforth his plot inevitably involves the consequences of an act of creation that he regards as a triumph in and of itself" (p. 510).

3. In *The Reproduction of Mothering*, Nancy Chodorow's central thesis is that women have symbiotic relationships with their daughters but not with their sons. Because they are the same gender, women tend not to experience their daughters as separate from them in the same way that they do their sons. Women as mothers then go on to produce daughters with mothering capacities and a desire to mother. Chodorow claims that most of our problems will wither away if men are brought into child-rearing.

Works Cited

Chodorow, Nancy. *The Reproduction of Mothering: Psychoanalysis and the Sociology of Gender.* Berkeley: University of California Press, 1978.

Cixous, Hélène. "Le rire de la Meduse." *L'Arc* 61 (1975): 3–54. Trans. Keith and Paula Cohen. "The Laugh of the Medusa." *Signs* 1/4 (Summer 1976): 875–93.

Daly, Ann. *Women Under the Knife: A History of Surgery.* New York: Routledge, 1991.

Ortner, Sherry. "Is Female to Male as Nature is to Culture?" *Woman Culture and Society,* eds. Michelle Zimbalist Rosaldo and Louise Lamphere. Stanford: Stanford University Press, 1974.

Rich, Adrienne. *Of Woman Born.* New York: W. W. Norton, 1976.

Singer, Sam. *Human Genetics: An Introduction to the Principles of Heredity.* San Francisco: W. H. Freeman & Co., 1978.

Spacks, Patricia Meyer. "Women's Stories, Women's Selves." *The Hudson Review* 30 (1977): 29–48.

Weldon, Fay. *The Cloning of Joanna May.* New York: Penguin, 1989.

Winnett, Susan. "Women, Men, Narrative, and Principles of Pleasure." *PMLA* (Summer 1990): 505–18.

JULIE NASH

"Energy and Brashness" and Fay Weldon's Tricksters

And the woman said, "The serpent beguiled me and I did eat."
—The Book of Genesis

Not my fault that what is true can also be ridiculous.
—Fay Weldon, *Life Force*

In her novels *The Life and Loves of a She-Devil* (1983) and *Life Force* (1992), Fay Weldon invites us to reconsider traditional conceptions of the trickster figure to reflect and even improve female experience, specifically the experience of the restless, unhappy housewife. Rather than portraying the trickster as a naturally male-centered, preconscious being, Weldon uses the archetype to expose the trickster as an artificial creation of restless women.

The trickster figure in myth and literature is a marginalized creature who functions outside society's accepted norms and values. Given the trickster's inherent marginalized position, it is curious that C. G. Jung and other archetypal critics closely associate the trickster figure with masculinity, whereas women have more typically existed on the cultural fringes where the trickster operates. As Estella Lauter and Carol Schreier Rupprecht point out in *Feminist Archetypal Theory,* early archetypal criticism, while valuing feminine behaviors in males, "did not value the actual experiences of women themselves" (p. 7). Lauter and Rupprecht discuss the findings of critics such as Naomi Goldenberg, who "pointed out that Jung's followers had come to see archetypes as 'unchanging and unchangeable'" (p. 7). Obviously, women writers such as Fay Weldon, Alice Walker, and

Louise Erdrich, who consciously use myth to frame their works, must revise this rigid conception of archetypes to make them reflect more accurately the experiences of women. As Lauter and Rupprecht write, "In the
case of feminist theory, if we regard the archetype not as an image whose
content is frozen but . . . as a tendency to form and reform images in relation to certain kinds of repeated experience, then the concept could
serve to clarify distinctly female concerns that have persisted throughout
human history" (p. 14).

Fay Weldon accomplishes this "forming and reforming" of formerly
rigid archetypal patterns in her novels and short stories. In a 1989 interview, Weldon denies using any direct literary or mythological sources for
her novel *The Life and Loves of a She-Devil*, "although she said she was of
course familiar with European folktales and classical myths. She suggested we consider the book in terms of psychoanalysis instead" (Johnson). Yet, despite Weldon's assertion that *She-Devil* is not a modern
retelling of an ancient story or myth, the novel clearly operates within a
mythological framework. The trickster figure, particularly, offers a key to
understanding *She Devil*'s complex, angry heroine, Ruth, whose dual impulses to destroy and redeem correspond to the outrageous behavior of the
trickster figure.

According to Jung, the archetype of the trickster reflects a primitive
stage of human consciousness, "corresponding to a psyche that has hardly
left the animal level" (p. 260). Jung characterizes the trickster by his "fondness for sly jokes and malicious pranks, his powers as a shape-shifter, his
dual nature, half-animal, half-divine, his exposure to all kinds of tortures
and—last but not least—his approximation to the figure of a savior"
(p. 255). In *The Life and Loves of a She-Devil*, Ruth consciously creates
herself as a trickster figure (or "she-devil"), deliberately deciding to abandon her role as a dutiful wife and mother. As opposed to the traditional
trickster whose consciousness is "naturally" in a predeveloped or nonexistent state, Ruth's efforts to lose her social consciousness (and conscience) are deliberate and painstaking; for example, she admits to being
"wounded" when she first leaves her children (p. 87). But despite this
important deviation from the traditional archetype, Ruth's description of
the she-devil closely resembles that of a trickster figure: "There is no
shame, no guilt, no dreary striving to be good. There is only, in the end,
what you *want*. And I can take what I want. I am a she-devil!" (p. 48).
Perhaps Ruth's adoption of the archetype seems so unnatural and difficult
because most famous tricksters (Brer Rabbit, Bugs Bunny, Stagolee, Satan)
are male, and Ruth distinctly attributes her power and "success" to her
womanhood. As Ruth embarks on her pursuit of revenge, Weldon writes,

"she laughed and said she was taking arms against god Himself. Lucifer had tried and failed, but he was male. She thought she might do better, being female" (p. 94).

Throughout the novel, Weldon draws parallels between Ruth and Satan. If Ruth is indeed a female Lucifer figure, it follows that she embodies characteristics of the trickster as well; the serpent in the garden is certainly a classic embodiment of the archetype, with his malicious, seductive behavior and his talents as a shape-shifter. In *She-Devil*, Ruth consciously aligns herself with Satan's power, knowing that as a woman, she may succeed where her predecessor has failed. Ironically, Ruth sees her womanhood as an advantage. After all, her misery largely centers around her powerless position as a suburban housewife. But Ruth subverts the stereotypical drawbacks of female existence—submissiveness, powerlessness, helplessness, dependence—locating these "weaknesses" as the source of her power.

Ruth possesses the trickster's shape-shifting abilities, regularly changing identities in order to enact her revenge; and years of mistreatment and humiliation by Bobbo prepare her for the various personae she adopts as a she-devil. Weldon implies that Ruth, as a former housewife, has been "trained" in menial and degrading tasks, training that becomes essential when Ruth needs to integrate herself anonymously into a household or business. As Weldon's narrator points out,

There is always a living to be earned doing the work that others prefer not to do. Employment can generally be found looking after other people's children, caring for the insane, or guarding imprisoned criminals, cleaning the public rest rooms, laying out the dead, or making beds in cheap hotels. [P. 125]

Ruth moves effortlessly from one menial position to another. As a nursing home orderly, she gains access to Mary Fisher's mother; as a nanny, she moves into a judge's household and influences her husband Bobbo's prison sentence. Ruth's plans require that she remain marginalized and unnoticed. By placing herself in a low social position, she is virtually guaranteed anonymity—and as a woman, Weldon implies, Ruth is automatically halfway there. Despite her large, unusual appearance, Ruth is so successful as a shape-shifter that even Bobbo fails to recognize her when he passes her on the street.

Ruth thought that that was not at all strange: they now inhabited different worlds. Hers was unknown to him: those on the right side of everything like to know as little as possible about those on the wrong side. The poor, exploited, and oppressed, however, love to know about their masters, to gaze at their faces in the paper, to marvel at their love affairs, to discover their foibles. . . . So Ruth would recognize Bobbo, lover and accountant Bobbo would not recognize Ruth, hospital ward orderly and abandoned mother. Convenient, indeed essential, as it was to her plans, still she resented it. [P. 134]

If it weren't for her gender-specific experiences (housework, caretaking, etc.), Ruth would be unable to blend so easily into the "wrong" side of society. Ironically, success as a trickster depends not on the adoption of *male* behavior, but on the emphasis of conventional *female* conduct such as humility and servitude. The trick lies in Ruth's usage of these behaviors for her own empowerment.

"Creative by nature, in some ways a helper to humanity" (Leeming, p. 163), the trickster traditionally combines his misdeeds with productivity. Though Ruth's motives are almost always completely self-serving, she is the only character in the novel who leaves a positive legacy. Warwick Wadlington explains this apparent contradiction as the trickster's embodiment of two antithetical human experiences: "On the one hand, a force of treacherous disorder that outrages and disrupts, and on the other hand, an unanticipated, usually unintentional benevolence in which trickery is at the expense of inimical forces and for the benefit of mankind" (p. 15).

Ruth's most cunning motives unintentionally lead to her most benevolent actions. When she opens the Vesta Rose employment agency for women, she does so with the intention of infiltrating Bobbo's office with two of her clients—one who agrees to tamper with his financial records, and another whose subsequent affair with Bobbo and later disappearance implicate him in his criminal case. Although the Vesta Rose employment agency exists solely to execute Ruth's revenge, it also benefits hundreds of women who use its services:

The women on its books—and they emerged out of the suburbs on bus and train by the hundreds—were grateful, patient, responsible, and hardworking; and for the most part, after a little training by Ruth, regarded office work as simplicity itself; as should anyone who has dealt daily with the intricacies of sibling rivalry and the subtleties of marital accord, or discord. Vesta Roses, as they came to be called, were soon in great demand by employers throughout the city. [P. 139]

Not only has Ruth provided jobs for these women, she has also enhanced their opportunities and self-esteem. As Vesta Rose, Ruth tells Nurse Hopkins that "we can tap our own energies and the energies of women like us—women shut away in homes performing some menial tasks, sometimes graceful women trapped by love or duty into lives they never meant" (p. 137). Ruth's own miserable experience as a housewife has opened her eyes to the plight of other women, but Weldon emphasizes that it is by no means Ruth's central concern, merely a fortunate product of her plan. As she explains, "Each woman for herself, I cry!" (p. 192).

Yet there is no denying that Ruth's malicious actions, while disrupting order on one level, establish order on another. Thus, while Ruth's physical transformations defy God and nature and destroy the lives of Bobbo and Mary Fisher, the small steps she takes on her way to this transformation result in countless improved lives. The trickster's creative tendencies even in the midst of destruction support Jung's theory that the trickster figure is "the forerunner of the savior, and, like him, God, man, and animal at once. He is both subhuman and superhuman, a bestial and divine being" (p. 263). Jung focuses on the dual nature of the trickster that Ruth embodies so completely; though she calls herself a devil, she acknowledges another connection to the savior:

I am a she-devil. I wouldn't be surprised if I wasn't the second coming, this time in female form; what the world has been waiting for. Perhaps what Jesus did in his day for men, so I do now, for women. He offered the stony path to heaven: I offer the motor way to hell. I bring suffering and self-knowledge (the two go together) for others and salvation for myself. . . . If I'm nailed to the cross of my own convenience I'll put up with it. I just want my own way, and by Satan I'll have it. [P. 192]

Though Ruth stresses her amoral nature and her resolve to have her own way "by Satan," she hints at a larger social purpose, particularly directed at women.

Nowhere is Ruth's role as both savior and demon more clear than in her actions toward her enemy and victim, Mary Fisher. Ruth destroys Mary Fisher's complacent life in her high Tower, causing her to feel the pain of Bobbo's infidelity, the realities of motherhood, and a profound sense of failure. As Ruth tells us triumphantly, "Mary Fisher lives in the high Tower and wishes she didn't. She doesn't want to live anymore, in fact. Quite frankly, she wants to be dead. . . . She believes in hell now. She is in it already and knows she deserves it" (p. 243). Ruth has succeeded in destroying her enemy, yet Mary Fisher's ruin is also her redemption. Thanks to Ruth's actions, Mary Fisher stops living a lie; she accepts responsibility for her life and is finally redeemed. Mary Fisher wonders, "what was there ever to be frightened of, except coming face to face with her own guilt?" (p. 244) Though she is dying of cancer, Mary Fisher finally takes responsibility for others, Ruth's children and her own mother: "Mary Fisher, without knowing it, is almost happy. If happiness is anything, it is a feeling of being essential" (p. 245). As Ruth stated earlier, the deliverance she offers other women involves "suffering and self-knowledge." Ruth imposes suffering on Mary Fisher for her own satisfaction, not for Mary Fisher's sake; yet according to her own words, she is aware that such suffering leads to self-knowledge and therefore redemption. Willing to undergo her own sufferings, Ruth faces a type of "cruci-fixion" in her final act as shape-shifter. Despite her constant assertions that she is divine and invincible, and despite the demonic red glint of her eyes, Ruth is just partially superhuman or divine. Like the archetypal trickster, with his "exposure to all kinds of torture" and "self-imposed sufferings" (Jung, 255–56), Ruth must undergo unbearable plastic surgery to complete her transformation. She willingly accepts this torture as nec-essary for her salvation, and argues that "The more you want the more you suffer. If you want everything, you must suffer everything" (p. 187).

The result of this suffering is her "success." Looking exactly like Mary Fisher, she moves into the high Tower and reunites with Bobbo. Yet, de-spite her assertion that "Life is very pleasant," Ruth's happiness now de-pends on her ability to "cause Bobbo as much misery as he ever caused [her]" (p. 277). The final lines of the novel reveal a disillusionment with her power and role as a trickster. For the first time since her transformation into she-devil, she describes herself in human rather than divine or satanic terms: "I am a lady of six foot two, who had tucks taken in her legs. A comic turn, turned serious" (p. 278). While Ruth has previously changed identities with ease, she cannot "become" Mary Fisher with the same fa-cility that Satan "becomes" the serpent, for example. Ruth's ironic final words emphasize her realization that she "[is] not all she-devil. A she-devil has no memory of the past—she is born fresh every morning. She deals with the feelings of today, not yesterday, and she is free" (p. 187). Being driven by memories of the past, Ruth is never completely free, but her adoption of trickster characteristics has certainly given her power if not freedom. Toward the end of her transformation, Ruth says of Mary Fisher, "She is a woman: she made the landscape better. She-devils can make nothing better except themselves. In the end, she wins" (p. 266). Yet Ruth, despite her own acknowledgment, is both a trickster figure (she-devil) and a woman. The difficulty in reconciling this apparent contra-diction leads to a rather bittersweet victory for Ruth; yet this same duality enables her to achieve all of her original goals and redeem other women in the process. In the end, Ruth has improved much more than the land-scape—and she wins.

All of Weldon's tricksters are not women characters; some closely re-semble the more "traditional" tricksters of folklore and fiction. In Life Force, Weldon presents us with a seemingly classic example of the male trickster figure in the philandering Leslie Beck. Yet with Leslie, as with Ruth, Weldon employs the archetype only to subvert it. Leslie Beck can be read as the trickster in his ultimate preconscious state. He seems to possess naturally the attitudes and lifestyle that Ruth has cultivated painstakingly. According to him and his lovers, he is the incarnation of the Life Force, "the self of the night . . . that creature of engorged delight" who, like the trickster, is "irrational, uncontrolled, universal, shameful" (p. 16). It is Leslie Beck's utter lack of consciousness that makes him irresistible to the bored neighborhood women who, like the narrator Nora, need to believe they are capable of being more than good wives to good husbands.

Like the archetypal trickster, Leslie is at times more animal than human, and this animal aspect—emphasized by his ten-inch penis—draws the women to him. As Nora says, "Leslie Beck brandishes his giant phallus and women lie wounded all around" (p. 142). His lover Marion likens him to the trickster's bestial alter ego, the fox:

Once [his teeth had] put me in mind of some small, agreeable, nuzzling animal, or, as he became more imperative, something dangerous, some glossy fox, perhaps, rooting around and above me—a vision which would occasionally change, even in the middle of lovemaking, to one of the fox loose in the henhouse, tearing and slavering, blood and feathers everywhere. [P. 8]

As Marion's and Nora's comments indicate, Leslie's animal nature is linked closely to his dangerous, even deadly, yet nevertheless "imperative" sexuality. Like Ruth, Leslie Beck seems to possess a supernatural ability to manipulate any situation. The neighborhood women who succumb to the Life Force are driven by an urgent desire, though, like Marion and Nora, they are aware of the risks they face, the least of which is losing their families. As Nora admits, "copulating with other women's husbands in secret, no matter how the self esteem rises, no matter how exciting secrets are, is also in some way to lower the self" (p. 84).

According to Nora, Leslie's Life Force is rooted in the present in the same way that Ruth's true she-devil can forget her past:

The Life Force is not about futures; it is all here and now. Leslie Beck could plan a building, plan a marriage, plan a site for a seduction, and achieve his plan simply because he didn't worry about the consequences. He looked ahead but never too far ahead. [P. 99]

This ability to exist completely in the present, with no thought to future consequences or past responsibilities, characterizes the trickster figure in traditional archetypal criticism. Statements like these by Nora and by Leslie himself invite us to read Leslie as a clear representation of a trickster figure. Yet just as Ruth veers from this paradigm by obsessing about her past and her future revenge, so does Leslie have a side to him that is driven by more than immediate pleasure. Though Nora says that Leslie could "plan a marriage" because he never considered the consequences, she ad-

mits that his marriages were made to further his social and business stand-
ings: "Leslie Beck felt it was his duty to get on in the world. His aspiration
was to be ruthless" (p. 100).

As the novel progresses, we begin to understand the real source of Leslie's power. His appeal is not based on his innate animal sexuality, or even
his "magnificent dong," but rather the imaginations of women like Nora
who need to create a trickster figure in Leslie in order to animate their
own unsatisfactory lives. Nora insists on her own view of Leslie Beck—
the Life Force, the trickster without a conscience—and refutes any suggestion that Leslie may be other than as she has defined him. Rosalie, Nora's
friend and one of Leslie's lovers, suggests to Nora that Leslie may be motivated by more than just animal passion, asking her to consider,

That Leslie Beck felt inadequate when we talked about political details he
couldn't follow, books he hadn't read, plays he hadn't heard of? So what, he'd
say; so I don't run my own telly program like Wallace, so I don't publish books,
like Ed, or write them, like Vinny, so I'm a Philistine. But I can have your
wives at will and make money. Sneer at me if you will. [P. 118]

Rosalie's understanding of Leslie is an insightful explanation of his need
to have sex with the wives of his "friends." But Nora refuses that more
complex, psychological interpretation in favor of her own image of him as
the Life Force: " 'I don't want to think it was because of anything,' I say, 'I
think it was just for itself; just for his body and my body' " (p. 118).

Whereas Ruth *becomes* the trickster figure as she abandons the role of
submissive housewife, Nora (along with Rosalie, Susan, and Marion, to
lesser degrees) *imposes* the role of the trickster onto Leslie Beck in her
attempt to escape the monotony of her marriage. Leslie is pleased to play
the role, but it is no more "natural" for him than it is for Ruth. In both
novels, the trickster figure is a construct created by women who need to
infuse their lives with aspects of the irrational "self of the night" in order
to break free from the confines of their unhappy marriages and lives. Once
Weldon has moved away from the trickster figure's traditional masculine
qualities, the archetype becomes a useful frame for her characters. The
use of the trickster archetype—which is generally exaggerated or larger
than life—helps illustrate women's desperate need to escape their re-
stricting lives. Explaining that she and Ed "live with a certain formality,"
Nora apologizes for what is essentially her "self of the night"—"it's just
that sometimes I long for the energy and brashness of what is random and
to the common sense" (p. 66).

This longing leads Nora to regard Leslie as "Tarzan to my Jane" (p. 92),
an uncivilizing presence in her civilized world. Describing the women in

her circle, Nora says, "We were all flesh and hot dinners, baby poppers, nest builders. Our men had dongs of conventional size, and lived within the rather wide norm of conventional existence" (p. 95). Just as Ruth becomes part-human, part-divine, Leslie too transcends the mere human in Nora's mind. While Leslie Beck is in reality a rather conventional man, albeit an adulterous one, Nora imagines him to be a super human to satisfy her own restlessness. Prior to their first sexual encounter, which takes place several stories high at an unfinished construction site, Nora remarks: "He stood in his natural state in his natural place; he was meant to poise between heaven and earth; he had elevated me and I was honored" (p. 98). Nora cannot see that Leslie is "naturally" just a man, and a rather ordinary one at that. In her imagination he is her savior, rescuing her from her life with her husband.

In one of Weldon's classic "comic turns," Leslie Beck the magnificent becomes a victim of his lovers' imaginations. By allowing himself to be reinvented as a trickster figure and a superhuman he is no longer thought of as a human. Despite her claim that "the dimension of his prick was neither here nor there" (p. 98), Nora comes to view Leslie only on her own terms: "He was a fool, he had no taste, he would swim around out of his depth and be laughed at; but his one great attribute he used and used it well. God will forgive him" (p. 100). Yet part of Nora understands that she is blinded by her own need for excitement, for secrets "which are to true love as artificial sweetener is to sugar. . . . A cheat. Everything costs. Nothing is for nothing. Fewer calories, more cancer" (p. 174). The personal costs of her affair with Leslie are almost expected: the loss of her family, friends, and respectability. Yet there are costs for Leslie Beck too.

The novel opens and closes with an older, faded Leslie Beck. His power, unlike that of a "natural trickster," has diminished with the passage of time: "He was not the man he had been. His face was shriveled in upon itself. The hair was now sandy, not red; it no longer flourished, as once it had. The full mouth had narrowed" (p. 186). Because Leslie Beck had so fully accepted his role as an invincible trickster figure, a devouring animal, he is perplexed as the inevitable loss of his sexual abilities leads to the loss of his own identity. Referring specifically to his dead wife, Anita, Leslie comments on the way women have "used" him: "she needed me, she used me. It was her life force, not mine. I was nothing. Just a kind of brush she used" (p. 189). Just as Anita needed her image of Leslie Beck the trickster to inspire her art, so Nora needed to project her own "life force" on to Leslie in order to justify her restlessness and her own discontent. Leslie's realization that he "was nothing" is sadly accurate. What appeared to be his Tarzanlike conquering of the women he knew was

merely an artificial role that was imposed upon him the day that Marion
reported she had spied his enormous penis as he stepped out of the
shower. When we understand Leslie in this way, he loses his "impera-
tiveness" and becomes more pathetic than powerful. Ironically, he becomes the trickster in a different sense. As Sharon Marybeads Bowers
observes, "One of the trademarks of a cultural trickster hero . . . is that he
is often the one who gets tricked" (p. 136).

Fay Weldon has been concerned with the real and potential misery of
the suburban housewife since her first novel, The Fat Woman's Joke (1966).
Her fiction overturns the conventional romance plot by replacing "happily
ever after" with, at best, "happily together for now," and at worst, "miserably ever after." In reforming a familiar archetype like the trickster
figure, Weldon contextualizes her works in terms of the "energy and brashness" repressed by married life, and the extreme forms the "self of the
night" will take if continually repressed. In typical Weldon style, we are
given no easy answers—there are none because, as Nora says, "Everything
costs." The ambiguous conclusions to both novels allow us to make our
own judgments, but warn us not to make them too hastily. Before putting
away her manuscript, Nora wonders:

Well there you have it. Did we do right, did we do wrong? Forget Leslie Beck.
Were we good women or bad? I suppose we'll never know, unless there's a
Day of Judgement, and we'll find out then. There certainly seems to be a human
craving for such a day; but alas, the needs of humanity at large, like the needs
of the individual, are seldom satisfied. [P. 221]

Weldon's ambiguous moral judgments, her "forced" happy endings, and
her malicious destruction of the romance conventions we hold dear, render
her what Bonnie Tu Smith has termed " 'trickster' par excellence" (p. 249)
in her article on the woman writer as trickster figure. By combining the
anger and wit of a she-devil with the energy of the Life Force, Weldon
creates in her novels what Ruth and Leslie Beck create in their lives. As
Sharon Marybeads Bowers writes, "The trick is how the story is told"
(p. 135), and the trickster is found wherever women writers like Fay Weldon are reforming the way we perceive our roles as women and our responses to one another.

Works Cited

Bowers, Sharon Marybeads. "Louise Erdrich as Nanapush." New Perspectives
    on Women and Comedy, ed. Regina Barreca. New York: PUB, 1992.
Johnson, Jane McPhetres. Consider the Source: Old Tales. The New England
    Foundation for the Humanities, 1989.

Jung, Carl. *The Archetypes and the Collective Unconscious*. Princeton: Bollingen Series, 1959.

Lauter, Estella, and Carol Schreier Rupprecht, eds. Introduction. *Feminist Archetypal Theory: Interdisciplinary Re-Visions of Jungian Thought*. Knoxville, Tenn.: The University of Tennessee Press, 1985.

Leeming, David Adams. *The World of Myth*. New York: Oxford University Press, 1990.

Tu Smith, Bonnie. "Literary Tricksterism: Maxine Hong Kingston's *The Woman Warrior: Memoirs of a Girlhood Among Ghosts*." *Literature Interpretation Theory* 2/4:249–59.

Wadlington, Warwick. *The Confidence Game in American Literature*. Princeton, N.J.: Princeton University Press, 1975.

Weldon, Fay. *Life Force*. New York: Penguin, 1992.

———. *The Life and Loves of a She-Devil*. New York: Ballantine Books, 1983.

SUSAN JARET McKINSTRY

Fay Weldon's *Life and Loves of a She-Devil*: The Speaking Body

Isn't the final goal of writing to articulate the body?
—Chantal Chawaf

"Reader, I married him," claims Jane Eyre. Charlotte Brontë's 1847 novel provides readers with a conventional happy ending, but with some questions about the violent path we have taken to get there. Jane's husband, after first attempting bigamy, is blinded and crippled in the fire set by his mad wife, Bertha, an arsonist who attempts murder and commits suicide. Sweet Jane herself manages to reject a spiritual marriage that she claims would "kill her" and instead succeeds Bertha, replacing that "demon" as Rochester's literal "right hand," his "clinging vine," his wife. The textual violence of Bertha's imprisonment and death is often overshadowed by discussions of the conventional rewards the text provides to the heroine—money, family, and marriage. Jane is transformed from a plain, poor governess to an independent heiress. If a woman's body conforms to social and fictional expectations, transformations of the mind—growing up, usually, into social conformity—can beautify a plain woman and lead to a happy ending. Who can question Rochester's luck in exchanging the insane demon Bertha with the quietly sensible Jane? The novel rewards the angel in the house and destroys the monster.

Brontë's tale of triangular desire, textual violence, and transformations is revised in Fay Weldon's 1983 novel, *The Life and Loves of a She-Devil*. Instead of recounting conquering Jane's marital claim, Weldon turns the tale so that the monstrous wife is the narrative center, and winning the man is not a simple happy ending. Brontë's tale is the subject of many revisions, and several reconsider Bertha's role in the story; for example, Jean Rhys's *Wide Sargasso Sea* also offers Bertha a chance to tell her story. Weldon's darkly humorous novel does more than give a voice to a modern mad wife, however; through this voice, this version of the tale, Weldon raises larger questions about narrative transformations and the bodily violence they produce. Helena Michie complains that "in the attempt to produce and to reproduce the literal female body, contemporary feminists have only succeeded in creating a metaphor" (*Flesh Made Word*, p. 149), but Weldon proves that writing can, indeed, articulate the body. In this novel, the female voice is embodied—full-bodied, and speaking only through the body, in a sort of French feminist's nightmare. The monstrous female literally, physically, grotesquely transforms herself into the angel— a transformation that undermines conventional happy endings, just rewards, narrative process, and the moral development of heroines and villains. The transformation demands violence, just as it did in *Jane Eyre*. But the site of violence is narrowed from the husband or house—although the wife in *She-Devil* does indeed destroy her husband and burn her house down—to the female body itself.

Growing up, here, does not mean coming into possession of self, power, and money; rather, it means dispossessing the self, remaking the body into another body and, therefore, the self into another self, since the body stands as the symbol of identity. In "(Re)Writing the Body," Susan Rubin Suleiman claims:

The cultural significance of the female body is not only (not even first and foremost) that of a flesh-and-blood entity, but that of a *symbolic construct*. Everything we know about the body—certainly as regards the past, and even, it could be argued, as regards the present—exists for us in some form of discourse; and discourse, whether verbal or visual, fictive or historical or speculative, is never unmediated, never free of interpretation, never innocent (*The Female Body in Western Culture*, p. 2).

The discourse of transformations in Weldon's novel tells two distinct stories: one, the seemingly innocent desire to be better, to be an Ugly Duckling growing into beauty, to be a heroine; the other, the more violent tale of self-loathing, self-destruction as a means of improvement, where the body itself becomes the site of struggle. For Weldon takes the female body as symbol and turns that symbol back into flesh-and-blood, but flesh-and-blood dismembered by the symbolic demands on it.

The moral of the story is not learning to love the body you have, but fighting to have the body you can love. Unlike the Ugly Duckling story, this is not a natural process, but a surgical one. And the unnatural, bloody struggle to transform the physical body into the symbolized ideal of desire represents Weldon's view of the real cultural violence against women: not marriage to a Rochester, but desire to be his desire, desire to speak the self through a body that mirrors ideal models of femaleness. Such models are often beyond any possible transformations of the physical body. "And how, especially, do ugly women survive, those whom the world pities?" the narrator asks. "I'll tell you; they live as I do, outfacing truth, hardening the skin against perpetual humiliation, until it's as tough and cold as a crocodile's" (p. 7). Weldon's novel states directly what Brontë avoided: the violent cost of love and marriage for female identity in a world where women must be angelic beauties, where the body rather than the spirit must be improved, where violence is turned against women's bodies by women themselves in the name of self-improvement, transformation, beauty.

Jane Eyre outlives her rival, Bertha, but in Weldon's novel the rivals for the unhappy wife, Ruth, are fictional, mass-produced romantic heroines, so the ideal body is already a symbolic construct, not flesh-and-blood but a text: "In Mary Fisher's novels, which sell by the hundred thousand in glittery pink-and-gold covers, little staunch heroines raise tearful eyes to handsome men, and by giving them up, gain them. Little women can look up to men. But women of six feet two have trouble doing so" (p. 22). The novel is full of physical details: Ruth is six foot two, her handsome husband, Bobbo, is five foot ten, and his lover—the romance writer Mary Fisher—is five foot four. Ruth's physical body is not ideal. And the fictions of desire function in the world as in books, for the heroines are the beautiful women like Mary, as Ruth sees: "Mary Fisher has made her books come true. It can be done. She's done it" (p. 66).

Weldon's novel asks whether a woman who does not look like a heroine can do it. Ruth is not betrayed by her mind, as Bertha Rochester is, but by her body, by her size, by her failure to look and therefore be feminine. Ruth's response is not renunciation of her embodied voice, or of desire, but renunciation of her excessive self:

"And I tell you this: I am jealous! I am jealous of every pretty woman who ever lived and looked up since the world began. I am, in fact, quite eaten up by jealousy, and a fine, lively, hungry emotion it is. But *why* should I care, you ask? Can't I just live in myself and forget that part of myself and be content? Don't I have a home, and a husband to pay the bills, and children to look after? Isn't that enough? 'No!' is the answer. I want, I crave, I die to be part of that other erotic world, of choice and desire and lust. It isn't love I want; it is nothing so simple. What I want is to take everything and return nothing. What I want is power over the hearts and pockets of men. It is all the power we can have, . . . and even that is denied me." [P. 22]

Ruth's powerlessness has an ideological cause—she does not fit the rules for female bodies; her body is not the appropriate female symbol but instead is embarrassing, excessive flesh-and-blood. Bodily interventions determine her story; her husband seduces her because she is a "vast obliging mountain" (p. 28) and marries her because she becomes pregnant and he contracts hepatitis. Yet the novel makes it clear that to both Ruth and her husband, her body defines her self, and her self is unacceptably monstrous: "It was obvious to both of them that it was Ruth's body that was at fault. . . . He had married it perforce and in error and would do his essential duties by it, but he would never be reconciled to its enormity, and Ruth knew it" (p. 31).

Ruth tries disembodying herself, silencing her voice. She is initially so submissive that she does not consistently have her own voice; the narrative alternates between first and third person. In moments of doubt she recites the "Litany of the Good Wife," which articulates the double standard of unequal marriage, including such axioms as: "I must pretend to be happy when I am not; for everyone's sake"; "I must be grateful for the roof over my head and the food on my table, and spend my days showing it, by cleaning and cooking and jumping up and down from my chair; for everyone's sake"; and "I must build up my husband's sexual confidence, I must not express any sexual interest in other men, in private or public" because "I must render him moral support in all his undertakings, however immoral they may be, for the marriage's sake. I must pretend in all matters to be less than he" (p. 23).

It doesn't work. Ruth's voice is too strong. When Bobbo shouts, "How can one love what is essentially unlovable" (p. 40), Ruth is freed from the rules of the good wife, for she recognizes the inescapable body that defines her self. Ironically, her husband gives her a new identity: "I thought I was a good wife tried temporarily and understandably beyond endurance, but no. He says I am a she-devil. I expect he is right. In fact, since he does so well in the world and I do so badly, I really must assume he is right. I am a she-devil" (p. 43).

Having failed as woman and as wife because of her massive body, Ruth becomes a she-devil, a celebrant of female power. Like her other roles, it is based on another's view of her, another's naming of her. Even so, it allows her to give voice to her desire: "I want revenge. I want power. I want money. I want to be loved and not love in return. I want to give hate its head. I want hate to drive out love. . . . Peel away the wife, the mother, find the woman, and there the she-devil is. Excellent!" (pp. 43–44). This process of self-transformation through peeling away social constructions of womanhood is not painless: "The roots of self-reproach and good behavior tangle deep in the living flesh; you can't ease them out gently; they have to be torn out, and they bring flesh with them. Sometimes in the night I scream so loud I wake the neighbors" (p. 51).

This is indeed the embodied voice, speaking through the body by making feeling physical. Female behavior and female flesh are "tangled," and a transformation of one is a transformation—often, destruction—of the other. The symbolic construct and the flesh-and-blood body define the self, and they are inextricably, unhappily bound together. Deserted by her husband, who now lives with lovely Mary Fisher, Ruth leaves her two children with him. And her emotional pain is expressed physically, as bodily loss: "I must think of this grief as a physical pain. I must remember that just as a broken leg heals with time so with this psychic injury. There will be no disfiguring scar tissue: this is an inner wound, not an outer one. I am a woman learning to be without her children. I am a snake shedding its skin" (p. 77). The images are telling: the body represents the spirit. Emotional breaks parallel physical breaks. A cold-blooded serpent, able to renew itself physically, replaces the model of motherhood. Physical transformations can change women's stories, just as snakes can shed their skins. This seems to confirm the perception of the female body as symbolic representation of the self; Ruth's struggle supports the cultural view of her large body as wrong, as nonfemale, as unnatural.

Such a physical body is practically immoral, for its very existence breaks the rules for femaleness, the spiritualization of the fragile flesh. Asked about her plans, Ruth replies that "she was taking up arms against God Himself. Lucifer had tried and failed, but he was male. She thought she might do better, being female" (p. 83). Her site of battle is her body: she remakes herself, redefining herself in the bodily image she chooses. When a dentist, hired to remove her large teeth, claims that "we are as God made us," she replies: "That isn't true. We are here in this world to improve upon his original idea. To create justice, truth, and beauty where He so obviously and lamentably failed" (p. 115). Again, the text reconfirms the concept of the female body as the object of necessary transformations into the ideal; woman's body, as her self, cannot be accepted as natural or right, but must be remade. Part of Ruth's plan is to reject all her conventional female traits, since her unconventional body only asserts her failure to be female: "Any lingering spark of compunction, any trace of those qualities traditionally associated with women—such as sweetness, the capacity to forgive, forbearance, and gentleness—were at that moment quite obliterated" (p. 118).

The result of her self-transformation through emotional shedding is access to power. Able to leave her emotional life behind, she is capable of changing her self:

"Out there in the world everything is possible and exciting. We can be different women: we can tap our own energies and the energies of women like us— women shut away in homes performing sometimes menial tasks, sometimes graceful women trapped by love and duty into lives they never meant, and driven by necessity into jobs they loathe and which slowly kill them. We can get out there into the exciting world of business, of money and profit and loss, and help them, too. . . . And there waiting, too, is that other world of power— of judges and priests and doctors, the ones who tell the women what to do and how to think." [P. 120]

This sounds like a feminist claim, a resolution for equality, as Ruth suc- ceeds in these male worlds despite her body, yet she is still marked—and remarked upon—because of her body. Her jobs are menial, domestic, and demeaning, requiring physical strength but no mind or heart—aide in an abusive mental hospital and a dreadful home for the elderly, housekeeper for a priest and a judge. She starts an employment agency for women and becomes the disembodied telephone voice, the mysterious successful businesswoman "Vesta Rose" whose history is buried as her body is hidden.

Disguising her self, her identity, and her body, Ruth takes on male power with a vengeance. She destroys her husband financially so that he is jailed for embezzlement; she seduces the judge so the sentence is harsher; she seduces a priest and sends him off to seduce Mary Fisher. And she over- whelms her doctors, the plastic surgeons and reconstructionists she hires to remake her in the image she chooses. She seems to have power indeed, for she has written a self outside the definitions of the wife and the mother. Hélène Cixous writes in "The Laugh of the Medusa," "by writing her self, woman will return to the body which has been more than confiscated from her, which has been turned into the uncanny stranger on display" (p. 250).

But that is the twist of the novel. Rather than returning to the body, Ruth confiscates her own body. Ruth may destroy her husband, she may destroy her rival, but the power she takes on is the most conventional one: she kills her self, her body, so that she can be remade into the image of Mary Fisher, the beautiful woman, the heroine. "Isn't it rather ordinary?" one of the surgeons complains; the other replies, "If you have been ex- traordinary all your life, just to be ordinary must be wonderful. . . . [A]ll she has ever wanted is to be like other women" (p. 220). Like other women, then, she wants a body that fits the rules. She becomes, in the doctors' words, a "Venus," a "Pygmalion," "an impossible male fantasy made flesh" (p. 225). Impossible indeed; the body is surgically, painfully produced and maintained. And it is a male fantasy; she can desire no self other than the self designed by male desire. Her body remains her text.

During the process of transformation, Ruth—now naming herself Marlene Hunter—makes headlines, but no one can find out who she really is, because she erases her past along with her body, her identity, and becomes the new body. In "The Clinical Eye," Mary Anne Doane argues that in illness "the female body is located not so much as spectacle but as an element in the discourse of medicine, a manuscript to be read for the symptoms which betray her story, her identity' (*Female Body*, p. 157). Hiding her past identity, Ruth becomes a discourse of absence; as her body shrinks in every dimension—height, jaw, teeth, limbs and all—her story seems to represent the symptoms of femaleness itself. Her presence becomes absence—absence of self, of physical identity. She presents herself literally as the other woman. That painful, complicated surgical process—described in awful detail in the novel—makes the process of self-transformation answer a larger question. The female body in this novel is still a text to be inscribed, yet the woman herself controls the writing, revising herself physically into the image of the perfect woman. The dead body is her own; she is the murderer of herself as Ruth, and the creator of herself as a series of women: Vesta Rose, Polly Patch, Georgiana Tilling, Marlene Hunter, and, finally, Mary Fisher, her husband's lover.

That self-transformation is a form of sexual suicide, since it is essential self-destruction in order to fit the rules for female sexuality. Margaret Higonnet writes in "Speaking Silences: Women's Suicide":

To embrace death is at the same time to read one's own life. The act is a self-barred signature; its destructive narcissism seems to some particularly feminine. . . . The desire to control one's own life may extend into manipulation of the lives of the survivors—and women are thought to be particularly prone to this motive. The act may be dedicated, like a poem, to some one in particular. [*Female Body*, p. 69]

Note her language: the body becomes, through its destruction, a work of art, a linguistic act, a poem dedicated to another. The "destructive narcissism" that marks suicide also marks the female body as symbolic construct, for it is produced only by destroying the individual woman, the separate self. Higonnet claims that "When women represent the death of the self on their bodies, they do so in a gesture that remains open-ended" (p. 69). Ruth's gesture is certainly that: she can commit suicide, can kill herself off, and yet transform herself into the object of desire she could not otherwise be.

Thus the death of the self through self-directed violence becomes the transformation that allows the happy ending. Ruth is like the heroine of

Marge Piercy's 1973 poem "Barbie Doll," for whom success is measured
by self-destruction and self-mutilation in the quest for physical perfection:

> She was advised to play coy,
> exhorted to come on hearty,
> exercise, diet, smile and wheedle.
> Her good nature wore out
> Like a fan belt.
> So she cut off her nose and legs
> And offered them up.
>
> In the casket displayed on satin she lay
> with the undertaker's cosmetics painted on,
> a turned-up putty nose,
> dressed in a pink-and-white nightie.
> Doesn't she look pretty? everyone said.
> Consummation at last.
> To every woman a happy ending.

This physical dismemberment certainly undermines the promised
happy ending by illustrating the ironic consummation of achieving beauty
at the cost of life. Self-transformation is self-destruction, and its violence
transforms the mind as well as the physical body. Ruth discovers the repercussions of vengeance after she reclaims her husband with her revised
body: "I cause Bobbo as much misery as he ever caused me, and more. I
try not to, but somehow it is not a matter of male or female, after all; it
never was: merely of power. I have all, and he has none. As I was, so he
is now" (p. 241). And that is her equality.

This is a darkly humorous novel, as I pointed out earlier; Weldon is not
writing a murder story in the traditional sense, and the deaths of the characters are less simple than the stabbing of Alec D'Urberville, the blinding
of Rochester, and other violent acts explained by the "gentle" motives of
desperate women. Yet the process of *self*-destruction here is even more
direct, and since it is located in a hatred of the physical body it has much
in common with anorexia nervosa, as Noelle Caskey defines it:

It is the literal-mindedness of anorexia to take "the body" as a synonym for
"the self," and to try to live in the world through a manipulation of "the body,"
particularly as it is reflected to the anorexic by the perceived wishes of others.
Anorexia is the cultivation of a specific image *as an image*—it is a purely
artificial creation and that is why it is admired. Will alone produces it and
maintains it against considerable physical odds. [*Female Body,* p. 184]

Ruth's dramatic weight loss, plastic surgery, and willful insistence on surgically shortening her arms and legs, seriously risking her health both now
and in the future, make her the object of great admiration. She becomes

an artificial creation, a pure image; the surgeons work with giant photographs of Mary Fisher as their models, and Ruth becomes the image of Mary Fisher that is so admired by others—her husband, in particular. She changes her self by destroying her body. That reduction of self to body, the reduction of body to image, fulfills the perceived desire of the culture for female beauty.

Weldon's novel comments on the violence of cultural demands for female bodies resulting in self-loathing, in anorexia, in suicide. Written with a feminist swerve, the novel illustrates the speaking body that destroys both men and women, both the other and the self. By mastering female seduction and male deduction, Ruth violently revises the story of her life. In the process she kills herself, but gains her own voice, her own pen, as she writes the story of her transformation into the object of her husband's desire—and perhaps her own desire. But she does not tell a story with a happy ending, for she plays into the hands of the culture that equates body with self, and questions her narrative violence in transforming herself into the image of a heroine.

That is the larger issue the novel addresses: the appropriation of violence by women merely destroys women, remaking them but not in a better image. The violence is turned against the self in bodily transformations, and such transformations only rewrite the body as self without revising the conventions of the text. Weldon's novel illustrates that boldly. By revising the triangle of *Jane Eyre*, by illustrating the inequalities of male-female relations in marriage, and by transforming Ruth the vengeful giant into the physical image of a beautiful romance writer, Weldon contains the violence in very fictional terms, and in a perverse sort of domestic comedy. Ruth, at the end of the novel, even writes a romance and sends it to Mary Fisher's publishers, who want to buy it. She can indeed write the right fictions, produce the appropriate stories that will sell the romance that destroyed her. The novel comes full circle, with Ruth, now Mary, living in Mary's house with Ruth's husband/Mary's lover, living Mary's successful romance. But the process of writing the self is violent. Mary is dead, Ruth's children are gone, Ruth's husband is aged and confused, and Ruth suffers the side effects of the agonizing surgery she has undergone.

If the closure of *Jane Eyre* is frustrating to some feminist readers who are angered by Jane's self-satisfied reduction into a wife, the end of Weldon's novel is terrifying. Ruth does not challenge the rules for female bodies, the role of body as self and symbol. Instead, Ruth literally reduces herself into another woman in order to regain her place as the wife. She transforms herself into something smaller. She speaks only through the body. She employs her powerful mind—and her wealth—to command surgeons to recreate her body into one less powerful, more delicate, more desirable, more—as the surgeon complains—ordinary.

I think the novel can be read as an indictment of the violence women commit against their bodies in the production of an accepted ideal bodily self, and a warning about the potential for more active, outwardly directed violence against the men (and women) who demand that ideal self. Ruth's self-directed violence is horrifying, for she is intelligent, articulate, and aware of the power of her mind, yet is convinced that only the body articulates a self. The idea of self-transformation may be a common fantasy, often satisfied in romantic novels; but in Weldon's novel we are forced to face the violence of the model of female perfection that such novels reproduce by equating the female body and the female self. Ruth's last words remind us: "I am a lady of six foot two, who had tucks taken in her legs. A comic turn, turned serious" (p. 241).

Works Cited

Brontë, Charlotte. *Jane Eyre*. Oxford: Clarendon Press, 1973.

Chawaf, Chantal. "Linguistic Flesh." In *New French Feminisms,* ed. Elaine Marks and Isabelle de Courtivron. New York: Schocken Books, 1981.

Cixous, Hélène. "The Laugh of the Medusa." Trans. Keith Cohen and Paula Cohen. *Signs* 1/4 (Summer 1976): 875–93.

Michie, Helena. *The Flesh Made Word: Female Figures and Women's Bodies.* New York: Oxford University Press, 1987.

Piercy, Marge. "Barbie Doll." *Circles in the Water.* New York: Alfred A. Knopf, 1982.

Rhys, Jean. *Wide Sargasso Sea*. London: Deutsch Press, 1966.

Suleiman, Susan Rubin, ed. *The Female Body in Western Culture: Contemporary Perspectives*. Cambridge: Harvard University Press, 1986.

Weldon, Fay. *The Life and Loves of a She-Devil*. New York: Pantheon Press, 1984.

PAMELA KATZ

They Should Have Called It "She-Angel"

On page 43 of *The Life and Loves of a She-Devil*, Ruth cries out:

"I want revenge.
I want power.
I want money.
I want to be loved and not love in return."

In the Weldon universe, the last line could also have read: "All of the above." To be loved and not love in return is her definition of power. From a position of absolute power one can have all the revenge and money in the world. Ruth's transformation from victimized housewife to she-devil centers around the moment in which she stops loving her cruel and unfaithful husband, Bobbo. Her ultimate acquisition of power stems from this transformation.

"I cast off the chains that bound me down, of habit, custom, and sexual aspiration; home, family, friends—all the objects of natural affections. Not until then could I be free, and could I begin." [P. 162]

This is the beginning of Ruth's journey, the sealing of her pact with the devil, and her absolute removal from familial and social concerns. When Ruth stops loving, she can stop caring, and as a result gain access to the power that has always eluded her. Freed from the society that imprisons her, Ruth can finally laugh at the feeble institutions (such as marriage, motherhood, and community) that once "bound her down." And we laugh with her. The novel's comic effect is dependent upon its hilarious parody of society.

In the film adaptation, titled *She-Devil*, the main character, Ruth, has altogether different aims: in the short term, she wants to ruin her husband's home, family, career, and freedom. Please note that she doesn't, as she does in the book, want these things for herself. In the long term, we will see, she wants happiness, acceptance, love. She never stops loving her husband, she is simply very angry with him. She wants shallow revenge and cinematic apologies. She wants, it ultimately seems, to save her marriage. She never separates herself from the society and the world that imprisons her, and therefore never attains freedom or power. The film's Ruth never breaks free of her stereotypical status as a woman in a man's world and therefore constitutes no threat to its institutions. The film chooses to ignore the novel's irreverent view of society and people, and in so doing, it fails as a comedy. The story of this sanitized Ruth simply isn't funny.

Without Ruth's moment of transformation from housewife to she-devil, so explicit in the book, her ability to pull off elaborate plans for revenge seems entirely implausible, even in a comedy. When the film chooses to disregard the most pivotal moment in the book—when Ruth renounces the world and no longer lives by its rules—her subsequent attempts to destroy Bobbo's life seem hard to believe, difficult to understand, and, finally, not very funny. Ruth's transformation is the key to the book's meaning. In removing this element, and simply portraying Ruth as a pitiable and abused housewife (who gets very upset), the most important underpinning of the story's meaning is utterly destroyed. The book comments scathingly on the role of women in society, the effect of true love on women, and, finally, on the nature of humanity. The film insists on simplifying the characters and, moreover, it attempts to make Ruth more acceptable and likable. The result is dilution to the point of distortion. In trying to keep the movie on a light comic level, the film was forced to abandon the darker forces of evil which help to explain Ruth's re-creation into a she-devil.

I would like to compare the novel *The Life and Loves of a She-Devil* and the film *She-Devil* with regard to three basic themes: first, the Weldon claim that "not loving" is the first step to freedom; second, that once freed of the chains of love, a woman can entirely re-create her identity (we will see this to be true not only of the "heroine," Ruth, but also of her rival, Mary Fisher); and, finally, that it is necessary to interpret the novel as a feminist *Faust*, a deeply black comedy about the forces of good and evil. The film refused to acknowledge the evil component in the novel, and therein lies its final failure. Weldon's tightly bound universe can't be randomly dissected and ransacked for the "funny parts." It's all or nothing, or nothing works. As we will see, it is impossible to separate Weldon's comedy from her social satire.

The Plot: The Novel

A brief synopsis of the complicated plot of the novel will guide us through this analysis. The main character, Ruth, is tall (too tall to "look up to men"), heavy, and unattractive. She is married to handsome Bobbo, who was forced into the wedding because Ruth became pregnant. They have two troublesome children, a suburban house, and several pets. Bobbo is extremely unhappy with his domestic situation, and Ruth is constantly humiliated by her attempts to please him. The book opens by finding Bobbo falling in love with beautiful (and small) Mary Fisher, an extremely successful romance author. When Bobbo goes to live with Mary, having violently dubbed Ruth a "she-devil" upon his departure, Ruth's transformation takes place. First, she burns down the house and leaves the children with Mary and Bobbo. Second, she ensures that Mary Fisher's mother gets turned out of her nursing home, thereby sending old Mrs. Fisher back to live with Mary. In this way, Ruth brings domestic pressure into Mary Fisher's life, something Mary had avoided by remaining childless, hiring people to care for her aging mother, and employing servants to clean and cook. Third, Ruth ruins Bobbo's business and has him sent to jail for embezzling funds from his clients. She accomplishes this by starting an employment agency for women and planting an employee in Bobbo's office who deliberately alters his books. Next, Ruth goes to live with the judge in charge of Bobbo's case, and as she wields more and more influence over the judge, she manages to convince him to give Bobbo a severe jail sentence. As a mere side effect, Ruth manages to destroy Mary's career (after all, who can write romance novels with an unfaithful live-in boyfriend, two noisy children, a bitter old mother, etc. . . . ?). Mary's fortunes are depleted by hiring lawyers to free Bobbo. Mary ultimately gets cancer and dies. Alone. Just when we think that Ruth has gotten the revenge that she wanted, she uses the money she has earned to have drastic plastic surgery. She has her legs made six inches shorter (so she can, finally, look up to men) and her entire body and face restructured. She ends up looking exactly like Mary Fisher. When Bobbo's prison term is up, she picks him up and takes him to Mary Fisher's tower by the sea, which Ruth has bought, and they live together once more. Bobbo is confused and docile, and Ruth is sometimes nice to him, and sometimes not.

At the end of the book, Weldon calls her story: "A comic turn, turned serious" (p. 241). In the end, Ruth and Bobbo are back together. But not on any kind of conventional terms—she has altered herself to exactly resemble his mistress, and now she plays at the kind of cruelty he used to practice. The real Mary Fisher is dead. The children have grown up, left, and forgotten their parents. Weldon wreaks havoc with the conventions of good and evil, morality and immorality, and especially with the fanatical desire audiences have for a "happy ending." Here are all the broad ingredients for a happy ending—husband and wife reunited, virtuous wife triumphant, etc.—and yet it delivers the bleakest and blackest of messages.

The Plot of the Film

Take this black humor and just try lightening it up for a mass audience. Take short Roseanne Barr to play the mythically tall Ruth, leave out the really gritty parts, skip the plastic surgery because it's frankly too weird, and take what's left of the story. Then you will have the film: She-Devil.

The movie begins with Ruth as a pathetic, loving, cuckolded housewife. She doesn't know how to dress, or speak properly at pretentious receptions, or handle herself at a domestic dinner party. No wonder Bobbo falls in love with Mary Fisher, the glamorous romance novelist played by ever-glamorous Meryl Streep. Bobbo's affair is open and, needless to say, hurts Ruth very much. Bobbo lists his assets, terms Ruth a liability, calls her a she-devil, and leaves. Quite upset, she sits down to make a written list of Bobbo's "assets," as he called them: It goes like this: "HOME. FAMILY. CAREER. FREEDOM." (This is, presumably, what the filmmakers see as a literal translation of the novel's list mentioned earlier.) And quite industriously, Ruth follows the list: Ruth plugs in all the appliances, and burns down the house. She drops off the kids at Mary's, and goes her way. She goes to the nursing home, and sends Mary Fisher's mother back home. She changes Bobbo's books, and then starts an employment agency for women. She employs a woman to work for Bobbo who then changes the books further, and eventually Bobbo is caught and goes to jail. When Mary Fisher discovers that it appears Bobbo was trying to steal her money, she dumps him. (Not, as in the book, where she goes broke and dies for him.) Basically, the film ends there: Bobbo in jail, Ruth triumphant, and Mary Fisher going back to her old life. (With the small twist that Mary Fisher becomes a "serious" writer.) If we are looking closely, we will see a passing nod to the last third of the book, which concerns Ruth's extensive and ironic plastic surgery: a mole is at some point removed from Ruth's cheek. She also dresses better. In the final scene of the film, Ruth is seen bringing the

children to visit Bobbo in prison. He is more subdued now and asks to
come visit Ruth when he is freed. Perhaps, he offers, he can cook dinner
for them. "Yes," she says. "That would be nice."

These are glaring plot differences to say the least. But to our three
themes:

First, *not loving is the first step to freedom and power.* This point is
clearly made in one line from the novel: "I sing a hymn to the death of
love and the end of pain" (p. 163). Weldon shows how Ruth's progression
begins with her recognition of love as a destructive force in her life. Before
this revelation, she is miserable. Early in the book, we find Ruth dismal
and unhappy as Bobbo prepares to leave her for Mary.

"Mary Fisher writes about nothing but love. All you need is love. I assume I
love Bobbo because I am married to him. Good women love their husbands.
But love compared to hate, is a pallid emotion. Fidgety and troublesome and
making for misery." [P. 10]

Having discovered the relationship between love and misery, Ruth is on
her way. By page 24, Ruth's freedom is only just beginning:

"I look inside myself: I find hate, yes: hate for Mary Fisher, hot, strong, and
sweet: but not a scrap of love, not the faintest, wriggling tendril. I have fallen
out of love with Bobbo!" [P. 24]

And from this moment on, Ruth finds the energy and ability within herself—the strength to fight Bobbo and his unfair desertion, the nerve to
abandon her domestic obligations as wife and mother, the rebelliousness
to defy society's demands upon her feelings. When Bobbo calls Ruth a
"she-devil," he inadvertently gives her the key to her freedom and, simultaneously, his own destruction.

"This is exhilarating! If you are a she-devil, the mind clears at once. The spirits
rise. There is no shame, no guilt, no dreary striving to be good. There is only,
in the end, what you want. . . . I am a she-devil!" [P. 43]

Bobbo freed her. Released from the prison of her love for him, she can
do as she pleases. This psychological transformation is the book's most
crucial moment. The moment he calls her a "she-devil," Ruth begins immediately to change her identity and her relationship to the world. This
transformation is not instant, or painless. Old habits are hard to break.
Leaving her children, perhaps, is the hardest.

"I am a woman learning to be without her children. I am a snake shedding its
skin. . . . I twist and squirm with guilt and pain, even knowing that the quieter
I stay the quicker I will heal, slip the old skin, and slither off renewed into the
world." [Pp. 77–78]

By intentionally losing her ability to love, Ruth empties herself of the most human of emotions. In order to accomplish this, Ruth practically changes species. Her humanity is not helping her, she must try a different animal.

This renewal brings us to our second theme: *creation of a new identity.* As Ruth divests herself of her old feelings and behavior, it is left to her to decide what her new identity will be. It is an arduous process. Changing identities is complicated: "The roots of self-reproach and good behavior tangle deep in the living flesh: you can't ease them out gently; they have to be torn out, and they bring flesh with them" (pp. 50–51).

Ruth's transformation into a "she-devil" allows her to relinquish her slavery to the world—her place as an unattractive, unimportant, powerless housewife amongst a million others: ". . . since I cannot change the world, I will change myself" (p. 57). It is clear that Weldon is not subtle about the idea of Ruth's transformation. It is the driving force of the story. Ruth creates her own identity anew. She progresses from a woman with no feelings of self-worth to someone who thinks only of herself. She sees no in-between. Hand-in-hand with this act of creation is the move from good to evil. As Ruth discards the "dreary striving to be good" (p. 43), she embraces evil. "I want hate to drive out love, and I want to follow hate where it leads . . ." (p. 43). Ruth's love for Bobbo is what makes her forgive all. Once she hates him, she can do what she wants. She no longer has to please him. She can be "bad." If evil acts suit her purpose, so be it. This insistence on evil is important. It is, as we will see, discarded by the film, and it is, I will demonstrate, only when Ruth can embrace the she-devil's evil nature, that she can accomplish anything. Again, Weldon is not vague on this point. Ruth's ability to accomplish her arduous plans for revenge hinges upon it:

Only as a she-devil, she can give up ". . . those qualities traditionally associated with women—such as sweetness, the capacity to forgive, forbearance, and gentleness." [P. 118]

This all-important act of creation is spelled out explicitly:

"She-devils are beyond nature: they create themselves out of nothing." [P. 133]

"I will be what I want, not what He ordained. I will mold a new image for myself out of the earth of my creation. I will defy my Maker, and remake myself." [P. 162]

Before we turn to the film to see how these first two themes are relentlessly discarded, we will examine how these ideas affect not only Ruth, but the other major female character, Mary Fisher.

Ruth's rival is equally capable of creating her own identity, but in her case, she follows a descending path from triumph to misery. When we first meet her, she is beautiful, rich, successful, and sought after. Bobbo, Ruth's Bobbo, loves her uncontrollably. When we leave her, she has died a lonely, pitiable, and horrible death. She dies with no friends, no money, and no Bobbo. It is love that does her in, bringing with it the death of her power.

Mary Fisher's success in life is attributed to her ability to "invent" perfect love in her novels. Thus, Weldon begins her book: "Mary Fisher lives in a High Tower, on the edge of the sea: she writes a great deal about the nature of love. She tells lies" (p. 1).

These "lies" are Mary's tools for her own reinvention. She begins as a cardboard cutout, a personification of her own two-dimensional heroines, a woman incapable of real love. Therein lies her success. She believes these lies, and has the ability to make them come true in her own life. Bobbo loves her power, as he hates Ruth's dependence; loves her beauty, as he hates Ruth's ugliness; and loves her world of champagne and smoked salmon and elegant parties, as he hates the suburban drudgery that Ruth represents. Prior to meeting Bobbo, she slept with whoever she wanted, and never formed a strong attachment. "Almost, she became her own creation" (p. 109).

Mary's downfall comes when she truly falls in love with Bobbo. She is then as powerless and miserable as Ruth was at the beginning. Why didn't she throw Bobbo and his children out? Or her mother? Because Mary loves, she is engaged in life and society, and subject to its rules. In Weldon's novel, Mary's absolute devotion to Bobbo is explained as follows: "The more she has of Bobbo's body, the more she wants it. She desires his good opinion: she will do anything to have it, even look after his children, her mother, grow old before her time. His good opinion means a good night in bed. Sexual thralldom is as tragic a condition in life as it is in literature. Mary Fisher knows it, but what can she do?" (p. 98). To regain her old life, Mary must leave Bobbo, but she cannot.

"Mary Fisher must renounce love, but cannot. And since she cannot, Mary Fisher must be like everyone else. She must take her destined place between past and future, limping between the old generation and the new: she cannot escape. She nearly did: almost, she became her own creation." [P. 109]

Mary Fisher does struggle. Even in the face of the real truth of love, she attempts to keep up appearances:

"Mary Fisher tosses and yearns and waits to be filled, and writes about love. Her lies are worse because now she knows they are lies. . . ." [P. 183]

Mary sells her houses to pay for Bobbo's legal fees. Her books don't sell so well now that she "knows they are lies" (p. 183) and eventually she falls sick and dies. Bobbo had long since ceased to love her, and with that her love for him grew fiercer every day. Mary made the fatal mistake of loving at all, and lost the power she had. She had power and wealth because she could commit adultery and not care, take the children's father and not care, tell lies to a hundred hundred women and not care. Ruth took Mary's "ruthlessness" away from her. Mary became as much "ruth" as Ruth ever was.

Now, what does the film make of these themes? First of all, Ruth never really falls out of love with Bobbo. We can surmise this by seeing that she may accept him back in the end. Such a decision stretches the plausibility of the story even within the context of high farce. If you love someone, would you really put them in prison for years? In the book, Ruth has permitted herself to hate Bobbo, and therefore her revenge knows no bounds. The revenge of a woman who still loves would be far meeker by comparison. Second, how do we explain Ruth's transformation within the film? There is no point at which her entire relationship to either her husband, her society, or her world changes. When Bobbo calls Ruth a she-devil, what happens? This moment, as crucial as it is to the story, is dealt with in a slapstick manner. In rendering the "she-devil" moment as a cartoon, and not as a momentous transformation for Ruth's character, the film loses its ability to engage us in the story. The definition of Ruth as a she-devil needed to be serious, if only for a moment, in order to make us believe in Ruth's cataclysmic change. Instead, we have the following: As Bobbo builds up to dubbing Ruth a "she-devil," she sits in garish blue light, crying while Bobbo screams at her. When he leaves, she turns to the magnified side of a mirror and views a grotesque rendering of her already blunt features. Then comes the requisite lightning, which if it were not such a tired cliché, might at least pass for an attempt to signal some kind of "elemental" change on the planet, and, finally, we hear Ruth's piercing scream. Cartoon images, all of them. It is not coincidental that all the film's pyrotechnics take place *outside* Ruth, the blue light, the lightning, the mirror's reflection. Her scream of rage is also mechanical, not human and yet not the devil either—just another overused effect: the reverberation button in a sound studio. In using these literally "unrealistic" effects, the film interprets Ruth's transformation as a passage from real to unreal, or human to inhuman. In fact, it should be the reverse. When Ruth becomes the devil, she becomes real, she confronts her "real" nature. She is not an abused housewife, she realizes, she is a she-devil for whom anything is possible. The change is psychic: it is a journey within Ruth's consciousness, a progression in her image of herself. It signals a progression from the unreality of people's view of her to the powerful reality of her recognition of herself. The film reverses this essential order, showing the change to be outside her, to be as superficial and shallow as a momentary reflection in a mirror, or a disco-blue light.

In the film, Ruth's scream is a scream of rage and frustration. In the book, this is a calm moment for Ruth, a happy one. Remember: ". . . the spirits rise. There is no shame, no guilt, no dreary striving to be good" (p. 43). Ruth is finally *not* frustrated, she is uplifted and ready for action. Roseanne Barr shrieking on her doorstep gives anything but this impression. Roseanne's "Ruth" doesn't ever really change—on the inside—and therefore we want to ask *what* can propel her from victimized housewife to successful (and still forgiving) businesswoman? It is a basic question of story-telling. How does this character change? What motivates her? In the book, it is clear: hate and jealousy motivate her. Armed with the forces of evil, and its attendant lack of guilt, Ruth in the book can quite believably do anything. She has removed herself from the obligations of society and family. The Ruth in the film is never free. She never truly separates from her children (she is with them at the end), and we are given to believe that she ultimately forgives Bobbo as well.

Without her transformation, her subsequent journey seems unbelievable, and even tedious. In the film, her revenge takes the form of a list, to be executed by a lifeless mannequin. Her character is static, and the world she moves in is drearily familiar. In the book, it is Ruth's point of view that is interesting, her developing relationship to herself and to the world. She allows us to see the world differently, and her perspective is wildly engaging. In isolation from the book's view of humanity and society, Ruth's path of revenge is simply not very funny. You cannot change a black comedy into a white one—it doesn't work.

Finally, we can see Weldon's novel as a feminist *Faust*. In Weldon's conception, Ruth does not make a pact with the devil (who is, after all, a man), she *becomes* the devil. This is in keeping with Weldon's insistence on empowering the female through her own abilities. "She [Ruth] said she was taking up arms against God Himself. Lucifer had tried and failed, but he was male. She thought she might do better, being female" (p. 83).

Ruth has reason to be angry. She has not, when she considers it, been treated so very well by God's world. She has every reason to try something else. "His ways are far too mysterious for me to put up with them anymore" (p. 146). "We are here in this world to improve upon his original idea. To create justice, truth, and beauty where He so obviously and lamentably failed" (p. 115).

For her first competitive act with God, Ruth, as we have seen, re-creates herself, taking even the act of creation away from him. This is, not coincidentally, something women are also better at. "I do not put my trust in fate, nor my faith in God. I will be what I want, not what He ordained. I will mold a new image for myself out of the earth of my creation. I will defy my Maker, and remake myself" (p. 162).

As with all Faustian bargains, Ruth understands that she must pay a price in order to take on God. She lives a low and seamy life in preparation for her future. A servant in a nursing home, a housekeeper/mistress to the sexually sadistic judge, a nurse in a mental hospital. Finally, she undergoes years of excruciating pain for her plastic surgery.

She also gives up her children, her feelings, her identity, and, most of all, her ability to love. In return she gets power, money, revenge, and the ability to be loved without returning it—her original demands. But Not Loving ultimately limits her. As she grieves, in her own way, for Mary Fisher's death, she says: "She [Mary] is a woman: she made the landscape better. She-devils can make nothing better, except themselves. In the end, she wins" (p. 231).

And so this "comic turn, turned serious" (p. 241) delivers its own comeuppance. Without loving, you cannot live a full and happy life. If you love, you must accept its attendant misery. Ruth knowingly trades love for power. Weldon's novel is mired in irony, grief, and, mostly, the blackest, blackest humor.

Any story must bring with it certain rules. Weldon's novel shows a spiritual journey from helplessness to power, a transformation of Ruth as victim, to Ruth as the avenger, and she creates an ordered universe in which this change makes sense. Weldon's choice was to observe the rules of Faust. You cannot sell your soul to the devil (or become the devil) without paying a price. The price for Ruth is her humanity and, ironically, her womanhood.

In the film, Ruth pays no price. She ruins her husband's life, it seems, to teach him a lesson which he all too willingly learns. By the end, everything seems back on its way to being "normal." The drama is flat and stale. Nobody changes. Taken out of its spiritual context, Ruth's revenge is dull and plodding. Having abandoned the fictional logic of Weldon's story, the filmmakers failed to replace it with anything else.

In the film, Ruth merrily whips through her plans for revenge, succeeds, and then quite as merrily brings her children to visit Bobbo in prison. In Weldon's own words: "It was as if they were saying that all she had to do was put on a bit of lipstick, and all would be well." But you can't get something for nothing. Ruth must pay a price for her transformation or the story has no dramatic depth.

What was the film trying to do? Better put, perhaps, what did it *have*

to "do" to the book in order to get made as a big-budget commercial film?
I make the following suggestions:

Create a more acceptable Ruth: Is it even a coincidence that the film's
star is short? Size is often a visual equivalent for power, and Roseanne's
Ruth has neither. The film systematically creates a less threatening Ruth
for the screen. This smaller Ruth doesn't sleep around (in the book, her
subsequent sexual exploits are detailed, lurid, and seamy), therefore she
is more virtuous; doesn't ultimately abandon her children, so she is still
a responsible mother; nor finally, does she cease to love and desire her
husband, so she doesn't attack the fabric of society. Please notice specifically that she takes her children back, which does not happen in the book.
The movie-going audience apparently cannot be expected to identify with
a woman who truly abandons her children—or, for that matter, her husband, with whom she is now on congenial terms. She returns to the hearth
(even if it's Bobbo's prison yard) and reunites the family. She comfortably
fulfills our deepest (or what Hollywood assumes are its audience's deepest) feelings about mothers and wives. At the end of the film, just after
Bobbo has offered to come cook dinner after he gets out of prison, we hear
Ruth in voice-over: "People can change. That's why you can't give up on
them." Female forbearance defined.

This need to make Ruth a conventionally "heroic" heroine takes several
forms, not only with regard to her feelings about Bobbo and her children,
but also her subsequent business. In the book, Ruth's employment agency
is clearly a means by which she interferes in Bobbo's business. In the film,
they try to make this a more politically correct establishment: In voice-
over we hear Ruth say: "I would start an employment agency for the unloved, and the unwanted. Women . . . the world had thrown away. And I
knew just where to find them. . . . All these women needed was a little
support and encouragement to turn their lives around." We then see pictures of Oprah Winfrey, Mother Teresa, Gloria Steinem, and Jane Fonda.
Without commenting on the simplicity of this message, we can safely say
that the book makes no pretense about Ruth's commitment to the agency:
"The agency also organized day-care facilities for the babies and young
children . . . , and shopping and delivery service for their convenience. . . .
For these privileges they paid dearly, but were pleased to do so. . . . Nurse
Hopkins ran the day-care center on the top floor of the agency building,
and if from time to time she used tranquilizers on the more obstreperous
children, she was at least trained and qualified to do so" (p. 122).

The film's Ruth doesn't have the frightening desires of Weldon's Ruth.
Remember the beginning of the book: Ruth wants revenge, power, money,

and much, much more. The film's more timid Ruth simply wants to ruin Bobbo's HOME, FAMILY, CAREER, AND FREEDOM. By the end, it even seems she may give all of this back to him. This More Acceptable Ruth still identifies herself with her husband. She desires nothing for herself.

Create a more evil Mary: In keeping with the movie's tendency to simplify the story, as Ruth is made more "GOOD," Mary by extension must be made more "BAD." This simpler setup keeps the story in a more conventional genre. GOOD GIRL/BAD GIRL always works. Whereas the book ends with Bobbo and Ruth, the film ends with Mary Fisher in a scene Ruth describes in voice-over. This strengthens the notion of one woman against the other.

The film's Mary leaves Bobbo when she thinks that he tried to steal her money. But if Mary didn't truly love Bobbo, she wouldn't have put up with his kids and other troubles for such a long time. She would have thrown him out long ago. Her relationship with him made no sense if she were not senselessly in love with him. Her ability to dump him when she "really" gets mad invalidates all that went before in the film. But by showing money (and not love) as the most important thing in her life, Mary can be comfortably dubbed a truly "bad" woman. An adulteress, on film in any case, must be evil by definition, and the filmmakers went to great lengths to make sure we don't miss this point.

The book gives us no such easy outs. The book does not pit one woman against the other, but, rather, it shows love itself to be against a woman's best interest. And yet, in the end, "Mary wins." Because she loves. And only true love could make her castle crumble. In the book, she dies, penniless and powerless, and we are not allowed to simply hate her. We can sympathize with women who are ruined by love. So love is at once the "evil" force in the book, woman's enemy, and at the same time, it is the only way we can make the "landscape better." Such a complex point is impossible to make within the context of the film's simple rendition.

In the film, it was necessary to be utterly against Mary Fisher. She is an evil, greedy adulteress, no more, no less. Easily digestible.

Create a happy ending: The final simplification of the plot is, of course, the film's abbreviated ending. Perhaps this can be defended as a cut merely for the purpose of time constraints, but it fits in so perfectly with the film's other choices that this plea would seem hardly credible. The book's ultimate message was too complex and too confusing for Hollywood. In the film's effort to simplify, simplify, they throw out the part of the story that is ironic and confusing. In the book, Ruth's physical transformation into

Mary's image, her self re-creation, is complete. She gets what she wants: her rival's life. After her successful efforts to ruin her husband's life, it is the book's deepest irony that all she wanted in the end was to be the object of her husband's desire, even though, as we have seen, she is incapable of loving him as she once did. This ending has no easy answers. We are forced to contemplate the uglier sides of love and power and the uncomfortable trade-off between love and freedom. We are, as Weldon wants us to be, dumbfounded.

In the context created by the film, it would make no sense for Ruth to transform herself into the film's "BAD" woman, Mary. Ruth wants to be GOOD, and to get what she Deserves. And she does. The film is determined, against all odds, to deliver that most tyrannical of Hollywood requirements, a Happy Ending. And *She-Devil* didn't lend itself easily to this formula. Only drastic cutting, and a complete removal of the book's ultimate message, could secure these ends. We are left with Ruth forgiving her chastened husband, and given no reason to understand why this would happen.

A more acceptable heroine, a simpler bad "guy," and a happy ending. A happy ending is more life-affirming and more comfortable for the paying audience. Ultimately, it offers a confirmation of society's rules and institutions. Marriage is not humiliated. Unfaithful men are redeemable. Clearly, the film chose not to acknowledge the she-devil story as a humorous indictment of society.

It is interesting to look at Weldon's novel as a feminist comedy and to see how the film fought, consciously or unconsciously, to fit the story into a conventional patriarchal definition of comedy. For our purposes, classic comedy can be defined as one that deals with cycles of fertility and regeneration. It shows the old corrupt order being replaced by the new; it is characterized by the purging of anything distressful; it portrays a place where order is created out of chaos; and, finally, has a happy ending. Conversely, and as defined by this book's editor, Regina Barreca, women's comedy can be seen as follows: it does not necessarily have a happy ending; it destroys the social order; rather than purging distress, feminist comedy acts as a catalyst for women to take action.

Clearly, *She-Devil* fits perfectly into the definition of women's comedy. It is without a simplistic "happy ending." Ruth's decision to give up her husband, her family, and all of society's normal requirements for a woman illustrates perfectly the destruction of the existing social order. And, finally, it is as clear a portrait of a woman taking action as ever there was.

The film version ends up remaking the story into a classic patriarchal comedy. We have already shown the fact that the film has a happy ending: the evil husband repents and is reunited with his children. There is a possibility for him to get back together with Ruth, or, at the very least, he wants to be in her future.

Mary Fisher can be defined as the old corrupt order in that she has power, money, and worldly success, yet she is an adulteress, an insincere writer, and a successful hypocrite. Needless to say, she is undone. She loses her man and her invulnerability. She is no longer without a care in the world. Hard-working, victimized Ruth is triumphant. This can be seen as the corrupt order being replaced by new. Virtue will win out. And as for regeneration, what is nearly the last scene in the film? The happy children. The husband offering to feed them. The perfect symbol of regeneration—and they seem happier and more cooperative than before.

We have seen how the film adaptation attempted to lighten the text and turn it into popular entertainment in an inoffensive manner. We have seen how the story's meaning is utterly subverted by these attempts to parcel out pieces of the story. On a deeper level, now, we can see that the film, wittingly or unwittingly, managed to take a woman's story, a comic turn, turned tragic, and make it into a man's. Reinvented it so that it would fit the patriarchal definitions of comedy.

This is the final turning upside down of all that the book attempted to portray. An examination of many classic films shows that the pattern set by the film of *She-Devil* fits perfectly into the history of Hollywood film adaptations. There is a striking similarity among the films that attempt to put powerful literary heroines on the screen. In these films, in general, as much power as possible is removed from the women; virginity remains at all costs, or some semblance of physical purity; and, finally, women are rarely loved without loving in return. It is interesting to note these points when discussing such adaptations as *Great Expectations*. It seems that Charles Dickens expected his audience in 1861 to be more accepting of "certain" kinds of women than David Lean thought an audience could handle in 1947. Hollywood always expects their audience to have less moral tolerance, and a more narrow definition of women, than books have expected from their readers throughout time.

Weldon deals with this theme when she describes the work of Mary Fisher. When she describes the formula behind Mary's romance novels she could equally well be speaking of the Hollywood tradition: "Now. In Mary Fisher's novels, which sell by the hundred thousand in glittery pink and gold covers, little staunch heroines raise tearful eyes to handsome men, and by giving them up, gain them. Little women can look up to men. But women of six feet two have trouble doing so" (p. 22).[1]

The very power that heroines of classic novels have is the power that Weldon gives to Ruth. And the movie took it away. Weldon acknowledges the issue of power quite bluntly toward the end of her novel: ". . . it is not a matter of male or female, after all; it never was: merely of power. I have all, and he has none" (p. 241). It is this raw power that films are still unwilling to grant to women on the screen.

To sum up, what have the thematic differences between the movie *She-Devil* and the novel *The Life and Loves of a She-Devil* enabled the movie to do in its quest to be conventional, commercial, and popularly successful in Hollywood terms?

First of all, the movie clearly fits into the classic Hollywood tradition of smoothing out the heroine, virginalizing her, making her better, making her Good. Second, unwittingly or otherwise, the film adaptation transformed a black feminist comedy into a light patriarchal conventional comedy complete with a happy ending.

And last, the film has attempted to portray a more politically correct Ruth. It seems that this is also a requirement for a contemporary Hollywood movie. You can't portray a truly powerful woman, but she shouldn't be "dated" either. You don't want anyone accusing you of trying to remake "Father Knows Best," not after the success of *Thelma and Louise*, or, for that matter, after Anita Hill. And *She-Devil*, don't forget, was directed by a woman, and proper feminist politics would be "expected" by the audience the studio is counting on her to draw. These days, in the context of a commercial, conventional Hollywood film, the heroine must also be politically correct. She should be a woman with a reasonable gripe trying in her own small way to correct a wrong, and thereby fix her marriage. Along the way, she also employs women who have difficulty getting jobs. She identifies with these women, "the unloved and the unwanted." By running this agency, Ruth gets a job herself, which maybe, in the film ideal of a politically correct world, was her real problem, after all. Perhaps they even expect us to believe that Ruth became more interesting to her husband because she joined the professional world. (Near the end of the film, Bobbo compliments Ruth for the first time. As she stands there in her professional businesswoman clothes, mole removed, he says (and means it), "You look great!"). But this political correctness is a shallow requirement. On a deeper level, the film *She-Devil* made sure that our male-dominated institutions and societal rules were all confirmed and supported. What began as a novel about a woman became a film about a woman finally receiving her husband's approval.

The real Ruth, the Ruth of the novel, is not such a socially respectable creature. She serves no one except herself. She has only her own interests at heart. Her ideas about reuniting with her husband are bizarre. Her employment agency is anything but a "do-good" operation designed to help women. She abandons the agency after it accomplishes its purpose and we never hear about it again. In the film, it seems as though the organization took on a life of its own, and she is still the president.

This brings us to the title of this essay. Ms. Weldon described the problem with the film adaptation in two sentences: "They should have called it 'She-Angel.' They tried to make Ruth nice and politically correct. And you see, she just isn't."

Notes

1. In this quote, Weldon also explains much of the mentality behind the Hollywood film. A heroine is heroic by gaining her man. That is her key to happiness. To attain this exalted plateau, a woman must be good, virtuous, and almost always a virgin. Power for women is what little their hero willingly bestows upon them. Women are not powerful in their own right. Sound exaggerated? Let's take a brief look at some adaptations of classic works.

The play *Pygmalion* by George Bernard Shaw (1914) and the film *My Fair Lady* directed by George Cukor (1964)

Since many found the play ambiguous concerning whom Eliza marries, Shaw wrote an essay to make his intent clear. According to Shaw, Eliza marries Freddy—Freddy, the dull, silly, penniless aristocrat who adores her. In the film, we are led to believe that she marries Professor Higgins, her benefactor, who does not adore her all the time, but to whom she owes her ability to speak properly. In the film, a powerless woman (Eliza) who is helped by a powerful man (Higgins) would be unforgivably ungrateful if she refused to marry him. Even though Shaw went to great effort to ensure that the meaning of his play's ending be correctly interpreted, the film still chose to ignore him. At the end of the film, we hear Rex Harrison say the famous words "Where the devil are my slippers?" and we see Audrey Hepburn gleefully returning to Higgins's hearth. What more could a woman want? In the play, the power tables are turned: in the beginning, she wants his help; he gives it only for his own benefit, in the interests of an experiment; in the end, he wants her, putting her in the powerful position. She cannot marry him without losing herself, so she declines. And therefore remains powerful. It is possible to say that in the play, Eliza is loved without loving in return. Not so, in the film. This is something that Shaw anticipated by noting in his famous postscript to the play:

. . . people in all directions have assumed, for no other reasons than that she (Eliza) became the heroine of a romance, that she must have married the hero of it. This is unbearable, not only because her little drama, if acted on such a thoughtless assumption, must be spoiled, but because the true

sequel is patent to anyone with a sense of human nature in general, and of feminine instinct in particular. [Penguin Edition, p. 134]
Further, he notes:
    This being the state of human affairs, what is Eliza fairly sure to do when she is placed between Freddy and Higgins? Will she look forward to a lifetime of fetching Higgins' slippers or to a lifetime of Freddy fetching hers? There can be no doubt about the answer. [P. 138]
Or can there? Clearly, Shaw had a more liberal view of women in 1916 than the filmmakers thought audiences would accept in 1964.

A smaller point, but pertinent, is that in the play, Eliza kisses Freddy so fervently that they are chased off by a policeman. No such encounter takes place in the film.

In the film, therefore, we have a more virtuous, more ultimately submissive, and less powerful Eliza. She has fewer choices in life as so defined, and flocks gratefully back to Higgins. This is the "happy" ending. Happy for Higgins, in any case.

Wuthering Heights: The book by Emily Brontë and the film directed by William Wyler (1939)

The final love scene in the book shows Catherine seven months' pregnant, near death, and having a mad, raging love scene with Heathcliff. Even as they tear each other to pieces, Cathy's savage love for Heathcliff is more than clear. As the book's witness proclaims: "My mistress had kissed him first." What are the repercussions of such a scene? First of all, it is a complete repudiation of Cathy's husband (who is seen as a nice enough person), and therefore makes a mockery of the institution of marriage. It also shows a physical and passionate love within a woman who is about to give birth. Cathy does in fact give birth only hours later, and she dies in the process. How does the film handle this female character, who is unfaithful, sexually alive, who spits upon marriage, and is unkind to her kind husband? The movie systematically removes her power. First of all, she never gets pregnant, keeping a more virginal air (even when married) around her. Second, after Cathy's death, Heathcliff begs her to curse him and to haunt him for the rest of his life. In the book, they threaten each other mutually in their last, passionate scene together. The movie leaves the power of Cathy's haunting to the discretion of Heathcliff's request. Finally, throughout Heathcliff and Cathy's last scene in the film, there is the constant overhanging fear of Edward's return—thus implementing some sense of his conjugal rights. In the book, they could care less about him. Again, we see the same themes: a more virginal heroine (they remove her pregnancy); a nicer heroine (the violence of her language when arguing with Heathcliff is decidedly toned down); ultimately a less powerful Cathy, who is begged by Heathcliff to haunt him. He commands her to do it, in fact. The film doesn't even allow Cathy the privilege of haunting him on her own.

Great Expectations: The book by Charles Dickens and the David Lean film (1947)

In the book, Estella marries and is widowed before she sees Pip again. Further, there is ambiguity over whether Pip and Estella will eventually unite. We may choose to interpret the book's ending to mean that they do reunite, but the fact of Estella's character would leave a healthy doubt as to their chances for happiness. For, in the novel, she does not relinquish herself, necessarily, to Pip. She remains aloof, still seems somewhat evil, and therefore retains her power over Pip, who desires nothing more than her love. Perhaps Estella is the classic female example of a woman who is loved, without necessarily loving in return. This, as Weldon and others seem to claim, is the true source of power: to be desired not just sexually, but totally, and to be unavailable, at least partially.

In the David Lean film, Estella is *still a virgin* when she finds Pip again, her husband-to-be having deserted her. In addition, she has become *nice*. Freed from Miss Havisham's spell, seemingly glad to be rid of all the teachings which she took so willingly at one time, Estella has undergone a transformation. She is good and virtuous and desires a relationship with a man. "In the film, she comes to Pip broken-hearted but with everything else intact. This much was demanded by a 1947 film audience, although apparently a reading public nearly ninety years earlier was tolerant enough to accept Estella as Pip's future wife despite the fact that she had been married and divorced" (from a lecture by Regina Barreca). Further, the film's romantic ending not only shows them getting together, but leaves little doubt of their happiness.

The film has provided what Shaw called "the ready-made and reach-me-downs of the ragshop in which Romance keeps its stock of 'happy endings' to misfit all stories" (p. 134). Surely, Dickens would be right in saying that no-where in his novel did he hint at such a transformation on Estella's part. Why, then, does David Lean make this change? The answer lies within the pattern I have been establishing. Seductive, unloving, powerful women have no place in Hollywood. Even when they bring with them the authorization of the world's great authors, every film director is called upon to "somehow" make these great literary heroines nicer, more virtuous, more submissive, and less powerful.

Somebody by now must be aching to bring up that most popular of "evil" heroines, Scarlett O'Hara, from *Gone with the Wind*. But there too you see the same typical translation from book to film. In the book, Scarlett not only marries Charles Hamilton (her first husband), but she has several children by him. Later, she has more children by her second husband, Frank Kennedy. In the film, she has no children until her third marriage with Rhett Butler. What is the overall impact of this? Virginity. Or at least there's no proof of the opposite. Her marriages are necessary to move the plot forward; they can't be dropped as Estella's was dropped in *Great Expectations*. But the children can be de-leted. And so the audience can be made to feel that Scarlett loses her precious innocence with the true romantic interest in the film, Rhett Butler. Early on in their epic "courtship," he says to her: "You need kissing badly. That's what's wrong with you. You should be kissed and often, and by someone who knows how." If we must acknowledge her past marriages, Rhett can still assure us that Scarlett has never "really" been touched. Finally, when Rhett Butler does kiss her, it is as if for the first time in her life. He even makes this point: "You've been married to a boy and an old man, why not try a husband of the right age, with a way with women?" (They kiss passionately.) She begs him to stop, threatening to faint. He responds: "I want you to faint. This is what you were meant for. None of the fools you've ever known have kissed you like this, have they?'' And she accepts his offer of marriage, begging for more kisses, thus confirming that this twice-married woman has never really been kissed. Her swooning response to Rhett's first kiss confirms the image of Scarlett as a physically innocent woman.

Surely, you will now cry out that this analysis is outdated. It only applies to "old" movies. Look at the seductresses in *Presumed Innocent*, in *Fatal Attraction*, in *Basic Instinct*—sexually active, ambitious, somewhat evil career women all of them. Well, look at them. The lawyer in *Presumed Innocent* is violently murdered by the outraged wife. After hearing about her evil deeds, the film often cuts immediately to photos of her bloody head. Does this indicate a causal relationship between her "bad" behavior and her eventual murder? The same thing happened to Glenn Close in the finale of *Fatal Attraction*. The seductress is killed by the "good" wife. And in *Basic Instinct*, the true murderess is unveiled and murdered as well. While there is some ambiguity at the end (however contrived) concerning the Sharon Stone character, it is clear that she is safe as long as she truly loves Michael Douglas.

Yes, such evil heroines are now allowed on screen, provided they die there. When it comes to adaptations of books, where such wanton and capricious killings might not be practical, it is best to alter the heroine's basic character. Obviously, twentieth-century film audiences are even more conservative and demanding than nineteenth-century readers. Or so the major Hollywood studios believe.

Works Cited

Shaw, George Bernard. *Pygmalion*. New York: Penguin, 1957.
Weldon, Fay. *The Life and Loves of a She-Devil*. New York: Ballantine Books, 1983.

JOHN GLAVIN

Fay Weldon, Leader of the Frivolous Band

Part One: Caveat [Cannibal] Lector

Fay Weldon's *Leader of the Band* (1988). A book I think I'm not supposed to read. I hear myself warned off in passages like this one: Sandra recalling "male medical hands inside me, rubber gloved if one's lucky, feeling a this or feeling a that. What can they *know*? What can they be feeling for? Some ritual here that is beyond rational understanding, but part of the male desire to be in on the female act of creation" (p. 103). This "male interest in female insides," including, surely? the insides of females' fiction, "the determination to be there helping," the novel insists, "gets us nowhere, except increasingly to indicate that we are all without guide, leader, Prime Mover" (pp. 103–104). Concede, it seems to say, that obstetrics, now an overwhelmingly male specialty, poaches on *obstetrix*, the Latin word for midwife. And conceding that much, get your gynecological hands off of and out of this book.

But then, you may recall, the male doctor in the novel does hold the long-withheld answer to the plot's puzzle. He does, as Sandra puts it, "have something of importance to impart" (p. 152), when—ironically— he reveals the secret that both settles Sandra's future and concludes her tale: "*puis-je vous offrir mes félicitations . . . vous êtes certainement enceinte.*" And there is also the curious last moment of the book as a whole, the conclusion of the third appended story, "Falling in Love in Helsinki," which isn't about falling in love at all, but about the recovery of the father. Or rather about "falling into love with life" (p. 196), apparently through a recuperative reunion with the father. And—I'm almost sorry to keep doing this—it's when "Listening to Jack" play the trumpet that Sandra "perceived all of a sudden that there might well perhaps be another way" to live, other—that is—than duty or madness (pp. 96–97). And, finally, it's clearly Sandra's attempt to recover at least the memory of her father from his own monstrosity that turns her from flight to life: "if you are determined to be proud of your father. Forget your mum. . . . the stains are gone" (p. 107). Can a Weldon novel really turn on getting back in touch with Dad, "the Bastard" (p. 155) that he is now, always has been, and probably ever shall be? Can such a Mum-refusing heroine really come from the pen that inscribed the She-Devil, that told the Fat Woman's Joke, that wondered and wandered Down and Out Among the Women? Remember Greta Garbo's response to the end of Cocteau's *Beauty and the Beast*? Watching Prince Charming's pretty face emerge, she was heard to sigh: "Give me back my beast." Do we, even the men among us, really want a responsible, reasonable heroine in the pages of a Weldon novel? Surely not. And that's not what we get. We get Sandra, "tough and frivolous." Which brings me back to where I began: my title.

Finding the Frivolous

Admit. Reader, you felt put off, finding frivolous in the title. (If I were more modish I'd win you at once with discipline or surveillance or scrutiny, or just plain police.) It won't help if I say that by frivolous I don't mean minor, silly, insignificant, or slight, as in the traditional usage: having little weight or importance, trifling, having no basis in law or fact. That is merely melodrama's way of reading and deflating what it means to be frivolous. And it's unlikely to ameliorate your distaste if I add that I mean frivolous as a compliment. Or even that I'm pretty sure Fay Weldon herself would accept the compliment.

But, in *Leader of the Band*, Sandra does define herself as hero with just that term: "I have become both tough and frivolous" (p. 34). That frivolity, that particular toughness of mind and feeling combined, is what I search for in fiction. Rarely do I find it; in fact, I don't find it in recent work by men. Sandra talks about that when she asks if we: "remember Sophie, of the Styron novel, who was told to decide by a Nazi officer which of her two children was to live? It was seen (by a man) as a hard and beastly choice, but if you ask me it was better than none. Why didn't she just grit her teeth and get on with it, or kill herself and both children with the material at hand if she couldn't bear it? Moan, moan, moan, Sophie!" (p. 105). The recent male imagination can't seem to avoid melodrama. (Perhaps because it's generally women's bodies, even in men's fictions, that endure the pain, and therefore spawn the toughness that distinguishes between the frivolous and the facile.) When men try to swerve, they tend to become arch (David Lodge), or mean (Malcolm Bradbury), or merely sad (J. R. Ackerley). Yet an astonishing company of (though by no means all) British women writers seem to find the frivolous their natural voice: Angela Carter, Penelope Fitzgerald, Mary Wesley, Jeanette Winterson, to name only a few.[1]

And from this frivolous group Fay Weldon emerges, this essay argues, "the leader of the band." She leads this talented band, in part because she generates so intelligent a metafictive discourse about the kind of writing she practices, and in part because she and her characters are so boldly eager to face head-on the difficult (read: tough) choices frivolity demands. It's that combination of discursive analysis and eager boldness that makes *The Leader of the Band* a paradigmatic text in the history and theory of frivolity. No recent novel, even by Fay Weldon, takes on more clearly or more successfully the frivolous imperative of "falling into love with life," nor reveals more frankly how nearly impossible it is to evade the automatic sadness bourgeois society imposes, and bourgeois fiction encodes.

Vamping Till Ready

So, in his male knowing, he's going to enlist this woman's book *Leader of the Band* as a paradigmatic text in his male-generated category, the frivolous, a genre no one else has ever even heard of. Except—I could rush to point out—Jacques Derrida. Which hardly improves—you say—the situation.

Actually, the frivolous does have a history, though not a place in history. A history that can suggest its claim to be taken seriously, if that does not seem too oxymoronic, as a sort of metagenre stranding its way through the other and more familiar taxonomies of the last two centuries.[2] Historically, the frivolous has meant everything the good bourgeois is not. Even now, lawsuits the courts do not respect they will dismiss as "frivolous." "As the social power of the bourgeoisie grows," Norbert Elias argues, "Bourgeois groups emphasize more and more their specifically bourgeois self-image. . . . Above all they counterpose [their] 'virtue' to 'courtly frivolity'" (p. 315). This kind of distinction has been ongoing at least since the nineteenth century. The dawning age of *laissez-faire*, to distinguish itself from what had preceded,—so argues Jean Starobinski, the inimitable historian of liberty—"had recourse to a falsified image of a 'frivolous' eighteenth century . . . solely intent on the culpable and delightful pursuit of unrestrained enjoyment" (p. 9). But even in the eighteenth century itself, as Derrida points out in his essay on Condillac, *The Archeology of the Frivolous*, it functioned as a key term to distinguish the bourgeois values of the useful and the serviceable, cardinal values of empiricism, from what seemed superfluous and excessive.[3] With its near neighbor, the carnival-esque, the frivolous shares "an attitude of creative disrespect, a radical opposition to the illegitimately powerful, to the morose and monological" (Stamm, 55). But unlike carnival, the scoff-law frivolous looks for more than a temporary suspension of the established order. It looks instead for an immortality and completeness of its own designation.[4]

Obviously, I am troping the term, turning it, like Black or Gay, to rein-flate a kind of experience the original usage attempts to degrade. Weldon's Sandra cuts to the core of this recuperated frivolous when she insists that frivolity means "Form, style, content—in that order of importance": *form*, "the intricate patterns which contain the key"; *content*, "the mere stuff of the universe . . . last and least" (p. 8). Such a resistance to the referent's dominion over signification continues, into *laissez-faire* and thereafter, that founding movement in British antiestablishment discourse: anti-nomianism, the powerful antithesis to the Calvinism of the "respectable bourgeois Puritan" (Hill, p. 276). Weldon heroes like Sandra, or earlier the furious Ruth of *The Life and Loves of a She-Devil*, parade clearly the key features of the antinomian spirit.[5] Not only do they interiorize authority until impulse becomes the only law to which they admit themselves sub-ject, but any earlier adherence to an institutionalized law becomes de-monized. The frivolous/antinomian is thus always a former law-abider—a law-abider whose conversion leads in turn to a radical willingness to act in and on time rather than to an intellectual or apolitical flight from his-tory. The Weldonian-antinomian becomes *radically* involved in acting upon, rather than "radically alienated from the secular order" (Pocock, p. 346)—the way of the Romantic sublime.

Learning from the She-Devil

Those features virtually outline *The Life and Loves of a She-Devil*. From all too willing, though sadly inept, "good wife" under the law (indeed that is what the Biblical allusion to Ruth insists on), Ruth is transformed to the she-devil whose will and desire are the only laws she need ac-knowledge, and before which every other life and history palls. "But this is wonderful! This is exhilarating! If you are a she-devil, the mind clears at once. The spirits rise. There is no shame, no guilt, no dreary striving to be good. There is only, in the end, what you *want*. And I can take what I want. I am a she-devil" (p. 43). Apocalyptically, Ruth uses this crucial change to mold not only the law (Judge Bishop) and religion (Father Ferguson) but even the truly sacrosanct modern profession, health (Dr. Black and Mr. Genghis) in the forms found by her large and capable hands. From the crucial moment of her conversion, she demonstrates vividly and wittily that crucial antinomian "conviction of a radically free natural capacity within [her]self [that] intensifie[s] h[er] ability to engage in radical action based on radical criticism of . . . laws and liberties in their inherited form," a "liberation amounting almost to divinization of human capacities" (Pocock, p. 375). If in the late twentieth century, divinization must alter to demonization, as the gender of the pronouns also changes, that is simply the mark of a fully secularized—fully frivolous—assimilation of what was earlier religious and male.[6]

The frivolous refuses the mainline form of bourgeois cultures, the melodramatic.[7] In *She-Devil* melodrama is represented by its sweetened, neutered form, romance: the life, loves, and writing of Mary Fisher. Since melodrama helps to disguise puritanism's transformation into capitalism, by no accident does Mary Fisher grow rich writing novels that deny all problems of epistemological economy and clarification. Instead, her books (unlike her creator's) fulfill "a desire to make starkly articulate" (Brooks, p. 4). She invites her readers to see, as she does, looking out from her High Tower, "the way the evening sun stretches across the sea onto the old stone and makes everything a warm soft pinky yellow. Who needs rose-tinted glasses when reality is so cozy?" (*She-Devil*, p. 66). Simultaneously moralistic and antimetaphysical, her vision can "'prove' the existence of a moral [read: melodramatic] universe, which, though put into question, . . . does exist and can be made to assert its presence and its categorical force among men" (Brooks, p. 290). Especially when that force performs as a kind of all-pervasive sympathy, generating a world where "the rain falls because she is sad, [where] storms rage because she is consumed by unsatisfied lust and the crops fail because she is lonely" (*She-Devil*, p. 161). Here, any problematic "excess of the signifier in relation to the signifiable" (Brooks, p. 67) vanishes. Her readers accept supine passivity as the valid price of narcissistic centrality. It doesn't matter if I'm bull's eye to the world's slings and arrows as long as that guarantees that I'm the main attraction.

Prizing this cynosure innocence, despite her sexual self-indulgence, Mary Fisher writes and reads herself like Styron's Sophie: a righteous subject whose choices, dictated and structured by a predestined power, are no choice at all. She is thus powerless when Ruth turns against her. Melodramatic imaginations like Mary Fisher's read need as a trace on the squeaky-clean slate of the subject, inscribed by others' withdrawal or ab-

sence. Her collapse thus unfolds not from a gap within her character but
from a rupture in time and space, engineered by the now frivolous Ruth,
who appears to Mary as an excessive, inexplicable, externalized cupidity,
before which melodramatic subjects, Mary herself or the Bobbo of the
Tower, can only experience her- or himself as prey. "How weak people
are!" Ruth realizes. "How they simply accept what happens, as if there
were such a thing as destiny, and not just a life to be grappled with"
(p. 240).

Frivolous Ruth, grappling with life, scarred into awareness by melodrama's self-squeezing regime of service and utility, cautiously conserves
her own, incessantly jeopardized, power to maintain it and herself beyond
the claims of any reference: the Swiss bank accounts. She has complete
mobility. She can change her occupation, even her name, at will, while
Mary and Bobbo remain stationed and targeted in the entirely vulnerable
High Tower. Weldon's great comic image for this difference is, of course,
Ruth's transformation of her own body, despite its enormous cost in suffering. She makes herself refer, quite literally, to the image she has chosen,
rather than to the image the natural and social orders conspire to impose
upon her. Frivolity displaces cupidity with obsession, centered on the
ability to fold back on oneself, both semantically and erotically, rather than
to point to a place within a fixed order of (suburban) identities. Frivolity
thus becomes a term for "need left to itself, need without object, without
desire's direction" (Derrida, p. 130). Ruth wants Bobbo back, not because
she any longer loves, let alone desires, him, but because "the seeming repetition of desire without any object or of a floating desire" (Derrida) marks
the essential triumph in the frivolous mind of the subject over her here-
tofore ordained subjugation.

This contest between melodrama and frivolity comes to a head on the
question of suffering. Aware that suffering is always indecent, and also
likely to improve the position of someone other than the sufferer, the frivolous prefers, whenever possible, to be heartless rather than to celebrate
heartache. But this heartlessness also allows frivolity to use rather than
to be used by suffering. Melodramatic culture, loathing suffering but finding it inevitable, offers to convert pain into the price of wisdom and the
bond that cements society. That's Styron's point, or pointlessness, if we
read him with Starlady Sandra. Ruth, entirely frivolous, reads suffering
in a very different way. *"Il faut suffrir"* (*She-Devil*, p. 162), she acknowledges. But her suffering she herself selects: "The more you want the more
you suffer. If you want everything, you must suffer everything." The melodramatic "suffer at random, and gain nothing." Not even dignity. Suffering
makes Mary Fisher merely "petulant," and Bobbo "depressed" (p. 161).

But the frivolous locates suffering as part of the achievement of, the plea-sure of, power. "I have all," Ruth boasts at novel's end, and Bobbo "has none" (p. 241).

But you are wrong, you will say. Fay Weldon doesn't approve of Ruth. She says that She-Devil is about envy and its corrosive power.[8] Ruth, at the end, has not liberated herself. In her fury she has merely converted herself into the image of everything she once, wisely, loathed. Ruth is not the answer.

Segue into Leading the Band

You're right. Of course. Which is why I focus on Leader of the Band. The later novel not only represents a key text in the development of the con-temporary frivolous, a model or Ur-text of what such fiction could be, but it also seems to signal a far-reaching change in Fay Weldon's own vision of self-liberation. At its core, Leader of the Band quite literally renounces fury, purging frivolity of its contaminating double.

At first, it seems to make such good sense that fury opens the way to frivolity. Doesn't the frivolous turn mark a subject's furious rejection of imposed identity in favor of an identity she chooses to enact? In what else does the toughness of the frivolous root if not in its steady refusal to be read by any public order of utility? Isn't that why bourgeois society has insistently dismissed the frivolous with such derision? Because it can't believe in a viable meaning outside a socially constructed order?

Weldon answers this argument with the entirely admirable Mum in "A Libation of Blood," the first of the three stories appended to Leader of the Band. "You're so frivolous," complains Alice to her mother (p. 162). What has her mother said or done that merits the term? She's merely told Alice she's the result of a faulty condom, and "whoever liked"—the frivolous narrator immediately asks—"to believe they sat thus accidentally in the world?" If we are all here, men and women alike, accidental in an acci-dental world, (and not essential to an overdetermined universe, as Mary Fisher would have it), then what sense does fury make? What good can fury do? Alice has just suffered a miscarriage. Mum consoles Alice for her recent miscarriage by recalling—the first time her daughter's ever heard of it—"the time I miscarried the first lot of twins," said Mum, who was, as ever, full of surprises.

"Just as well. They weren't your father's. Now drink a lot of water, and re-place the lost blood, and here's to better luck next time. It'll happen." [Pp. 172–73]

Fury, as we'll see, can only subvert the enlargement promised by frivolous conversion: downscaling comedy to that "comic turn, turned serious" which finally summarizes *She-Devil* (p. 241).

Replacing fury, no matter how righteous its claim, *Leader of the Band* centers Starlady Sandra's "turn" on an unimpeachable commitment to enjoyment. "What else was there to do," Sandra asks, "but get through [life], enjoying yourself on the way" (p. 96). And that commitment to enjoyment, in turn, opens the way to the return of all that fury represses: of the father, of what the father knows and unknowingly misrepresents (classics and science), and even of the patriarchal family. This frivolous book argues that, beyond gender, ideology, class, injustice, and strife, it's "Luck of the draw, all luck of the draw" (p. 167). Using luck, then, not inviting or refusing suffering, turns out to be the way to liberate both the self and the knowledge the self needs to sustain itself. How frivolous.

Part Two: Leading the Band

The dynamic of that frivolity helps me, as the impossible reader of *Leader of the Band*, to sense the possibility of a pertinent male voice, of a not-irrelevant male reader. It makes me want to try to set going now a frivolous dialogue between the novel itself and what I know: the kinds of traditionally male knowledge the book subverts and revises, classics and sciences, or more specifically mythology and genetics. (Or does that simply mean older and contemporary mythologies?) Sandra's choice to accept her pregnancy opens a process that rethinks both the pseudo-tragic glamor of guilt-through-inheritance (the classical Furies that haunt her), and the semitough science of identity-by-inheritance (the mad, modern pursuit of genetics that originally caused her). By the end of the novel, the genetic and, more notably, the classical, each in its own way furious, have been not surpassed but sublated by the frivolous.[9] All unknowing, the frivolous imagination recovers what the furious heart leaves out or behind, retrieving a buried past to secure a dawning future.

Reviving the Classics

Sandra, discoverer of the planet Athena, maintains she is driven to France by "*Harpies *Furies *History" (p. 2). "In my veins," she claims, "runs the blood of the past" (p. 31), but networked through the capillaries of the Antique. Her story, like the stories hers adumbrates, works out the revenge of "the God Eros" (p. 12). Discovering and naming Athena, interpreting the Universe to thousands, ganged up on and ultimately discarded by the band, Starlady Sandra seems, on the one hand, a contemporary Cassandra. And yet, as the rejected, fury-haunted daughter of a "mad" and murderous mother, "Driven mad by my father" (pp. 30–31), she is also Electra to Tamara's Clytemnestra, to Oscar von Stirpit's murderous Agamemnon, and to her brother Robin's Orestes, the revenant, mad son of a mad mother. But of all the forms of classical revival working through the novel—"revive with the revivers" is the motto of the band she follows, the wonderfully named Citronella Jumpers (p. 4)—the most suggestive allusions cluster about the Furies, the novel's other (and, of course, female) band, "wielding their stick, their many-thonged whip, from behind" (p. 18).

Who are the Furies? What passion or position do they inscribe? And what do they tell us about Fay Weldon's relation to the classical, and to her own, past?

I can locate three major stages of Fury as figure or trope. The most recent, that of the Renaissance, is human, heroic, and male. It is also frequently, if only temporarily, insane. And admirable. Always admirable. Earlier, in *The Aeneid*, there is a Latin, or maybe just a Vergilian, Fury: Olympian, antiheroic, ambiguously gendered. And detestable. And earliest, a Greek Fury, which is chthonic, antiheroic, but definitely even defiantly female. And loathsome. (I'm going to skip over the Vergilian here, fascinating as it is in itself, because it doesn't seem particularly relevant to Fay Weldon or her book.)

Heroic male fury emerges in the Renaissance: Macbeth's "sound and the fury, signifying nothing." It's what Prospero dismisses, when at the peripeteia of *The Tempest* he decides: "with my nobler reason 'gainst my fury / Do I take part: the rarer action is / In virtue than in vengeance." The pattern text: Ariosto's *Orlando Furioso*. Its paradigmatic moment, the fulcrum of that epic. There Orlando enters the cave where his beloved Angelica has made love with Medoro, and where the lovers have carved their names:

> Three times, four times, six times, he read the script,
> Attempting still, unhappy wretch!, in vain,
> (For the true meaning he would not accept)
> To change the sense of what was clear and plain.
> Each time he read, an icy hand which gripped
> His heart caused him intolerable pain,
> Then motionless he stood, his eyes and mind
> Fixed on the stone, like stone inert and blind. [XXIII: 111]

And then he's promptly driven *furioso*.

Macbeth's, Prospero's furies both effect an erasure. Whether for good (Prospero) or ill (Macbeth), their fury wipes out some kind of crucial text, annulling a signification that has become unbearable. Like Orlando, they refuse to read, specifically to read history. What really has happened is too intolerably painful to remember. Its clear, plain, and ugly inscriptions must be annihilated, if not from public witness then at least from the mind. Even madness is preferable to the debased narration the contemporary scene allows human expectation. (And here we hear fury's founding gesture toward what will become the Sublime.) This fury is neither Erasmus's (Greek-ish) insanity, "which the Furies let slip from hell, each time they release their serpents" (Foucault, p. 27), nor the "desperate passion" Michel Foucault hears in Ophelia's last, sad song (pp. 30–31). Neither moralistic nor pathetic, heroic fury centers on the strong self. It works to deny the new age of the world-picture, with its all-dominating grid of univocally disciplined perspectives (in Heidegger's image), to retrieve an expanse of feeling that acknowledges no external restraint. Which is why, as Furor, fury soon becomes a more or less positive term for poetic inspiration. What Orlando reads on the cave's walls can't be, his fury insists, what his life really means. If that's what language and history now frame as the possible, it's clearly better to rage and to roam. Prospero, hero of literary, not martial, Romance, can surrender his fury because, through the magic of proto-imperialist technology, he's already gotten history to replace him as he'd like to be. (He's also already let his fury unleash the tempest that regains him power.) But "Lay on, Macduff," cries out Macbeth, refusing his knowledge that Macduff is prophetically promised victory. And Orlando's "rage and fury mount to such a pitch / . . . so now the Count / Rips forests up as if of no account" (XXIII: 134–35). Whether with Birnam Wood or Italian forests, heroic fury refuses axiomatically to let history, literally, account.

In a completely different direction, the Greek Furies, the Erinys, attempt to align history and truth, to tell what really happened. Their name derives from eris, the Greek for strife, quarrel, and contention. In Greek culture, especially in early Greek, they fulfill a particularly complex function, a complexity Liddell and Scott trace in the difference between Homer's earlier metros erinues, "the curses from one's mother," and Hesiod's later erinus patros, the blood-guilt of the father (p. 314). The Erinys thus voice family history in all its horror: at the earliest, history as the memory of crime; later on, history as the contentious past's deadlock on a fresh present. Finally, Athens breaks with domestic history, as the antithesis of cultural progress, displacing the family with the polis. Thus, if modern male fury refuses to read history, runs mad away from it (as in the Latin root, furo: to run mad, to rave[10]), then classical, that is, Athenian, male history, refuses to hear fury, refuses to hear what it consistently marginates as the shriek of the demonic female.

Curses from One's Mother

As a number of feminist scholars have argued, that marginalization is the particular cultural burden of Aeschylus' *Oresteia*. Conflating, as Froma Zeitlin suggests, "the myth of matriarchy and the myth of dragon combat" (p. 164), the play refuses the Furies' claims against the ephebe Orestes as "blind, archaic, barbaric, and regressive," the enemies of every structure or argument with any claim to be considered civilized (p. 162). This dismissal, however, is accomplished not by a male figure but, paradoxically, by a female, the goddess Athena—and here is where we return to Starlady Sandra, Athena's modern discoverer.

A female astronomer naming a new planet Athena might at first seem a gesture of feminist moment. We see this when Sandra fends off the hostility of the sexist Jumpers, apologetically claiming that she could make such a discovery "Only by mistake, . . . Well, almost by mistake" (p. 66). Indomitable, self-sufficient, virginal Athena represents everything the Jumpers' kind of woman is not. Except that Athena, for the Greeks at least, was always Daddy's best girl. She is Zeus's own child, produced apparently on his own, from his prodigious brain, and carrying on her father's wisdom. Thus, when at the climax of the *Oresteia* she rejects the Furies, and their proto-feminist insistence that Orestes suffer for murdering his mother, the goddess grounds her reply on nothing but her simple preference for men—in all things except (always Daddy's girl) marriage. In effect, in the founding gesture of Athenian justice, and virtually of Athenian tragedy, the archetypal father's daughter refuses a mother's enduring claim on her son.

Athena then turns out to be exactly the kind of female figure the Jumpers would approve. If that is so, then perhaps we have to re-read Sandra's crucial discovery as a kind of counterfeminist gesture. Not only does she repudiate any feminist taint in denying her originality to the Jumpers, but the discovery itself, or at least naming in Athena, seems almost a cryptorepudiation of feminism. And this is not merely a Derridean play on supplementary (read: classical) erudition. (Though it is that, or would like to be considered that, also.) The plot of the novel encases crucially the same discovery. Allying herself with Athena, Sandra inevitably boxes herself into playing Electra, that other, lesser and mortal Daddy's girl, the woman who plots her own mother's death. Electralike, Sandra grows up the daughter of an executed officer father, Oscar, vised between a mad murderous mother, Tamara, and an equally mad brother, Simon, "copying the behaviour of invisible masturbating demons, as my mother did . . . flesh of her flesh, brain of her brain, mad of her madness" (p. 36).

An Electra lives out Freud's fantasy of the castrated female. She enters
the Oedipal scenario merely by proxy. Only by depending on Orestes has
she any hope to satisfy her fantasies of revenge. And even with a brother
to act for her, she still cannot establish a self, behaving "not as a person
in her own right but as a mass of responses to other persons and their
deeds and wishes, whether true or false" (Grene, p. 136). But, as Sandra's
story begins, Robin, her Orestes, is dead. An Electra who can no longer
even borrow the family phallus, she's left with nothing but its domestic
demons. "And the furies buffeted me too, saying this is your punishment,
this desolation, put up with it. Pride goes before the fall" (p. 45).

Sandra responds to Simon's death by casting jaunty Jack Stubbs in the
empty role of protector, subordinating herself to the "well-hung" male
whose "carrot I'd followed south" (p. 18). Yet even when most infatuated
with Jack, Sandra senses that carrot's insufficiency. Having been "powerfully and briskly fucked," "truly colonised" (p. 27), she immediately has
to satisfy herself with the brass handle of the doorknob. Only then does
she feel "involved in the patterns of the changing universe" (p. 29)—those
forms that found the frivolous. Flight does nothing to protect her from the
past: the harpies "shrieking in my head . . . no, no, no, run, run: you can't
look back" (pp. 44–45).

Athena's discoverer must run from Athena's crime: disowning maternity. Defending himself, Orestes denies Clytemnestra's maternal rights,
insisting he and his heart belong only to Daddy. But Sandra-Electra's crime
against the mother goes Orestes one worse. "I remember the moment when
I discovered Athena. . . . All she did was whirl about in her own rather
unexpected orbit; a simple thing, a lump of stone, incapable of reproduction, helpless in the grip of her own qualities, which kept her suspended
there between heaven and hell, and not so different, when I came to think
of it, from myself" (pp. 144–45). Sandra believes that in becoming *a*
mother, she can only replicate *her* terrible mother. And so she denies not
only the mother but maternity itself. "I mean to help the evolutionary process along by failing to reproduce" (p. 85).

Running away with Jack, Sandra thus mimics heroic, male fury, the fury
that refuses history, that flees anywhere, anyhow, even to, or perhaps especially to, a ruined *hôtel de ville*, to escape seeing and admitting a connection to that terrible narrative that claims one for its own. At the same
time, she continues buffeted by the ancient Furies who clamber to revenge
her primordial crime against the mother. Commingling furies, ancient and
modern, leaves Sandra simultaneously, confusedly, both mad man and bad
woman, not leading the band, merely chasing the leader's member. Just as

earlier, in reading *She-Devil*, we saw Ruth's fury lead her not to discover her own real self, but merely to become the indolent clone of her former nemesis. In both cases, fury leads only to impasse.

The Blood-Guilt of the Father

Ironically, release from this maternal dead end comes through the father. When Sandra thinks, or rather, rethinks her father, "the Mad Sadist of Bleritz" (p. 85), and the father's science, eugenics, in the pivotal chapter 16, "Truth Being Stranger Than Fiction," she counters and finally deflates the constraining force of her mother's furious madness, releasing herself from her bed of mysterious, debilitating pain. Sandra executes this self-liberation by an eminently frivolous bid—here is the "scandal" of Weldon's text, and the heart of the frivolous—to "establish him in my own mind," this Nazi beast, this executed Nuremberg criminal, "as a reasonable and well-motivated man" (pp. 109–10).

We can probe this liberation by stressing its parallels in performance theory. Moving from Ruth to Sandra, Fay Weldon pushes beyond fury to the frivolity that undergirds Stanislavsky's insistence that actors continue performing even when someone else's chair unexpectedly collapses. "Once you learn to accept offers . . . you are suddenly in contact with people who are unbounded, whose imagination seems to function without limit" (Johnstone, p. 100). The She-Devil's insistent refusal of her subjected status clearly outflanks Mary Fisher's characteristic pattern of denial of anything even vaguely unpleasant. But even furious refusal never escapes the seesaw reversal of a master-slave dialectic. However, as Keith Johnstone insists, "the actor who will accept anything that happens seems supernatural" (p. 100). Supernatural because ultimate power (read: integrity *and* integration), generous power that rests on and regenerates serenity, such power roots in never permitting yourself to feel outpowered, in taking anything and everything that happens, planned or not, wanted or not, as part of what you can and should use. This acceptance has nothing to do with quietism. For the frivolous hero, every accident incorporates extraordinary opportunity. Thus the last lines of the last narrator of this book: "Anyway, sufficiently enamored of just the sheer dignity of creation to realize I shouldn't offend it the way I had been doing. I think everything's going to be all right now. I'll make out" (*Leader*, p. 196).

For Sandra, that frivolity requires her to accept as serious science, in all their horror, Oscar's eugenic experiments, the monstrous experiments that caused her being. That acceptance suddenly, shockingly deprives her of criminal abnormality. Oscar emerges a compeer not only of figures like

"Edward Teller, Father of the Bomb. Innovator. Saviour" (p. 110), but of
Sandra herself, the Astronomer Royal, his fellow-scientist and thus, in a
double way, heir to his "genuine spirit of scientific enquiry" (p. 105). "I'm
my father's daughter" (p. 105), owing to him not only atrocity, but in a
more important way, intelligence and distinction. Acknowledging herself
as "a perfect little replica of my father" (p. 111) thus, unexpectedly, nor-
malizes Sandra's previously unique monstrosity: "We are all misbegotten,
by one form of monster or another" (p. 111).

As she struggles to recuperate her family history in *all* its horror, Sandra
recuperates her own genetic complexity, and her innocence in cooperating
with its continuity. Her achievement parallels Orestes' release from the
Furies through the divine establishment of the Athenian justice system.
In this frivolous novel, however, enfranchisement comes not from sub-
mission to a transcendently mandated political order but by the self's
pleasure-saturated realization of her own accidental, fortuitous, and therefore innocent identity. This is the way everyone's life is. There's nothing
to be angry at, and plenty to laugh about. Sandra may be Byronically "the
point where the mad, the bad, and the infamous meet." But that means
she is also a nexus of scientific genius, extraordinary sexual energy, and
a marked ability at fiction (p. 137). Her new sense of self and the self's
history maintain her clear right to continue her own scientific and sexual
experimentation, including carrying "this baby" she has conceived with
Jack, to "allow it its passage into daylight" (p. 155).

Nevertheless, in taking from her own father's and from Jack's potential
for paternity as much as she needs and no more, Sandra sublates, she does
not replicate, patriarchy and the male voice. Even a reputable patriarchal
genetics, for example the Nobel Prize–winner François Jacob's *The Logic
of Life: A History of Heredity,* insists, despite its emphasis on flexibility,
that "A genetic code is like a language: even if they are only due to chance,
once the relations between 'sign' and 'meaning' are established, they cannot be changed" (p. 316). For Jacob, history moves "In spite of errors, of
dead ends, of false starts." But *Leader of the Band* comes to rejoice in a
frivolous history, history that moves accidentally, luckily, *because* of errors, dead ends, false starts. Running away from a dull marriage, Sandra
finds herself for the first time pregnant with a child she wants to have,
while at the same time happily able to send her lover back to his dull wife.
So much for unchanged and unchanging relations. This is a history that
breaks off with a question—"Who doesn't, these days?" (p. 155)—that is,
who doesn't these days worry whether a fetus will turn out he, she, or it?
And then, leaving that question open-ended, goes on to append three stories that deconstruct the novel's primary narrative. So much for "established" meaning.

Metis: An Epiphany

Bearing the child while sending Jack back to his dreary marriage, and spurning any claims on her even drearier husband, Sandra reverses Athena, mother and maternity repudiator. Early on, goaded by the Furies, Sandra saw herself as an Orpheus, forbidden to look back: "and he was a man, what hope is there for you, a woman?" (p. 45) But she has looked back, and as Orphic narrator redeemed her own Eurydice-self, from the hellish shadows that claimed her for an underworld of infertility and frenzy.

But we can perhaps go even further than the myths Weldon names, to one her frivolous inventions seem to adumbrate and renew. Behind the conventional narrative of Athena's "virgin-birth" from all-knowing Zeus, there's a feminist myth, long overlaid in the patriarchal myth-kitty. Hesiod claims that Zeus produced Athena apparently on his own only because he had actually swallowed up her pregnant mother, Metis, of whom he had become terrified. Metis meant terror to the all-ordering patriarch because, as Jean-Pierre Vernant suggests, she represented the "future understood as risk" (p. 1): "She tells the future not as something already determinate but as a possibility—either good or ill; and at the same time she offers the use of her stock of wiles to make it turn out for the better rather than for the worse" (p. 1). Metis, lo and behold, is Alice's Mum! the Ur-goddess of frivolity! Reader, are you surprised?

Mum-Metis, urging our accidental nativities and luck-struck lives, prescribes Weldon's antidote to fury. Fury can only make most of us merely and noisily ineffectual. Think of the sad mess Ruth ends up, in that tower with "artificial copses and granite-fountained fish ponds" (She-Devil, p. 241), rewriting Mary Fisher's mindless, bloodless books. But relinquishing fury, the Starlady moves from "passing presenter" (p. 66) to "fulcrum where the past and future balance" (p. 155). Who then needs the boy-god Eros, petulant and obtuse, all overdetermination and depression, presiding over the sober "collectivity . . . who" strive and tirelessly fail to "communicate with each other by means of sex" (Jacob, p. 23). Not I! Not while Fay Weldon points frivolously beyond Athena to Metis, the mother-star, tricking again her lucky, long-extinguished beams. A leader about whom even her male devotees can band.

Notes

I am delighted to acknowledge a deep debt to my learned colleagues in the Georgetown University Classics Department, Joseph O'Connor and Victoria

Pedrick, who pointed the way toward many of the arguments of this essay. And I wish especially to thank Fay Weldon for her typically generous response to my frivolous endeavor.

1. Of course, not all contemporary British women writers of distinction are frivolous. Margaret Drabble started out promisingly frivolous in novels like a *Summer Bird Cage* but seems to have lost heart about the time of *The Waterfall*. Doris Lessing is never frivolous and never less than magnificent. But that dark Sybil, Muriel Spark, has been frivolous during all of her distinguished career, except immediately after the Arab oil embargo (*The Takeover*, 1976) when it was understandably trying for anybody to remain frivolous. And the frivolous also includes much of the fiction of the incomparable, and entirely underrated, Sylvia Townsend Warner, whose "A Love Match" may be counted the supreme frivolous short story.

2. Its clouded history at times overlaps and other times parallels what Peter Sloterdijk calls the *kynical* (*Critique of Cynical Reason*). Sloterdijk locates in classical figures like Diogenes and Lucan the practice of *kynicism*, the revolt of self against domination by power, including the power-seeking, disillusioned, and pessimistic rationalism of so much contemporary theory. In the simplest terms, he posits an opposition between a totalizing, idealistic cynicism, or enlightened false consciousness, which insists that we forget to laugh, and the survival of an earlier kynicism, which reminds us to laugh through an individual and happy refusal of, or at least resistance to, all forms of universalism. The frivolous I'm defining shares much with Sloterdijk's kynical, but differs significantly in refusing its obsessive and Teutonic obscenity. In some ways, following Sloterdijk, one might call kynicism the German frivolous—or frivolity the British kynical.

3. My understanding of the frivolous, indeed my use of the term, depends heavily on Derrida's remarkable essay. But, for this chapter, I have decided to stress native British rather than pan-European sources and analogues. After Foucault, rewriting the history of a now much constrained British liberty requires increased and informed concern for the long, vibrant tradition of eccentricity that forms a vital feature of the British national and in many cases individual character. Especially of working- and lower-class eccentricity, a world virtually extirpated between the Blitz and the Telly. Dickens, for example, needs to be relocated even more insistently in the lower-middle-class urban world in which his antinomian moral imagination and his frivolous taste in entertainment was formed. No location for such study would prove more fruitful than the Music Hall, where figures like the inimitable Marie Lloyd represent heroines of a liberation Ibsen's women couldn't even die to achieve.

4. What follows assumes what I can't argue here:

• That the frivolous descends at least from the eighteenth century, continuing and redefining that most misunderstood of modern regimes, the rococo. And, even before the rococo, that we can locate a kind of proto-frivolous in the beginning of modern consciousness: in mannerism.

• That mannerism, the rococo, and the frivolous all three share an eccentric delight in, a disciplined deviation from, but not an explosion of, the norm, resisting an evolving bourgeois order, which founds its aesthetics and its ethics in a recovered and recuperated classicism.

• That the frivolous is fundamentally British, as Mannerism is essentially Italian, and the Rococo is quintessentially French.

• That, from the late eighteenth century on, a series of frivolous texts has resisted the hegemonic virtues of caution, prudence, and the fear of power. That these novels include some of the key titles in the Victorian canon: novels like *A Tale of Two Cities*, *Barchester Towers*, *Cranford*, *What Maisie Knew*, and *The Ordeal of Richard Feveral*. (Critical resistance to the frivolous may well be the principal cause for Meredith's contemporary eclipse; that and the fact that his prose sometimes seems like a labored and exact transcription from an original in Eskimo or Gorilla.)

• That the triumph of the Great Secular Inquisition—what the academy calls Modernism—left Beerbohm the last but not the least in this line. Perhaps the final frivolous gesture of the nineteenth century, Zuleika Dobson's Eights Week hetacomb of happily suicidal undergraduates. Probably because they anticipated the kinds of books they'd soon have set for their study.

And finally,

• That an extraordinary resurgence of the frivolous has been one of the great joys of the contemporary renaissance in women's writing.

5. My understanding of antinomianism relies heavily on J. G. A. Pocock's illuminating discussion in *The Machiavellian Moment*, pp. 346ff. Both Pocock and Christopher Hill stress the crucial way in which the historical thrusts of English antinomianism separate it from the more apocalyptic stress of continental, for example Genevan, Calvinisms—a distinction Americans especially have reason to note, since that historicism resulted in the founding of New England. This is a dimension worth stressing because it helps clarify why so much contemporary, continental theory, universalizing and apocalyptic in its own way, misreads the particular complexity of British culture.

6. A much-needed study of Fay Weldon's intellectual training, especially in the intellectual precincts of St. Andrews, would trace out the connections between her education and the continuing emphasis on antinomian individualism fundamental to Scottish culture. A culture as important to her as it is to the writer whom she in so many ways resembles, the Edinburgh-born and -trained Muriel Spark. Indeed, in some ways, Fay Weldon is the twentieth century's Thomas Carlyle—or vice versa.

7. My presentation of melodrama relies heavily on Peter Brooks's magisterial analysis in *The Melodramatic Imagination*. Though there are some grounds for quarreling with his history of the genre, and particularly of his understanding of the theatre-history of melodrama, he is unsurpassed in helping us see what melodrama has meant for the past two hundred years to the culture at large. For a supplementary reading of melodrama, see Louis James, *Fiction for the Working Man 1830–1850*, and Michael Booth, *Theatre in the Victorian Age*.

8. This was Fay Weldon's reading of *She-Devil*, offered during her response to the MLA Session on her work, "A Comic Turn, Turned Serious": *Fay Weldon's Wicked Fiction* (29 December 1989) in Washington, D.C.

9. Without chagrin I acknowledge that my argument about the novel's frivolity is itself deeply frivolous. It makes no claim that Fay Weldon knows either the classics or the genetics to which it alludes. (And which I know because of a typically patriarchal liberal education.) Indeed, in her response to the ver-

sion of this paper read at MLA, she insisted she knew nothing of the classical mythology I discuss here. She named the Starlady's discovery Athena simply because that seemed the most likely choice a female astronomer might make. Indeed, what choice did Sandra have? Except for Ceres (who is in many ways already associated with Earth), Athena-Minerva is the only major deity not named in the gradual enlargement of the solar system. Which says something, doesn't it?

10. *Furo* in turn transliterates a Greek verb *phuro* (which is not of course *eris*, the root of the Erinues). *Phuro* originally meant to make a dry element moist, and thus to mix, to confuse (Liddle, p. 875). Fury thus always muddles. In flight, it can't make—it can only refuse—meanings.

Works Cited

Ariosto, Ludovico. *Orlando Furioso.* Trans. Barbara Reynolds. Part I. New York: Penguin, 1975.

Booth, Michael. *Theatre in the Victorian Age.* Cambridge: Cambridge University Press, 1991.

Brooks, Peter. *The Melodramatic Imagination.* New York: Columbia University Press, 1985.

Derrida, Jacques. *The Archaeology of the Frivolous: Reading Condillac.* Trans. John P. Leavey, Jr. Lincoln: University of Nebraska, 1987.

Elias, Norbert. *Power & Civility: The Civilizing Process.* Vol. 2. Trans. Edmund Jephcott. New York: Pantheon, 1978.

Foucault, Michael. *Madness and Civilization: A History of Insanity in the Age of Reason.* Trans. Richard Howard. New York: Vintage, 1988.

Grene, David. "Introduction" to The *Electra.* In *Sophocles II.* Vol. 2. *The Complete Greek Tragedies,* ed. David Grene and Richmond Lattimore. New York: Modern Library, 1957.

Hill, Christopher. *The World Turned Upside Down: Radical Ideas During the English Revolution.* New York: Viking, 1972.

Jacob, François. *The Logic of Life: A History of Heredity.* Trans. Betty E. Spillmann. New York: Pantheon, 1973.

James, Louis. *Fiction for the Working Man 1830–1850.* Oxford: Oxford University Press, 1963.

Johnstone, Keith. *IMPRO: Improvisation and the Theatre.* New York: Routledge, 1981.

Liddell, H. G. *An Intermediate Greek-English Lexicon Founded upon the Seventh Edition of Liddell and Scott's Greek-English Lexicon.* Oxford: Clarendon Press, 1959.

Pocock, J. G. A. *The Machiavellian Moment.* Princeton: Princeton University Press, 1975.

Sloterdijk, Peter. *Critique of Cynical Reason.* Trans. Michael Eldred. Minneapolis: University of Minnesota Press, 1987.

Stamm, R. "On the Carnivalesque." *Wedge* (1982): 47–55.

Starobinski, Jean. *The Invention of Liberty 1700–1789.* Trans. Bernard C. Swift. Geneva: Editions d'Art Albert Skira, 1964.

Vernant, Jean-Pierre. "The Union with Metis and the Sovereignty of Heaven."

In *Myth, Religion & Society,* ed. R. L. Gordon. Cambridge: Cambridge University Press, 1986.

Weldon, Fay. *Leader of the Band.* New York: Viking, 1988.

————. *The Life and Loves of a She-Devil.* New York: Pantheon, 1983.

Zeitlin, Froma I. "The Dynamics of Misogyny: Myth and Mythmaking in the Oresteia." *Arethusa* 11 (1978): 149–84.

Journalist of the Heart

The invitation was proffered by the editor of this volume. Would I (Gina asked) like to look into the "journalism" of Fay Weldon? My answer mirrored the question: Would I. As in *Would I!* First, as Gina knew, I was a big fan of journalism generally: a card-carrying member of the Fifth Estate, disciple of Mencken and Murrow, firm believer that Tom Wolfe's and Joan Didion's best stuff was done long ago, back when they were *journalists*. As Gina knew, I'd stay up till two to catch a rerun of *All the President's Men* or, even better, *The Front Page* or *His Girl Friday.*

And second, as I may or may not have told Gina previously, I was a big fan of Weldon. I'd read *Puffball, Praxis, Joanna May, Life and Loves of . . .* and the short stories in *Moon over Minneapolis* (a fine collection; go find it). I found Weldon's fiction witty, incisive, entertaining, and down right significant—y'know, *important*—to boot.

What I hadn't known was that Weldon was a journalist. I knew she had written on Jane Austen and Rebecca West, but I surmised this was literary criticism, not journalism. I thought the same about that volume entitled *Post-Rushdie, Pre-Utopia.* You see, I figured Weldon for one of those relatively late-blooming British fiction writers who create a large and impressive oeuvre between age forty and the grave. The English seem to have a better idea about this nurturing of novelists than we Yanks do. There's a dearth of *wunderkinder* over there as most writers are out learning their chops before displaying them to the masses. Then, by the time these scribblers start trotting out public prose, they are pretty fine scribblers indeed, and trot out prose of high quality. Thus do the Brits embark upon distinguished careers in writing. Pym did it this way. Stevie Smith, the poet. Weldon.

Sorry: That's a tangential theory and I apologize for . . . well, for trotting it out. It has little to do with the subject at hand.

Which is: Fay Weldon, Journalist.

I mulled this for a while—*Fay Weldon, Journalist*—and came up empty. I hadn't had a clue that Ms. Weldon journalized . . . journaled . . . journayed . . . reported on stuff.

Now, I tried to envision it. I conjured the elegant Ms. Weldon in fur-felt fedora, press card in place, taking notes. Didn't work. I saw her sleuthing *à la* Woodward, meeting shadowy figures with deep throats in parking garages and eventually bringing down Thatcher (whom I assumed any liberal London cultural-elitist detested). Nope: History told me this hadn't happened. I tried to fit Ms. Weldon into the Rosalind Russell role: batting out the murder story on deadline on her rickety Royal, then dashing off with editor-in-chief Cary Grant in the film's final frames. I figured Ms. Weldon might seek me out and shoot me for that one, and erased it from memory.

So I was having trouble with this "Fay Weldon, Journalist" thing. Then the pile of FW Journalism arrived from Gina. Journalism it was, and a good substantial hunk of it. But it wasn't *that kind* of journalism.

It was, I realized pretty quickly, Fay Weldon's nonfiction: essays and sketches and musings and arguments and polemics and proddings about things that are true. (Not that Weldon's fiction isn't about true things. It *is*, of course. Hey—You know what I mean.)

So then: Fay Weldon's Nonfiction. That was the real assignment.

Fine. My task was now clear: Discuss Fay Weldon's nonfictions for a volume entitled *Fay Weldon's Wicked Fictions*. That I am the black sheep among Gina's contributors is evident, a point I'll raise with Gina later, and privately.

Well then: Weldon's Nonfictions. Are they, too, wicked? If so—Are they too wicked? Wicked enough? And more: What's wicked? Which wicked will we whack around? A teenage boy thinks Motley Crue is wicked, as in *wicked*, while his parents think the Crue is wicked, as in they-should-burn-in-hell!

Weldon's nonfiction is *wicked* and wicked both—by turns and even, sometimes, simultaneously. It is, for the most part, every bit as sharp, provocative, and fun to read as her fiction is. Every bit as pointed, too. As with the novelist Weldon, the journalist Weldon clearly feels there are those who should—or at least will—burn in hell.

As an operative theory for our examination, I would offer that the burn-in-hell essays, as opposed to the burn-in-hell novels, are less effective. When you're dealing with true folk you run the risk of sinking to their level by shouting at them, even if you're shouting perfectly sensible stuff. When you're dealing with fake folk, you control the explication of their vile behavior and thus, if you deal deftly, you maintain a firm upper hand. You manipulate events to make your point elegantly. When you get outraged with the real world, it is usually because you *can't* manipulate events. Your frustration is sometimes unseemly on the page.

But this will come through. Let's dive into the pile.

Its topics are several and varied. "On Censorship" resides hard by "Ladies Who Don't Lunch," which follows closely on the stomp, stomp, stomping heels of "Twenty Years Older and Deeper in Debt" (about Britain's failure to treat women equally in the workforce), which shares the covers with "God and the Creative Imagination." And then there's a commentary on the Anita Hill–Clarence Thomas dustup.

My goodness.

But think about it. Every one of these essays concerns either (a) women today, (b) literature today, or (c) both. And thus are they all material fit to be commented upon by the author of *Female Friends, The Hearts and Lives of Men* and the other aforementioned books. Weldon, when she chooses well, chooses topics she knows of, and Weldon's concerns in her novels are reflected in her essays.

Essays these are, mostly. A few are speeches, and they read somewhat less well, as speeches usually do. The speeches are more strident in argument and broader—less eloquent—in humor. But most items in this collection are essays, and good sound ones. Well worth reading.

Take Weldon's take on the Hill-Thomas affair ("Sex and Paradox Across the Atlantic"). It helps us Americans, I think, to get a view from afar: "The Affair settled down, or so it seemed to us here in Britain, into a dispute as to whether racism was worse than sexism: racism won by a hair. A sign of relief, I fear, ran through the male intelligentsia of the international community: and a sigh of sorrow through the female." Some would argue, perhaps, that the situation was a bit more complex than that, but the good essayist focuses on one point before traipsing off to the next one, and this is what Weldon does, always. Don't ever think she won't get to the next one. After she has examined Thomas-Hill from the sexist angle, she finishes with this provocative thought: "It is tempting to find a parallel in the Rushdie Affair, in which the sacrificial victim to a different paradox— that freedom of thought and freedom of religious belief are mutually exclusive—is still two years later dodging the assassination squads. The centuries are littered with such victims, from Socrates onward—as we creep miserably towards self-knowledge and the civilization that, with any luck, comes in its train." Make it *four* years later and let the lament stand.

The essay, with this last allusion, becomes rounded and worthy. It has added not just a lucid appraisal but an original thought to the heap of opinion built during Thomas-Hill. This is what E. B. White used to do: come up with a new way of looking at a thing, but a way that always, once digested, seemed no less valid or obvious than the standard way of looking at a thing. If an essayist's argument is forced, it's invalid. If an argument's usual, it's pointless.

I found the short Thomas-Hill essay the best of Weldon's no-jokes, Po-litical-with-a-cap-P pieces. I found, by way of contrast, her essay on the feminists Susan Faludi, author of *Backlash*, and Marilyn French, author of *The War Against Women*, much less fine.

In this piece Weldon doesn't forward a single thought that is incorrect. She starts by pointing out how much harder it has become to openly pro-claim oneself a feminist. She goes on to applaud Faludi and French for delineating the recent backlash against women. She continues by con-demning job bias. She finishes this way: "These are books for men as well as women: but let men answer the charges. They're pretty telling."

Well, sure they are. Weldon at one point calls *The War Against Women* an "unfunny, impassioned, angry and powerful book." Hers is an unfunny, impassioned, and angry essay that lacks the power usually inherent in a work by Fay Weldon, who is an impassioned, sometimes angry, and very funny writer. She would say (I would guess): "Some things just aren't funny." I'm not arguing that point. What I'm saying is: Weldon has such an acuity for seeing the funny—the quirky, the odd, the bizarre even—in a subject, or for skewering through humor, that when she does not do so, she is not at her very best. The Thomas-Hill essay had a Long Dong Silver joke, for goodness' sake—*and profited by it*. We were in Weldon country. In the Faludi-French piece, Weldon is a home-run hitter bunting. She's a serve-and-volley tennis player forced to the baseline. She has sheathed a part of her weaponry, and maybe the best part of it, for it is a part she wields as well as anyone in the trade. Imagine Navratilova forced to serve underhand.

And, again: In this essay, there isn't much that's new. There's nothing that's wrong, but not much that's new.

In her best essays, original thought after original thought comes marching.

I would argue that Weldon is as astute a categorizer—a labeler—as Mencken or Wolfe, who are justly famous for their dubbing of society. To be such a be-knighter, a writer must have a keen eye (the writer has to spot a type before labeling it). In "On the Reading of Frivolous Fiction" Weldon comes up with classifications for literature: good good books (tried and true classics like *Vanity Fair* and *Madame Bovary* that astound you anew with their quality), bad good books (those that aspire to be great through various devices and poses, and that are therefore "unendurable"), good bad books (these "can be terrific. *Hollywood Wives*, Mills and Boon, the thriller, the horror, the sci-fi romp: it is true they can take you out of the real world, but what's the matter with that? The real world isn't so hot. Read the good bad books while you gather strength for the good good books: the illumination of the vision, the shift of focus in the psyche that the good good book provides is strong stuff. You can't be open to it all the time."), and finally, bad bad books which are, basically, bad books. I finished the essay and said to my self, "She's right!" Now I will go forth and plagiarize Weldon's very original good good books theory, and I hope she takes this as a sincere form of flattery.

Another essay with labels: "Ladies Who Don't Lunch" would, I figured, be a lark. And it was, sort of. But as Weldon explained about midday women, it dawned on this reader that there really *are* differences of substance between ladies who lunch ("elegant, wealthy, fastidious, never drop food on their silk or cashmere clothes; empires crumble for them. They are timeless. Queen Nefertiti, Cleopatra and Helen of Troy were, I imagine, ladies who lunched.") and ladies who "do" lunch ("always busy. They plot, plan, conspire, radiate confidence, pick and choose lovers and organise empires. Elizabeth I and Florence Nightingale would have 'done' lunch.") and ladies who "meet for" lunch ("really nice and often covered with crumbs. They do good works and people are sorry when they die. They improve the lot of empires. Eleanor Roosevelt and Marie Stopes were the kind to meet other ladies for lunch.") Weldon enjoys, as you might expect, some high hilarity with her premises. (Overheard in "the Great Celestial Restaurant in the Sky [were] Nefertiti on Eleanor: My dear, for all the good she did in the world, did you see that *hat*? Marie on Elizabeth I: Such an unrestful, noisy person! No wonder she isn't married. Florence on Helen: Well, you can't deny her looks, but she's no better than a call girl. Everyone on Cleopatra: But Anthony was *married*!")

Weldon has her fun, but all the while she is going someplace. She is heading toward a discussion of how personal substance and style, sometimes seemingly at odds, can coexist. Weldon is an intellectually brilliant woman and yet she is one, she concedes, who suffers from "shopping disturbance." She explains: "I was born to shop. Some are, some aren't. I am totally at home, indeed almost at my happiest, in a department store. If this is a sin, I am a self-confessed sinner: if it is a vice, I am vicious: if it is an illness, I am ill." What she's getting at here is this: "Yes, yes, the personal is the political, all that, but the trivial must also be the immortal." In a way, it certainly must. The smaller a thing—the more interior it is— then the larger. It's a joke, but it isn't. It is, in fact, Weldon's defense for her status as a contributing editor of *Allure,* in which the essay appeared. She answers criticism "that it ill befits a 'serious writer' (me) to write for the readers of *Allure* (you)" with a paraphrase of Flaubert: "*Allure, c'est moi.*"

C'est elle, indeed. *She-Devil est elle,* but *Allure est elle aussi!* People are of many parts. And the Alluring aspects of Weldon are, I think, more central to her *being* than the angry-polemicist aspects. She's *not* Rush Limbaugh, and she needn't mud wrestle with him.

I found the "Lunch" essay immensely appealing and thought-provoking. I felt the same way about another piece for *Allure,* "Infidelity." This is a primer for the soon-to-be adulterous. "There's what ought to happen, and what does happen, and they're different," Weldon begins. "There's love eternal, couples walking hand in hand into the sunset of old age, and you and I know how seldom that happens, and how we go on hoping against hope that it will.

"There are theories of life and there's real life, and a great black tearful pit in between which it's all too easy to fall into. So be careful about theories. . . ." That's the lesson to be taught today: Be careful about theories, don't hang your hat on them. That life isn't always what it seems is a very ordinary dictum. Weldon, essayist, puts a spin on it. It's not an earth-moving spin, but it's a spin sufficient to propel the essay, to make this lesson her own: a Professor Weldon lesson in life.

"[I]f anyone tells you it's okay to have an affair, that it will enrich your marriage, don't listen. Or at any rate, if you do, if you're meeting this man out of hours, be careful, be secret, tell no one. And if you want to cry to the world I'm happy, it's so wonderful, I'm in love—don't do it." Weldon depicts, in this piece, the consequences of not heeding this advice. There's a hilarious sketch about an idealized husband, Dean, chancing upon a lover-ly phone message to his wife from one "Bob," who is, more unfortunately, her sister Frieda's husband. Dean takes this new circumstance of interfamilial intercourse absolutely in stride, and the sketch ends with him and his wife declaring in unison: "Hand in hand into the sunset!" Then Weldon depicts what really happens: Bob ripping apart his wayward wife's office; two families wrecked; Bob running off with the sister, etc.— all the stuff you might read in a Weldon novel. "The penalty for discovering your erotic self may be extreme," says Weldon. "So watch it." She is the bravest and most helpful of feminist journalists: One who reports not merely on the war between men and women, but on the tensions that drive actual men and women to do what they actually do. Joanna May may have found herself quadruple cloned, but I call Weldon a realist. Her launching pad is always firmly grounded in the real world.

There's reality aplenty in "The Wilder Shores of Self," which deals with the reality-altering practice of plastic surgery. The essay discusses from several angles the "whys" behind a woman's desire to remake her appearance. Weldon mentions early, "And of course our particular brand of feminism being what it is (I sometimes see it as a revival of the old puritanism) the sisters look particularly wrathfully upon plastic surgery; it is ideologically unsound, it smacks of vanity, of *pleasing men*. We call it cosmetic surgery, what's more, just to show it's frivolous." Then she runs through the awkwardness and unpleasantries associated with nipping and tucking. Then she gets to Ruth, hero of *She-Devil*, and Ruth's extraordinary makeover. The piece is essentially a defense of Ruth, and a well-reasoned one. Whether you agree with Ruth (Weldon?) or not—"The means of subsistence arriving not because of what you *do* but what you *are*."—you must admit, by the time Weldon charges "To the Clinics!" in the essay's final sentence, that the woman (women?) got you thinking about several aspects of pride, self-image, and life in the age of mutability. Weldon's pieces about personal matters are uniformly as provocative as they are, in fact, political.

There are in this collection some short takes that are . . . well . . . ephemeral. They aren't necessarily about ephemeral topics. In "Thoughts We Dare Not Speak Aloud" Weldon addresses our distrust of science. In "The Great Egg Mystery" she ruminates upon contamination in the food supply. Both essays are interesting to a point, but lean. They reflect an intelligent person's quick ideas on these things. They're the kind of discourse you'd get from a thrice-weekly op-ed columnist when that person needs to write about *something*, and there's just not much to write about.

I would say: Weldon is a novelist of the first rank, not a hired-hand journalist, and she doesn't *have* to do short takes, and maybe she shouldn't. I found the ephemera even less engaging than the polemics. At least, say, Faludi-French was in the great British angry-intellectuals tradition that saw the likes of Graham Greene forever writing (and mailing!) letters to the editors. The ephemera are ephemeral.

Especially when set alongside the personal, as in "Personal View." This essay begins: "Let me tell you what it's been like this summer, down here in Somerset in the South West of England." It's a lovely essay—a sort of pastoral—with a knife's edge. In looking about her world, Weldon finds it simple to comment upon real-estate costs, population swell, urban flight, the communication revolution, pesticides, cats, poverty, homelessness, drugs ("Don't think we escape"), and the question of who owns England. "And then this year we had our mad axe murderer, a serial killer as bad as any you get in New York or Los Angeles: a satanist, or so he thought, poor tragic wretch." One of Weldon's children was among "a group of vegetarian young" who found the body of one of the murder victims. Suddenly and shockingly (despite, or perhaps because of, the lulling prose of this piece), "Personal View" has its context. The texture of the essay is, oddly enough, the perfect one to set an axe murderer against, and imbue him with maximum impact; Shirley Jackson did a similar trick in *The Lottery.* "[I] look straight ahead," Weldon sums up, "past the cat sleeping on the fax, through the tendril fringed window, to the willows, and the variegated poplar—grown another two metres this season—and the green, green lush grass, and the pond with its graceful reeds and the languorous water lillies, and see the parading geese, and the grazing sheep, I might almost think, well yes, this is rural England, this is my view of it, and all is well with the world. Just keep your eyes straight." The reader can almost hear the lambs screaming.

The central point here—that Weldon is a world champion when looking inward, even if to comment about our larger world, and merely another competent critic when focusing at longer range upon the impersonal or exterior—has become, by now, redundantly made. But I'd like to stress before going further: Weldon is at her best far, far more often than she is at less than her best. "When the Writer Visits the Reader," "Night Life in the Acre" (about caring for her animals), "The Creator, A Profile" (God v. Science) and "God and the Creative Imagination" are all stimulating pieces, and these constitute the bulk of what's left of this nonfictive pile I've been sent. They are each sufficiently intriguing that I could discuss each at length, and would relish the task. But such discussion would add little or nothing to the theories being expressed here; it would merely reiterate. When one starts to treadmill like this, it's time to stop spouting and push forth toward some kind of conclusion.

So then: The least of Fay Weldon. Nonfiction Writer—in a reader-edification sense—includes her (happily few) toss-offs, and her overtly political essays. I am not saying she should leave the purely political realm to others. What she says needs to be said. But sometimes in saying, she produces un-Weldonesque essays. Think of the no-laughs Woody Allen films. I don't mean *Hannah and her Sisters,* I mean the really dour ones. Remember *Interiors?* I think the reason *Interiors* didn't work was because the director was denying a part of himself as he crafted his film. Woody Allen, despite the recent tabloid ugliness, must be a guy with a rarefied sense of humor; he made *Bananas,* and I rest my case. This humor is part of his character. To make a film like *Interiors,* he has to closet part of himself—his essence, his being, his Woodiness. Now, *Interiors* is a proficiently done bleak-as-death movie, but it was a forced bleak-as-death movie.

As for Weldon: She retains her keen eye when she writes outrage, but I feel she scores her points better when she puts her whole soul on display: the incisive, tweaking, funny Weldon that we know from the novels. She's best when she doesn't deny all that she is. My evidence for this lies in the mass of her nonfiction, which is terrific and, I would argue, no less political than the Political—cap P—writing. I think Weldon's take on lunch ladies, to return to a favorite, says as much about working women as does her broadside attack on Britain's Equal Opportunities Commission. And it says what it says with engagement and wit.

Moreover, in the former essay Weldon deals with women—people—and in the latter she deals with a panel and with statistics. All of Weldon's novels, it should be noted, are thick with flesh-and-blood (read: passion). This, as much as the felicitous writing and the entertaining plots, is at the heart of their considerable strength. And Weldon, nonfiction writer, is at her best when using all of her tools as a quick-witted *seer* looking at *human beings.*

It strikes me, ultimately, that the assignment as first put forth by Gina was on target: Fay Weldon, Journalist. Weldon is this, and in spades. Her assignment isn't 10 Downing Street or Parliament, but the hearts and minds of her fellow world citizens—particularly the hearts.

A figure lurks in the shadows of several of the best essays—in the forceful "On Betrayal" and the elegiac "The Changing Face of Fiction." His name is Professor Knox, late (we presume) of a Scottish university where Weldon once studied—"more time ago than I care to remember." Weldon writes in the essay about fiction: "I got along best with Moral Philosophy. . . . But alas, I was not my professor's favourite pupil. I found Kant, frankly, difficult. And besides that I was female. So on the whole he ignored my existence, apart from returning my essays unmarked and failing me my end of year examinations—which proved he must have at least known, somewhere in his stony heart, that I and a couple of others like me, that is to say female, were there in his class. Otherwise he looked through us and round us. This Professor Knox of ours would remark, from time to time, during lectures, that women were incapable of rational thought or moral judgment—a view held by many then and some now—and the young men would nod sagely and agree. And we young women, those being the days they were, did not take offence: we thought that was the way the world was and there was no changing it: we just assumed there was something wrong with us; we could not be properly female—that must be it."

Focus on that line "a view held by many then and some now" for just a moment.

Pause.

Now let's proceed with Knox.

Weldon went forth from that Scottish school (it was St. Andrews, by the way) into a world that was, as we know, changing, evolving, growing and diminishing by turns. She became a writer. "All I can do, when considering the changing face of fiction, is to look back on my own life and, using my novels as evidence for and against me, give an account of a political and fictional journey through the last twenty years: taking, as it were, the feminist route: no other, or so I always felt, being open to me."

By taking the feminist route, and by being a writer, she did her part to effect change—to gradually wrest societal standards and expectations from Professor Knox and all the Professor Knoxes while learning, herself, to take offense . . . or offence (as the Brits have it). So now she is delivered to the 90s a famous feminist writer and we expect that her expectations for Professor Knox are that he, if he is indeed *late*, is burning in hell. *As he should be!* Moreover, the "many then" but—much more importantly—the "some now" will (and should!) someday roast with him.

Ah, but there's this, as the essay draws to its close: "Most of us these days know that racism is 'wrong'; a few of us know that sexism is 'wrong.' With good Professor Knox's saner words still ringing in my ears decades later, I could take a deep breath and begin to define 'wrong' but I will spare you. Moral Philosophy is no longer taught in British universities: philosophy itself is an endangered subject: it is enough just to teach us to read and write. So what we do read is the more important. Fiction carries now a weight of responsibility: it must teach us to think. Who else, what else, is going to? Governments, these days, and funding bodies, would rather we were informed than wise; that we learned how to clone and work computers than studied Kant, the incomprehensible: but we, writers and readers, must get the better of them. Professor Knox, in more senses than one, was the last of a breed, and I mourn for him. He taught me a lot in spite of himself, and what is more, against all reason and self interest, I *liked him.* How very female, he would have said.

"Not feminine, female, and nothing wrong with that."

It's interesting that Knox's subject was moral philosophy. He was, we might guess, a very good teacher after all. And wouldn't he be surprised that his "saner words" are being purveyed in the 90s by that former young woman in the corner, the one he thought incapable of rational thought or moral judgment. And that she was the only one left to do it, because his dear course had become an anachronism.

All of this knocking around of Knox leads me to amend the answer to another question that was raised near the top: The best of these essays are *not* wicked. They are incisive and even prickly but not, I think, wicked. They are kinder than that. They are helpful and understanding. They are not arrogant (we're talking about the best ones now). They're not arrogant, but they *are* knowing. They are the products of one of our age's keenest . . . moral philosophers.

And they are, as was just recently mentioned, the products of a journalist. A crusader's instinct is to ignore the Knoxes, condemn them as the crusade presses forth. A journalist's instinct is to keep the ears open, and to query both sides. Weldon, obviously, has thought about why Knox felt the way he felt, and said what he said. Journalism gains what validity it has only when the journalist sees a whole. Weldon has bothered to look not just inside herself, but inside Knox. This female (not feminine) journalist whose assignment is the human (not just female) heart has bothered to investigate the heart of the perceived enemy. And she has delivered her report.

The heart. Weldon covers that waterfront like Runyon covered Broadway, like Drew Pearson covered Washington. It's her job. She's a pro. I see her now, finally, in fur-felt fedora. Her press card bears the particulars: Fay Weldon, Journalist. Beat: Heart.

LEE A. JACOBUS

The Monologic Narrator in Fay Weldon's Short Fiction

Some time in 1946, after "drinking just enough to make his thought processes churn," Samuel Beckett took a "late night prowl" on a jetty in Dublin harbor and had a vision. It changed his life because it changed his writing. In 1960 he advised John Montague, who was having trouble writing a poem, to use the method he had devised for himself that night: "Ah, Montague, what you need is monologue—*monologue*!" (Bair, p. 351). Fay Weldon might have overheard that conversation. Readers of her short stories, especially those in *Moon Over Minneapolis*, find themselves in the grips of women narrators who impress themselves relentlessly in a stream of one-sided narration whose angst is arresting and whose intensity grows almost unbounded.

Fay Weldon's monologic narrator is less gloomy than Beckett's cadre of Molloy, Moran, Murphy, and Watt, but she is just as aware of her audience. When giving us a picture of Romula in whose heart is engraved the phrase "I do what I can and I am what I am," in the story of the same name, the unnamed narrator resembles the spectator in a seventeenth-century painting, the figure that peers out at us from the canvas apparently quite aware of our enduring gaze: "Let me tell you more about Romula" (p. 15), she says, telling us a great deal about the former winner of the Miss Skyways Competition. As with any narrator aware of her audience, this one speaks complicitly, as if we were gossip partners counted upon to keep the secret. For instance, the narrator has kept Romula's identity a secret: "Details have of course been altered to protect her identity" (p. 16), but we know of her dragon tattoo as well as her place of work, so we are warned that what we are told must go no further: "Should you come across her, when you travel Skyways, should the little lace half-glove on the hand of the girl who brings your coffee, tongs out the hot towels (Club Class only), slip back to reveal the macho stamp of the dragon, please keep it to yourself. I wouldn't want her to think a confidence had been betrayed" (p. 16). But of course the entire story is a confidence betrayed, showing us an intimate portrait of an "unbiddable" young woman who will do what she wishes despite a mother's hopes and plans, despite a mother's rules and expectations. A flight with her mother to the isle of Lesbos backfires, and when Romula decides to be an "air hostess, her mother just said, 'Okay. If that's what you really want. Do what you can and be what you are, and good luck to you" (p. 23).

Most of Weldon's narrators simply can't wait to tell us about themselves. Their level of intimacy resembles that of a person in a checkout lane who confides his distrust of the media, the government, the in-laws. One would ordinarily avoid such a narrator, but in Weldon's stories the fascination holds us on: "Sir, you have a nice face. I reckon I can talk to you. Tell you about myself? Why not! That's what you're there for, after all," the narrator of "The Year of the Green Pudding" tells us, and we realize she is right. We learn that she is a country person, a middling sort of person, "Did I mention I was a vegetarian?" (p. 26). She tells us she was once a vegan, revealing a pattern of close reasoning that typifies the Weldon narrator: "(that's someone who doesn't eat any dairy foods, never mind just the cow itself, both on health grounds and because if eating the cow is murder, drinking the milk is theft)" (p. 26). The "Pudding" narrator is unusual because not only is she aware of our presence, she imagines our questions. In a sense, just as some writers use the rhetorical question expecting no answer, the "Pudding" narrator employs the rhetorical answer, expecting no question. But of course in some instances the implied question is clear: "Concorde? I was working on the Liver Paté Account. They were serving it on Concorde, on little pieces of toast, with free champagne cocktails. The client offered me a free flight. Why are you so interested in Concorde?" (p. 27). Part of the reason for our interest is that just before, parenthetically, she told us her best friend Cynthia's eyes were "the blue you see when you look out of Concorde's window. (I have been in Concorde: I am full of surprises)" (p. 27). Indeed, she is full of surprises, this narrator who calmly tells us of Cynthia, who returning with her newborn from the hospital discovers the narrator in bed with her husband, Crocus. The narrator describes the resulting depression as if she had no responsibility: "Crocus went out to her, but she didn't stay, she just handed him the baby and left. And by the time I'd got myself together—I never

was a fast dresser—and he'd handed the baby to me and was gone after
her, it was too late. She went down the Underground and threw herself
under a train. The poor driver. I think of the poor drivers when anything
like that happens" (p. 28). She worked it out by explaining "that [Cyn-
thia'd] been on antidepressants and had threatened suicide in the past.
Neither of them had told me that. So what sort of friendship was that? Do
you think they were ashamed or something? Shouldn't you be frank, with
friends?" (p. 29).

In her zeal to do penance, she avoided married men only to meet Martin, whose wife (wanting a divorce) gave her the go ahead: "Martin cured
me of every sad, negative feeling I ever had. It's been a wonderful year, a
whole year of happiness. We became proper vegans" (p. 30). But disaster
struck. She was responsible for the Christmas pudding recipe for the Fresh
Ginger Account "read by tens of millions" and left the sugar out because
she didn't double check—she was too lovestruck with Martin. "Green.
Mould. Inedible. Green puddings by the million, sir, and my fault. A million family Christmases spoiled, because I was in love" (p. 31).

The narrator is a femme fatale. Her opening words to the listener are
"It must be possible to live on this earth without doing anyone any damage. It must be. I try to be good. I really try." We realize why she is a vegan,
why she saves wasps from glasses of cider, why she tries to avoid walking
on snails, and why she ends her monologue warning her listener not to
move his arm for fear of harming the nearby spider. She does her best: "I
do try to get by doing as little damage as I can. And I make a very good
onion and potato pie" (p. 26).

We are much more cheered by the narrator of "Ind Aff," also a femme
fatale, who frees herself from a hopeless situation in Sarajevo, revealing
all the while the first-class mind of the storyteller. She has run off with
her professor, aptly named Peter Piper, hoping that it is true love. But while
waiting for the wild boar and reflecting on the coincidences that brought
Princip to the café where, after having taken one shot at the Archduke
Ferdinand, he rested with a cup of coffee only to have the Archduke's
chauffeur bring the car to that spot to wait for instructions. His next shot
missed, the next killed the wife—"(never forget the wife), and the third
got the Archduke and a whole generation, and their children, and their
children's children" (p. 43). However, this femme fatale decides to take
fate into her own hands, having learned from Princip's lesson. As she reasons, maybe Princip had a second chance in missing the Archduke the
first time, and maybe he should have sat there drinking his coffee and then
gone home to mother.

As she rises to leave the aging Peter Piper, their dinner of wild boar (should she have ordered vegetarian?) passes her on its way to her table and she suddenly realizes "It was a sad and silly thing to do, in the first place, to confuse mere passing academic ambition with love. . . . A silly sad episode, which I regret. As silly and sad as Princip, poor young man, with his feverish mind. . . . If he'd just hung on a bit, there in Sarajevo that August day, he might have come to his senses. People do, sometimes quite quickly" (p. 43). Homme fatale or femme fatale, most of the time we have a range of choices. This narrator's monologue shows us that we need not always cause harm, that sometimes we can come to our senses.

Then again, the slightly paranoid transvestite narrator of "Down the Clinical Disco" ("I've talked too much") has not only come to her senses, but must keep on the lookout to make sure no one from the staff at the Broadmoor hospital for the criminal insane is poking about in the pub where she is talking. She wants to be sure she and Eddie look normal. Linda, whom she's just met, listens as the narrator worries over details: "Are you sure that man's not watching? Is there something wrong with us? Eddie? You're not wearing your earring, are you? Turn your head. No, that's all right. We look just like everyone else. Don't we? Is my lipstick smudged? Christ, I hate wearing it. It makes my eyes look small" (p. 78). She tells us how she met Eddie in Broadmoor, where one's behavior must veer toward normal if one ever hopes to be released. "And the men have to act interested, but not too interested. Eddie and I met at the clinical disco, acting just gently interested. Eddie felt up my titties, and I rubbed myself against him and the staff watched. . . . We were both out in three months." "Sorry. When we're our side of our front door I scrub off the make-up and get into jeans and he gets into drag, and we're ourselves, and we just hope no one comes knocking on the door to say, hey that's not normal, back to Broadmoor, but I reckon love's a talisman. If we hold on to that we'll be okay" (p. 79).

The narrator of "Pumpkin Pie" tells us a moral social tale comparing the pies of the poor to the pies of the rich. After a harrowing case of near arson—a specialty of Weldon's monologic narrators—the Thanksgiving pie is served to Honey Marvin, whose high standards insist on cholesterol-free pumpkin pie. " 'That was a *very* good pumpkin pie,' said Honey Marvin at ten o'clock that evening, when she came in to lock the fridge and Antoinette was on her hands and knees cleaning the kitchen floor" (p. 87). Obviously, Honey Marvin is oblivious to the unfairness of her standards, and the Cassandralike narrator has to end the story with a moral: "The rich do what they can to make the poor *mind* being poor to keep the differential going. And the poor do mind, and they consent to being poor less and less, and there are more and more of them about. Had you noticed?

And they begin to know that the pumpkin pies of the poor taste as good if not better than the pumpkin pies of the rich; so if you can't make your own, do without, and let the hired help stay home for a change. Or you'll find cholesterol in your pie and a knife in your back, and a good thing too" (p. 88).

Monologic narration develops with a few minor twists into a marvel of revelations in the "As Told to Miss Jacobs" stories, the unilateral "conversations" with Miss Jacobs, the psychotherapist. In "A Gentle Tonic Effect," the speaker is identified as Morna Casey, a woman with nightmares who has "very little time for people who go to therapists" (p. 147) and who is suspicious of those who can listen to others for an hour and be paid exorbitantly. All Miss Jacobs says to her is that the first hour is free and that if Morna Casey would lie on the couch she would not be disturbed by her writing things down. Meanwhile, the nightmare-ridden Morna Casey tells us that she is a PR person with a special task in restoring public confidence in Artefax, "a new vitamin-derivative drug hailed as a wonder cure for addictions of all kinds . . . considered by some to be responsible for a recent spate of monstrous births" (p. 152). She is sure that if she "changed [her] job the dreams would stop," but when she thinks about shifting careers, she tells Miss Jacobs that "I think I'd feel quite at home with radioactivity: it's like nicotine and Artefax—in reasonable quantities it has this gentle tonic effect" (p. 152).

A conventional authorial narrator intervenes with a few paragraphs of description, telling us that Morna Casey "was a willowy blonde in her late thirties: elegantly turned out, executive style" (p. 148) and that she worked with her husband in "Maltman Ltd, a firm which originally sold whisky but had lately diversified into pharmaceuticals" (p. 148). But the story is Morna's, speaking almost without interruption. She resembles other Weldon narrators in not needing to be prodded, not needing encouragement. Indeed, she observes that Miss Jacobs reminds her of "the owl in *Squirrel Nutkin*," silent, wise, and somewhat threatening, "But you won't get to gobble me up: I'm too quick and fast for the likes of you" (p. 148). She tells Miss Jacobs that she met Hector in a pub: "Who's that man with the big nose?" (p. 149). Hector followed Morna and her husband home, effectively replacing him because Hector's forte is "A word too crude for your ears, Miss Jacobs." The result of his forte is their son Rider, born on a toilet seat and fished out of the water by Hector, and "Now Rider climbs about in potholes—he actually likes being spreadeagled flat against slimy rock faces, holding on with his fingertips" (p. 150). This Calibanlike image may be a clue to the inner poet: "No one knows how poetic I am," she tells Miss Jacobs, and it may also be a clue to the nightmare that haunts Morna

Casey. Her dream comes in two parts: Rider "about twenty inches long—
and he's clinging on by his fingertips to the inside of the toilet, and crying,
so I lean on the handle and flush him away" (p. 150). In the second half
of the dream, deformed people rise out of the toilet and "loom over me
and that's the bit I don't like" (p. 150). The poetic Miss Casey has lent her
talents to an industry that produces monstrous births—and among them
are the monsters of her own imagination.

Rosamund, the narrator in search of "moral and mental health" (p. 161)
in "Moon Over Minneapolis," rushes from the agony of twinship at home
to the potential delights of the twin cities. Her first-class ticket to Tom
seems designed to provide her release from competition with her twin
Minnie. But she realizes it is a trap: that she was headed for yet another
success, another proof of her preferredness, her "good luck." So she has
decided to return Club Class and give up her good fortune. She always
"loses" the competition to Minnie because she is more beautiful, more
successful, luckier. When Rosamund's husband Peter died, Minnie accused her of wearing black because she looks good in it. As she tells Miss
Jacobs, "To those that hath shall be given; difficult to hand it back, saying
I don't deserve this. But that's what I did, Miss Jacobs. That's why I lie
here: a corpse in mourning for itself" (p. 161). When she met Tom's family
she "tried not to think of Minnie. They asked me if I had brothers and
sisters. I denied her. I said I was an only child. It was my new view of
myself" (p. 161).

But she could not go through with the wedding. She saw the inequities
as too great. Her children, "both born bright and beautiful," went to good
schools and got a good education. Minnie's husband Horace was a so-
cialist who "didn't believe in doctors," so their son Andrew grew up
"dragging a leg behind him" and developed "personality problems." Their
daughter Lois "is just hopeless," a plain girl Minnie called "Uglymug," of
whom she said, " 'Just my luck!' As if it was her misfortune, not poor little
Lois's" (p. 160).

With all the burden of success, Rosamund describes herself walking
next to the Mississippi with Tom. "To the left rose the elegant new towers
of Minneapolis outlined in blocks and spires of light: symbols of wealth,
aspiration and progress. To the right, across the river, huddled the brooding clutter of St. Paul. Unequal twins, growing more unequal day by day.
St. Paul has the problems: race riots, poverty, squalor" (p. 162). She tells
Tom she won't marry because "the moon's not full." It is a half moon,
neither waxing nor waning, "unsatisfactory as half-moons are." When she
returned home, "Minnie just said, 'Oh, you're back. Made a mess of it for
once, did you!' " (p. 162)

Like all Weldon's monologic narrators, Rosamund feels a world of relief having disburdened herself, even with the suspicion that Miss Jacobs had fallen asleep: "I can hear you snoring; little snores or little sniffs" (p. 163). Miss Jacobs has been a perfect audience—virtually silent. In the process of remaining silent, she has helped Rosamund develop her own insight about that evening with "a half-moon over Minneapolis, catching its skyscrapers in miraculous light, while St Paul lay low, dark and brooding. And it wasn't fair. God makes nothing fair. It is up to us to render it fair" (p. 163). Rosamund, a Dantean/Yeatsian rose of the world, does what she can to make the world fair.

No one could appear more reasonable than the narrator of "Un Crime Maternel," the wife—now widow—of Peter (a teacher who was frequently away—could it be Peter Piper?) whose failings as a father included a sex drive that drove him, with the narrator's understanding, to other women. The narrator's passion for her children, Janet and Harvey, was such that she could not share them with Peter and his girlfriend, a junk-food addict, who took Janet and Harvey to the zoo, "can you imagine, a zoo?—the torment of those wild creatures" (p. 168). She did not begrudge Peter his girlfriends, nor was he a bad father. "It wasn't Peter's *fault* that this was what he was. Blame God, if you must blame anyone, for creating parents and children whose emotional interests overlap but do not coincide" (p. 169). Something had to be done, and since divorce "is so crippling to the child's psyche" she "could see no other way out" (p. 69).

Like most of Weldon's monologic narrators, this one, too, is a "vegetarian and I never let the children eat beef because of the possibility of mad cow disease" (p. 169). The narrator's beef casserole—brewed for Peter and the girlfriend—includes a death cap mushroom picked during their country walk. "It proved as fatal as the books said" (p. 169). But the children "witnessed nothing nasty": the narrator got Peter and his girlfriend to the hospital where they died. Spare the children. They need a good home and a good mother. It only stands to reason that the courts "won't be so stupid as not to understand that" (p. 169). The logic may be insane, but it is insistent and strangely coherent. In "Un Crime Maternel" Miss Jacobs makes a house call—to Holloway prison—and once in "the horrid little airless green room smelling of cabbage" (p. 165) she never stirs. The narrator is surprised to hear Miss Jacobs is a psychiatrist: "What did they call you?" she asks, opening the story. In her passion to explain herself and clarify her motives, she does her best to convince Miss Jacobs—and us—that she did what any concerned mother would do. Like the narrator in "Down the Clinical Disco," she is almost convincing.

"Mother Mary," the sometimes insightful narrator of "A Pattern of

Cats," offers Miss Jacobs a clear-sighted analysis of neurosis worthy of Freud: "The human situation is at fault, Miss Jacobs. If only men gave birth to girl babies, and women restricted their output to boys, and each suckled offspring of the opposite sex, why then I imagine girls would be as cheerful and confident and positive as boys. They wouldn't have to creep around trying to please, forever looking for the satisfaction that men naturally have; of once having controlled, owned, taken total nourishment from a creature of the opposite sex, and then, loftily, discarded it" (p. 174). The problem of raising children is related to raising cats—there is a pattern. Holly is now the family cat, one hundred and five years old in human terms, now listless in its dirt bed waiting to die. Holly is related to Don's "vaguely Siamese" former cat called The Cat, the black familiar who made Mary think of witches and who now exists only as a spirit in memory.

Mary's daughter Jenny had gone the way of neglect and drugs "and nearly killed me with the distress of it" (p. 177). She blamed herself, but so did everyone else: "Poor little Jenny, all her mother Mary's fault, all of it. Mary was irresponsible, said everyone, Mary stayed out, went to parties, drank too much, took a job, had a career even after she married Don and settled down (so-called)" (p. 177). "I longed for Jenny to reflect credit on to me, be the proud child of love and sexual freedom, of kindness and cuddles: not this angry skinny devil who shot up heroin and would steal and borrow money from my friends to do it. This laughing buoyant child of the family photograph" (p. 177). Mary's insights are those of the middle class, aware, concerned, analytical, and totally astonished at the waywardness of its children. Is it possible the parents gave too much love? Was it a matter of too much freedom, too much privilege, too much concern? And who is to blame: "It was not my fault that she took to the dogs: it is to my credit that she survived" (p. 178).

Jenny survived through "Intervention by cat." Lying on a dirty mattress in a "squat," she felt a cat, a black cat, jump on her chest—"A very flat chest, Miss Jacobs"—and when it stared at her, Jenny thought it was The Cat, but The Cat was dead. And when she went out of the room into the air to stare after The Cat, somehow "instinct," not "reason," saved her and pointed her in the direction of Narcotics Anon. "Intervention by cat happened on a second occasion. . . . It's why I've come to see you" (p. 180). Jenny had picked up a boy she met at Narcotics Anon, and in her morning-after guilt, she lay in bed when suddenly a cat—Holly—thudded on her chest, and then went to sleep between her and the boy. This intervention saved them both: "And between them they worked it all out, and neither went back to the needles, which had been in the air" (p. 180). But, of course, it could not have been Holly, who was safe home in Hampstead. It must have been one of her relatives, a look-alike, part of a pattern of cats.

Mary had worried for ten years that Jenny would die, but now she would live. "Like something good I once did, once upon a time, just fed back into the pattern of events and worked out okay, and came back to rescue me. Us. Pow! So that phone call never came. Forget the cats. What are cats?" (p. 180). And for that matter, what are mothers? What are children? Is it reason or instinct that saves them all? In the case of cats—who gets run over and replaced—it is instinct. Mother Mary tells us the same about Jenny who by instinct and the intervention of cats saves herself, and about Carl the younger child who by instinct never was any trouble.

Weldon's monologic narrators are by instinct arresting, revealing, relentless. That their Coleridgean narratives are often told to Miss Jacobs is deliciously up to date, since the modern marriage guest may preside over the marriage of true minds in the manner of the psychiatric specialist. And when Miss Jacobs is not available, any reader will do.

Works Cited

Bair, Deirdre. *Samuel Beckett*. New York: Harcourt, 1978.

Weldon, Fay. *Moon Over Minneapolis*. New York: Viking Penguin, 1992.

———. "Down the Clinical Disco." In Fay Weldon, *Moon Over Minneapolis*. New York: Viking Penguin, 1992.

———. "A Gentle Tonic Effect." In Fay Weldon, *Moon Over Minneapolis*. New York: Viking Penguin, 1992.

———. "Ind, Aff." In Fay Weldon, *Moon Over Minneapolis*. New York: Viking Penguin, 1992.

———. "A Pattern of Cats." In Fay Weldon, *Moon Over Minneapolis*. New York: Viking Penguin, 1992.

———. "Pumpkin Pie." In Fay Weldon, *Moon Over Minneapolis*. New York: Viking Penguin, 1992.

———. "The Year of the Green Pudding." In Fay Weldon, *Moon Over Minneapolis*. New York: Viking Penguin, 1992.

———. "Un Crime Maternel." In Fay Weldon, *Moon Over Minneapolis*. New York: Viking Penguin, 1992.

REGINA BARRECA

It's the End of the World as We Know It: Bringing Down the House in Fay Weldon's Fiction

"I've just heard a song called 'It's the End of the World as We Know It, and I Feel Fine.' Do you know it? It's now my favorite song," declared Fay Weldon during a telephone conversation three years ago, in 1990. I knew the song, imagined that one of her sons had no doubt been playing it over the stereo, and recognized the gleeful sound of Fay's delight in the idea that we could all feel fine as the world was shattered around us. The ending of one thing can only signal the beginning of something new, and isn't that cause enough to celebrate? The end of the world as we know it sounded good to Fay Weldon, and somehow she made it sound good to me.

Weldon's ability to transform endings into beginnings, tragedy into comedy, comedy into tragedy, the familiar into the exotic, or the sacred into the profane is her signature. The term "Weldonesque" is invoked when one of her readers sees in life or literature the kind of reversals, revisions, wickedness, and wisdom that mark Weldon's chronicling of the absurdities of a woman's life in the twentieth century. Your sister telephones, feeling ill, the minute you've told your mother that you just got a promotion? Your cat refuses to enter the room when your new lover is there? You discover that the aged and needy woman you live next door to is your aunt's former school rival and enemy? "Weldonesque," we mutter, and get on with our lives.

I want to argue that Fay Weldon is a novelist, short story writer, and essayist who sees herself as writing—to use her words—"rather wicked" material. Enjoying her work, Weldon imparts to her loyal readers a sense of complicity and cunning, and offers them permission to laugh out loud at the sanctimonious. When I asked her about her narrative style and her apparent commitment to writing a particularly lethal form of deadpan humor, Weldon declared that "it would not be fair to make people feel safe when safety is, in fact, an illusion. It is dangerous to be reassuring."[1] She went on to explain that "humor allows the reader to feel pleasure even as something important is being passed onto them." Women have been driven so far from their genuine centers of pleasure that, according to Weldon, they must be introduced to the obvious audience for their particular humor: themselves. And that is why, as Weldon writes in *Letters to Alice*, "any seminar on Women and Writing, or Women Writers, or the New Female Culture, or whatever, is instantly booked up . . . we are not alone in the oddity of our beliefs. Our neighbour, whom we never thought would laugh when we laughed, actually does" (p. 74).

At what do women laugh? They laugh at the way women are systematically trained to misread their own perceptions of the world, as well as the way that they are simultaneously encouraged to ascribe power to any man, however feeble, dull, or impotent. For example, the twenty-one-year-old unwed mother Scarlet of *Down Among the Women* misreads her response to Edwin, an appalling man nearly forty years her senior. She kisses his dry, thin lips and feels something, but Weldon tells us that "[i]t is not desire that is stirred, it is her imagination; but how can she know this? She feels she loves him. When she thinks of him kissing her, she is simply enchanted" (p. 110). In this novel, which the author regards as her most autobiographical, readers are encouraged to laugh at the disjuncture between Scarlet's romance script and her choice of a leading man, but the laughter is not directed at Scarlet. Significantly, the humor of the passage resides in the cultural structure that would quite naturally pair an old man with a young woman. Weldon's humor does not reject Scarlet but instead questions the conventional notion of desire. Weldon instructs us that "we see the world as we are taught to see it, not how it is," implying that if we are taught to find old men attractive, then we will seek them out and subsequently rationalize our attraction (p. 34).

Even beautiful, successful, and worldly Mary Fisher, in Weldon's well-known *The Life and Loves of a She-Devil*, falls from worldly and wordy success the moment she relies on her new lover's opinions of her writing. Bobbo, once only Mary Fisher's accountant but now her lover—and, by extension, the supreme critic of her work—suggests that her wildly successful novels should be written with an eye toward the presentation of reality. Mary shows her manuscript in progress to Bobbo, "as any loving woman would her man, and he had even helped her with it. He'd wanted her heroes to be a little graver, a little less tall" (p. 103). Not seeing that Bobbo wants all heroes to be created in his image, Mary Fisher listens and subsequently tailors her writing to fit Bobbo's tastes. She gains his grudging approval but nearly loses her publishing contract. How and why does this happen: why are women so willing to forfeit success and personal happiness? Or, as Weldon asks, "Why does it take so long? Why do we stay so stubbornly blind to our own condition, when our eyes are not only open, but frequently wet with grief and bewilderment?" (Praxis, p. 229). Perhaps it is "our passivity" that "betrays us, whispering in our ears, oh, it isn't worth a fight! He will only lie on the far side of the bed!" (p. 229). "Whereas the male humorous figure . . . seeks escape from the moral domination of women," argues Walker in her article "Humor and Gender Roles," "the female figure in women's humor struggles vainly to live up to expectations for her behavior emanating from a culture dominated by men" (p. 101). Weldon shows the impossibility of achieving perfection in the eyes of a man who will only lie on the far side of the bed when confronted with any requirements from his partner. In addition to passivity, in women's disparagement of their own sex lies powerlessness. "We prefer the company of men to women," wryly observes one of Weldon's characters (Praxis, p. 229). Women's identification with and desire to please men even as they fear them, coupled with an inherited fear of independence, keep women at one another's throats. "We betray each other," writes Weldon in an early novel. "We manipulate, through sex: we fight each other for possession of the male—snap, catch, swallow, gone! Where's the next? We will quite deliberately make our sisters jealous and wretched" (Praxis, p. 229).

As Judith Wilt has noted, women have also been encouraged to turn humor against themselves in order to render neutral an experience that might otherwise cause them to act to the detriment of the system. Women in Weldon's novels do so at their own risk (usually high) and then only for those periods in which they are going through what Weldon calls a "stupid patch" of attempting to live "an agreeable fiction" (Down Among the Women, p. 127). Praxis, for example, at her most self-denying stage:

turned the meeting with the Women's Libbers into a joke, into a dinner-table story, and presently could stop trembling when she thought about it. [P. 237]

When Gwyneth in Female Friends uses the cliché "you have to laugh . . . it's a funny old life," the third-person narrator responds only with an ironic "Ha-ha" (p. 47). Gwyneth is using the phrase as the system would have her use it, to continue justifying her own powerlessness.

It is when women begin to use comedy not to justify the ways of god/ man but rather to expose the folly of such ways, or when women's comedy is misread by convention, that it gains its real power. By understanding the social and economic basis for women's exclusion from the patriarchal structure or, as Weldon defines social structure, "the government, the church, the civil service, educational and caring organizations, lobbies, societies for this and that, quangos and so forth and so on" (Darcy's Utopia, p. 18), women can undermine the system by refusing to participate within their assigned roles. Weldon humorously but unrelentingly exposes the myths that have helped keep women in their place. For this reason, in part, she establishes her right to be called a feminist author. Indeed, Weldon has been said to "create a work whose very structure is feminist." In "Feminism and Art in Fay Weldon's Novels," Agate Krouse goes on to say that Weldon "may be unique among the new feminist novelists in developing such a structure" (p. 5). Weldon's carefully constructed characters rarely present themselves as role models. Weldon is not of the let's-present-the-best-possible-images-of-the-modern-woman school; her women are, well, no better than her men, although they are usually more complex, interesting, and important. Her novels are intricate weavings of politics, aphoristic commentary, romance, and satire. One recent novel, Darcy's Utopia, published in 1990, fulfills expectations for a Weldon work: the reader must pay attention to every curve in the narrative to stay in control of the tale or risk being taken in by the false prophets whose words line the pages. Darcy's Utopia is a disturbing and fascinating comic novel requiring enormous attention. Her particular brand of humor laces these pages in a particularly wicked manner, to borrow Weldon's own term, because it plays on the role of the reader as well as the roles of the characters. On the face of it, the novel deals with Eleanor Darcy and her ideas for a new society where "we have to start again, rethink everything, from how and why we brush our teeth to how and why we bury our dead" (p. 185). Eleanor is an example of the sort of ambitious, if not ruthless, protagonist Weldon created in She-Devil, but this time instead of changing herself to suit the world, Eleanor wants to change the world to suit herself. The characters who meet her are uneasy around Eleanor and their experience mirrors our response as readers: Eleanor is hardly a heroine, given to pronouncements such as "all babies will be automatically aborted unless good reasons can be shown why they should be allowed to proceed to term," and "it's only women who can't find lovers, who only have husbands, who have to make do with babies" (pp. 133, 163). This is hardly the talk of a heroine; Eleanor commands center stage, but Weldon offers the reader clear caveats concerning the various seductions of her vision. In other words, it is dangerous to approach this novel believing that Weldon is providing a blueprint for a desirable social order, however superficially appealing Darcy's thought of a "unicultural, multiracial, secular society" (p. 135) might be; seeing the split between the author's voice and the voice of the protagonist was never more important than in this ironic tour de force.

Eleanor Darcy preaches in order to convert journalists Valerie Jones and Hugo Vansitart to her doctrine. Like Weldon's other works, *Darcy's Utopia* concerns itself with the distribution of, right to, and uses of power. As in her other works, humor undercuts what first appear to be the most serious declarations; Eleanor's closest friend tells the journalists that it's "hard to tell when she's joking and when she isn't" (p. 188), reminiscent of the much-commented-upon last line in *She-Devil*, "A comic turn, turned serious" (p. 241). Nearly every character in these novels ends by questioning the right of any society to govern; indeed, questioning the very idea of society itself: "Rules? You want rules? You really can't survive without a book of rules? . . . Can't you decide, one by one, what's right, what's wrong? Do you have to continue to believe in groups?" (p. 225).

Weldon's satire encompasses everything from high culture—"museums will be very boring places indeed. If you want to subdue the children you only have to take them on a visit to a museum, and they will behave at once, for fear of being taken there again" (p. 171)—to elections—"there will be elections, but people will be expected merely to vote for people they personally like. It will be a popularity contest. An annual 'boy or girl most likely to run the country' jamboree" (p. 87). A structuring principle for all Weldon's fiction is an unevasive acknowledgment of the mutability of perception and definition. Only the worst are full of unconsidered conviction.

Individual characters more than announce prepackaged convictions; they attempt to live by such falsehoods. When a physical education teacher announces proudly that "female fidelity . . . is the cornerstone on which the family, the heredity principle, and the whole of capitalism rests" (*Down Among the Women*, p. 196), we hear echoes of Cixous and Clement, as well as echoes of Marx and Levi-Strauss. Tellingly, Weldon, who can certainly be identified as a writer concerned with materialist analysis, holds degrees in both economics and psychology, and her novels reflect both these influences. In addition, Weldon writes frequently on the hard sciences, and offers conclusions drawn from her knowledge of structural anthropology. In fact, Levi-Strauss's concept of woman as sign is converted into everyday language by Weldon when a character from *The President's Child* explains that "men . . . pass girls on, you know. They're forever doing each other favors. They like to share the good things of life, whilst making sure the less privileged don't get a look-in. They're the same sexually as they are financially. Capitalist to the core. They hand around the wives too . . ." (p. 74). This may be the point at which we should qualify Aristotle's claim that comedy typically "aims at representing men as worse . . . than in actual life" (*Poetics*, 2.4). Though Weldon's comedy is often described as an exaggerated and humorously distorted picture of our culture, it actually offers an unnervingly accurate portrait of contemporary life. Weldon's humor, like the humor produced by other women writers, often works by providing what at first might seem like hyperbole ("men pass women around") which is then revealed to be a transcription of the everyday life of a number of her characters. Those characters or actions that would seem to be "an imitation . . . of a lower type" turn out to be simply median (*Poetics*, 5.1). What is perceived as exaggeration is actually the product of an uncensored vision; the lower types are indeed running the system.

Comedy, however, can also disrupt the system by providing a context for women's refusal to participate while still allowing them to remain within the confines of accepted discourse. Weldon gives evidence of a woman's power, through sexuality and through humor, to refuse to be part of the masculine game. For example, the following anecdote from *Down Among the Women* prompts us to laugh at the figure of authority, not at the sexually active, socially marginal woman: "Reminds me of the story of Royalty visiting the maternity hospital. Royalty inclines towards young mother. 'What lovely red hair baby has, mother. Does he take after his father?' Answer: 'Don't know, ma'am, he never took his hat off'" (p. 21). Weldon implies women refuse to act as the currency of the dominant system when they realize the system has been constructed on a false basis. When women understand, as Elsa does in *Little Sisters/Words of Advice*, that for them, at least, sex is "not for procreation, it is for the sharing of privilege," they can abandon the rules and seek their own limitless pleasure and power (p. 134). Elsa, in fact, realizes that sex, outside the rules laid down for women's morality, proves fortifying rather than depleting, proves exhilarating rather than shameful. It proves, in fact, comedic. Shame, perhaps, is the province of the male, since sex proves to be his "loss" under these terms: "Man! Come to bed. Handsome, young, rich, powerful, or otherwise fortunate—is that you? Excellent? Come inside. Because what I know and perhaps you don't is that by some mysterious but certain process of osmosis I will thereupon draw something of these qualities into myself . . . gaining my pleasure through your loss" (p. 134).

This realization, Weldon suggests, is what has created the figure of the sorceress, the hysteric, the witch. Once the first rule is broken, all rules crumble. For Weldon, "the first step . . . the breaking of the first rule" (*She-Devil*, p. 54), is often the rejection of discrimination: one learns to reject the false assembly of values. The second step is realizing that "when male power and prestige are at stake the lives and happiness of women and children are immaterial" (*President's Child*, p. 163). This leads to the ultimate realization that the public world, which is supposedly created in order to protect the vulnerable, actually sets about systematically to destroy the powerless, but only after those in authority have profited from them. "Let us now praise fallen women" demands Weldon in *Down Among the Women*, "those of them at any rate who did not choose to fall, but were pushed and never rose again . . . truckloads of young Cairo girls, ferried in for the use of the troops . . . lost to syphilis, death or drudgery. Those girls, other girls, scooped up from all the great cities of East and West, Cairo, Saigon, Berlin, Rome. Where are their memorials? Where are they remembered, prayed for, honoured? Didn't they do their bit?" (p. 185). The most significant part of women's recognitions in these matters is to see that reality and nature are arguments used by men against women, used by men to enable themselves to keep the power they have asserted—and, most importantly, that power and authority are constructs of language, not forces reflecting the inherent order of the universe.

Language permits those in authority to do exactly as they please. Even women's understanding of themselves has often been designed by men who have been "prepared to generalise about women, and women would not argue, but would simper, and be flattered by the attention paid" (*Praxis*, p. 217). The cost of this attention, however, is astronomical. Weldon writes in *The President's Child* that men "murder and kill with impunity: not so much in the belief of the rightness of their cause, or even telling themselves that ends could justify means, or in their own self-interest, but simply not realizing that murder was what they had done" (*President's Child*, p. 62). This occurs, as Isabel says, because they have the authority enabling them to change "language itself to suit their purposes. If . . . anyone had to go, she would not be killed, let alone murdered; she would be liquidated, wiped out, taken out, obliterated, dealt with . . ." (*President's Child*, p. 62). Women's marginality is written into the language, as feminist critics have pointed out. Monique Wittig, for example, writes that personal pronouns are "pathways and means of entrance into language," and that they mark gender through all language, "without justification of any kind, without questioning" (p. 65). Weldon confronts this in her fiction. "I know you have a low opinion of your own sex," says one woman in *Praxis*, "it is inevitable; our inferiority is written into the language: but you must be aware: you must know what's happening" (p. 154).

In *She-Devil*, Ruth indicates that it is not surprising that women are not offered easy access to traditional authority given their exclusion from language: "we are powerless, and poor, and have no importance. We are not even included in everyone" (p. 50). If women subscribe to the conventional role assigned to them within the traditional system, they are stripped of their humanity. "Human beings rant and roister, fuck and feed, love and smother, shake their fists at the universe in thunderstorms and defy a creator who is sure to get them with the next lightning bolt," explains Weldon in *Female Friends*. "These little English girls, with their soft, uncomplaining voices, and their docile hearts, whose worst crime has been a foul on the hockey pitch, are quite alien . . ." (p. 130). Women have not been permitted to participate as human beings and so are perpetually alien to the world of men while creating distance between themselves and other women. On the other hand they can realize that, as Esther says to Phyllis in *The Fat Woman's Joke*: "Any woman who struggles to be accepted in a man's world makes herself ridiculous. It is a world of folly, fantasy and self-indulgence and it is not worth aspiring to. We must create our own world" (p. 83). While not a separatist feminist in her personal politics, certainly Weldon would advise women to leave behind the masculine model and find a vision that accommodates a woman's perspective. Women must, to begin with, see themselves and all women as human beings, and as guardians of their own integrity and fate. This simple agenda is at the heart of Weldon's feminism.

This leads to Weldon's assumption that although "you could advance the view that all good writing is bound to be feminist . . . it depends on how you're going to define feminist," claiming that "it took me a very long time to believe that men were actually human beings. I believed the world was female, whereas men have always believed the world is male. It's unusual for women to suffer from my delusion."[2] As Weldon illustrates in her novels, however, the apparently vigorous world of men pales in comparison to the world of women: "affairs of state . . . are child's play compared to the affairs of the home . . . of the intricacies of a marriage and the marriage bed," she writes in *Remember Me* (p. 203). In this way, Weldon illustrates one element identified by Nancy Walker as characteristic of women's humor, that "[m]en are nearly extraneous to the 'real' lives of women; their experiences outside the home are so remote as to seem nonexistent, and their lives within the orbit of the home are trivial, insignificant, or mysterious" (p. 113). Weldon sees the tasks designated as women's work—the primarily emotional responsibility of caring for other human beings on a day-to-day basis—as far more dangerous than work in the corporate world. Weldon argues convincingly that "if a corporation had to decide at what point it was feasible for a small child to ride its bicycle in the road, they would hire a dozen consultants and probably be unable to arrive at any conclusion. A mother has to make that decision in one afternoon based purely on her good sense and instinct. And she has to accept responsibility for her decision herself."[3] For Weldon the traditional cliché is inverted; she regards "men as, for the most part, decorative." The real weight of the world's work falls on women.

If women are able to cope effectively with the world's emotional work, why are they so often so ill-prepared to care for themselves? Where did they learn to see themselves as failures or victims? From Mary Fisher, for one, who "writes a great deal about the nature of love. She tells lies" (She-Devil, p. 1). If we examine the philosophies of the aging barmaid Gwyneth of *Female Friends*, we see that she absorbs her platitudes from "dubious sources, magazines, preachers and sentimental drinkers," and that these "often flatly contradicting the truths of her own experience, are usually false and occasionally dangerous" (p. 45). And, of course, women get instructions directly from the state: "There was much talk of 'the bond' down at the clinic and a good deal done to foster it. It was less taxing on welfare funds to have mothers looking after their own progeny than leaving the state to do it" (She-Devil, p. 180). Weldon points out that women often begin from a false point if they start by "supposing there's a world in which there's a right way to do things." Nothing is obvious, least of all the truth. When Ruth of She-Devil takes her whining, clinging children to the high tower where Mary Fisher lives with Ruth's adulterous husband in order to leave the children there ("the only place they'll have a chance to witness" the primal scene, she dryly offers) she is confronted with a stock truth:

"It is obvious that the children can't stay here. They must go home where they belong, with their mother."
"Why is it obvious?" asked Ruth. [P. 72]

Just as there is no hard core of reality, since truth, as Weldon describes it, is like an onion where you simply peel away layer after layer only to find that there is no heart of the matter, there is also "no such thing as the essential self." So admits one of Ruth's many doctors when she asks about changing her physical self: "It is all inessential, and all liable to change and flux, and usually the better for it" (p. 221). When women recognize that the apparent orthodoxy is upheld by mere consensus, they can begin to acknowledge the powers of subversion which they have within them. Every prevailing notion is then held up for questioning, especially those as fundamental as the concept of nature itself. In one quintessentially Weldon passage, the author vivisects the conventional bond between women and nature by at first declaring that "[i]t is nature, they say, that makes us get married. Nature, they say, that makes us crave to have babies. . . . It's nature that makes us love our children, clean our houses, gives us a thrill of pleasure when we please the home-coming male," but then undoes the rhetoric by asking, "Who is this Nature?" (*Praxis*, p. 147). [As Weldon has said in various books, "*They* will say anything."] "Nature does not know best, or if it does, it is on the man's side . . . when anyone says to you, this, that or the other is natural, then fight. Nature does not know best; for the birds, for the bees, for the cows; for men, perhaps. But your interests and Nature's do not coincide. Nature our Friend is an argument used, quite understandably, by men" (*Praxis*, p. 147). Weldon's humorous framing of such universals as "Nature our Friend" indicates the way women's comedy borrows clichés only to undercut them, and her off-handed remark concerning the nature of oppression ("an argument used, quite understandably, by men") calls our attention to her understanding of the social and cultural basis for the powerless position of women. There is nothing inherently natural any more than there is any inherently right answer or right way to live. And besides, as Ruth petulantly declares, women-as-she-devils are "beyond nature: they create themselves out of nothing" (*She-Devil*, p. 133). Women have to invent themselves from the beginning if they reject the sexual script prepared for them by the self-appointed guardians of righteousness.

The righteous view of the world set forth by the status quo would, for example, have women understand and forgive what should remain monstrously baffling and unforgivable. If the cultural catechism would have us "understand furcoated women and children without shoes," we will then be taught to rationalize "Hitler and the Bank of England and the behaviour of Cinderella's sisters . . ." (*Female Friends*, p. 53). Constructing a classically Weldon mosaic of politics, economics, and emotion, the author underscores the reason we must combat the forces of generalization and justification. In addition, Weldon's unapologetic coupling of the supposedly important (Hitler, the Bank of England) with the supposedly trivial (Cinderella's sisters) is emblematic of the way her very prose encompasses her refusal to accept standardized systems of value.

Weldon's moral framework is based on the concept of situational morality, validating the multiplicity of experience against a drive for a unified vision. There is no one right way to live, women realize, if they do not accept the absolute, codified systems of their culture. Praxis recognizes this, for example, when she argues that there are a number of "different" worlds, "each with its different ways and standards, its different framework of normality" (*Praxis*, p. 190). This recognition eventually leads to laughter at standards arbitrarily imposed on women who can never meet them. But, significantly, these recognitions then lead to anger at the typically strait-jacketed definitions of femininity. In other words, humor is not merely a cathartic experience that purges anger or frustration. Instead, it is a catalyst, urging women on to anger and action. In Weldon novels, certainly, women are encouraged to harness and redouble their refusal and anger until it becomes an unholy transfiguration. They must see, like Ruth, that "it is not easy . . . to forgo the reassuring pleasures of servitude, to face the unknown. Don't think it doesn't hurt. The first sea animals crawling up onto dry land must have had an agonizing time: struggling for breath, burning in the primeval sun" (*Remember Me*, p. 246).

As if formulating a mathematical equation for a child, Weldon explains: "if everything is inexplicable, anything might happen" (*Praxis*, p. 19). And if everything is open to question, then women should question the basis for their institutionalized oppression. There are several ways to question and disrupt the system, with the creation of art being one among many. Art, for Weldon, "is invention and distillation mixed . . . it is fundamentally subversive."[4]

Art, given its subversive roots, may well provide a more effective tool against the dominant order than politics, whose fundamental nature is conservative. Weldon insists that the possibilities for overturning the system lie not in political revolutions but in revising the entire concept of power and construction. "You could go to Israel and fight Arabs and really start something. Build a new country," suggests Elaine to Praxis, who replies that "new countries are in your mind." Elaine, although she acknowledges Praxis's point, suggests that "they have to be, if you're a woman. . . . Personally, I'd rather carry a gun" (*Praxis*, p. 171). Carrying a gun is the easiest and least dangerous option; women are far more dangerous than weapons. When faced with the maxim "one comes to terms with this kind of thing in the end," in response to a miserable situation, a woman should reply, "I come to terms with nothing" (*Fat Woman's Joke*, p. 10). When truly marginalized, or in other words, when they have abandoned the attempt to naturalize their lives, women inevitably gain power from their exiled position. They secure for themselves the right to outright laughter and obvious outrage.

"Anger was better than misery," decides Praxis (p. 253). Weldon expresses her characters' rage through the apparently conventional forms of the domestic novel, but with subversive results. Weldon provides equally detailed recipes for dinner and for conflagrations. As one critic comments, Weldon "describes the modern all-electric kitchen with deadly accuracy,

then invests it with the occult resonance of a magic cave. Suburban dinners do of course get fixed, between bouts of hysteria and plate-throwing,
but behind them you can hear the thunder and smell sulfur" (Caldwell,
p. 52). Ruth's sorceress-recipe from She-Devil illustrates this union:

I make puff pastry for the chicken vol-au-vents, and when I have finished cir-
cling out the dough with the brim of a wine-glass, making wafer rounds, I take
the thin curved strips the cutter left behind and mold them into a shape much
like the shape of Mary Fisher, and turn the oven high, high, and crisp the figure
in it until such a stench fills the kitchen that even the fan cannot remove it.
Good. [P. 10]

In this passage, Weldon's humor is at its best: she is irreverent toward
domesticity and is shamelessly furious, yet relates everything in deadpan-
clean prose. In making a kitchen the scene of her anger, Ruth is playing
out an argument by Catherine Clement, who asserts that "Cooking badly
is also being badly married . . . there is a family, household, intimate
stench hanging over it all . . ." (p. 37). Ruth also acts out Clement's direc-
tive that the hysteric weeps but the sorceress does not when she reveals
that "I ran upstairs, loving, weeping. I will run downstairs, unloving, not
weeping" (She-Devil, p. 24).

Indeed, Weldon creates a number of characters similar to those described in The Newly Born Woman, women who "revolt and shake up the
public, the group, the men, the others to whom they are exhibited. The
sorceress heals, against the Church's canon . . . the hysteric unties the familiar bonds, introduces disorder into the well-regulated unfolding of
everyday life, gives rise to magic in ostensible reason" (p. 5). Ruth becomes expert at healing physical, emotional, and spiritual woes as she
progresses through her unholy transformation. She forces science to bend
to her wishes and relies on magic to secure her eventual triumph. She is
a great force of disorder and a powerful adversary to received wisdom.
Ruth, as a result of her triumphs, recognizes, however, that the usual field
of battle is misleadingly reductive. To reduce all women's struggles to a
mere fight between the sexes is to unify them into an absurdity of the sort
propagated by the dominant culture. It is a more complex battle than that
because "it is not a matter of male or female, after all; it never was: merely
of power" (Praxis, p. 241). It is the structure of power itself that needs
subverting; men, deluded and decorative, are dangerous to women because they try to make women into the sign that will permit the system
to flourish.

One of the ways, as we have seen, that women revise the constructed
order is by rejecting the typically happy ending and, by implication, rejecting the rewards for behaving within the rules. Women will, like Wel-

don, conclude that this is the end of the world as we know it, and still feel
fine. Yet happy endings in women's writing, as we have also seen, are the
triumphs of nonclosure, multiplicity, and limitlessness. Happy endings in
women's writings often replace "integration" and "reaffirmation" with
recognition and realization. As Weldon writes in *Letters to Alice*, happy
endings do not mean "mere fortunate events" but a reassessment or reconciliation with the self, not with society, "even at death" (p. 83). But part
of women's defiance, and one of Weldon's strongest comedic structures,
is the refusal of women to accept finality, even the finality of death or
marriage. Her novels often end with the dissolution of a marriage, with
the defeat of reason, with the triumph of the female Lucifer, with the abandonment of children, or with the laying to rest of a ghost. Weldon systematically inverts the normal happy ending, so that we applaud Chloe's
abandonment of her husband at the end of *Female Friends*. Chloe's triumph
rests on the fact that she has finally stopped understanding and forgiving
her infuriatingly narcissistic husband. "As for me," she says at the novel's
conclusion, "I no longer wait to die. I put my house . . . in order, and not
before time. The children help. Oliver says 'But you can't leave me with
Francoise,' and I reply, 'I can, I can, and I do'" (p. 311).

Similarly, at the end of *Praxis*, we have an old woman with a broken
toe, who laughs in delight at her own triumph. "Even here," says the heroine, "in this horrible room, hungry and in pain, helpless, abandoned by
the world in general and the social worker in particular, I can feel joy,
excitation and exhilaration. I changed the world a little: yes, I did. Tilted
it, minutely, on its axis. I, Praxis Duveen" (p. 50). Triumph at undoing the
structures, undermining the system, likens daily life to a battle, "an exhilarating battle, don't think it wasn't. The sun shone brightly at the height
of it, armour glinted, sparks flew" (*Female Friends*, p. 309). Weldon sheds
her particular light on what has remained shadowed in the typical happy
ending, the acceptance of mutability and possibility. As she instructs her
female reader: ". . . days can be happy—whole futures cannot. This is
what grandmama says. This moment now is all you have. These days,
these nights, these moments one by one" (*Female Friends*, p. 310). Therefore, she insists that women—and men as well—must "treasure your moments of beauty, your glimpses of truth, your nights of love. They are all
you have. Take family snaps, unashamed" (*Remember Me*, p. 310). Madeleine, soon to die in a car crash on the A-1, buys heather from a poor
woman, taking coins from the milk money: "'Never mind,' says Madeleine
from her heart. 'Never mind. Good times will come again. Or at any rate,
we had them once'" (p. 18). It is in *Remember Me* that Weldon's refrain

"recognition, realization!"—so very emblematic of women's comedy—occurs. What should women realize?

For a start, they should pay careful and constant attention to the stories of their sisters, mothers, and grandmothers. Women must learn to validate and value the experience of other women, patterning their lives and thoughts from the alternative text feminine wisdom provides. Weldon counsels that if attention is paid, then the listener, sitting on her grandmother's cushions, "may not end as tired and worn and sad as she. Be grateful for the softness of the cushion, while it's there, and hope that she who stuffed and sewed it does not grudge its pleasure to you. The sewing of it brought her a great deal of pain and very little reward" (*Female Friends*, p. 309). Significantly, the validation of relationships apart from those of the usual pair of lovers is the hallmark of Weldon's endings. This validation can concern, as does Elsa's in *Little Sisters/Words of Advice*, a woman who finally sees the full range of emotions she holds for her mother. Elsa realizes that she "loves her, fears her, pities her, resents her, escapes her, joins her, loves her" mother and therefore "is saved" (p. 137). The traditional happy ending of boy-gets-girl-and-forms-a-new-society is at best " 'like a happy ending,' Scarlet complains . . ." (*Down Among the Women*, p. 183).

Weldon, like other women writers, has cause to complain about the traditional happy ending and the subsequent fate of women at the hand of conventional comedy. The heroines of conventional comedies appear to be in as insecure a position as the one in which Gemma finds herself in *Little Sisters*:

Silence. The knife blade trembled at her throat.
Mr. First sighed and put the knife down.

A joke, after all.

Of course. Employers always joke with typists. [P. 94]

In Weldon, however, there is no such thing as "only" joking. " 'I was only joking,' she says. But of course she isn't," Weldon writes in *Down Among the Women* (p. 88). Joking is an important business for the very fact that comedy is part of the survival process for women. Praxis goes through the full range of responses when she "wrote, she raged, grieved and laughed, she thought she nearly died; then, presently, she began to feel better" (p. 280). Comedy and power are interlocked in Weldon's writing: the power of comedy is to undo expectations and revise women's view of themselves in the system.

Most significantly, joking is a divisive, not a unifying experience.

Chloe's laughter at the end of *Female Friends* is the laugh not only of the Medusa, of Medea, and of Clytemnestra, but is also the laughter heard in the wake of every woman's escape from any form of confinement:

Chloe finds she is laughing, not hysterically, or miserably, but really quite lightly and merrily; and worse, not with Oliver, but at him, and in this she is, at last, in tune with the rest of the universe. [P. 259]

Seven pages later, Weldon, as if to double-check, asks: "is she laughing at him?" The answer is "yes, she is. Her victory is complete" (p. 267).

It is no small victory. Why is comedy so important? Because laughter is as obvious a manifestation of refusal as the bite or the kick. The whole system of society and culture may, in fact, be set up by men in order to keep "women occupied, and that's important. If they had a spare hour or two they might look at their husbands and laugh, mightn't they?" (*Down Among the Women*, p. 54). And that laughter, Weldon implies, would bring down the house. Good for her, we say, and set about to help on this particularly Weldonesque project.

Notes

1. Unpublished interview.
2. Interview, "Me and My Shadows," *On Gender and Writing*, ed. Michelene Wandor (London: Pandora Press, 1988), pp. 160–65.
3. Unpublished interview.
4. John Hoffenden, *Novelists in Interview* (London: Methuen, 1985), p. 305.

Works Cited

Aristotle. *The Poetics*. In *Criticism: Major Statements*, ed. Charles Kaplan and William Anderson. New York: St. Martins Press, 1991.
Caldwell, Mark. "Fay Weldon's Microwave Voodoo." *Village Voice* (25 September 1984): 52.
Cixous, Hélène, and Catherine Clement. *The Newly Born Woman*. Trans. Betsy Wing. *Theory and History of Literature*, vol. 24. Minneapolis: University of Minnesota Press, 1987.
Krouse, Agate Nesaule. "Feminism and Art in Fay Weldon's Novels." *Critique* 20.2 (1978): 5–20.
Walker, Nancy. "Humor and Gender Roles: The 'Funny' Feminism of the Post-World War II Suburbs." *American Quarterly* 37 (1985): 98–113.
Weldon, Fay. *Darcy's Utopia*. New York: Viking, 1991.
———. *Down Among the Women*. Chicago: Academy Chicago, 1984.
———. *The Fat Woman's Joke*. London: Coronet, 1982.
———. *Female Friends*. New York: St. Martins Press, 1974.

————. *Letters to Alice: On first reading Jane Austen*. London: Hodder and Stoughton, 1977.

————. *The Life and Loves of a She-Devil*. New York: Pantheon Books, 1984.

————. *Praxis*. New York: Summit Books, 1978.

————. *The President's Child*. New York: Doubleday, 1983.

————. *Remember Me*. New York: Random House, 1976.

————. *Words of Advice (Little Sisters)*. New York: Random House, 1976.

Wilt, Judith. "The Laughter of Maidens, the Cackle of Matriarchs: Notes on the Collision between Humor and Feminism." In *Gender and the Literary Voice*, ed. Janet Todd. New York: Holmes and Meier, 1980.

Wittig, Monique. "The Mark of Gender." In *Poetics of Gender*, ed. Nancy K. Miller. New York: Columbia University Press, 1986.

FAY WELDON

Italy, March 1990

The Changing Face of Fiction

I never studied literature; I am no academic, no theoretician. All I can do, when considering the changing face of fiction, is to look back on my own life and, using my novels as evidence for and against me, give an account of a political and fictional journey through the last twenty-five years: taking, as it were, the feminist route: no other, or so I always felt, being open to me.

When I was a student at a Scottish university, more time ago than I care to remember, I took a course in Moral Philosophy, along with Economics and Psychology. I got along best with Moral Philosophy—an altogether less speculative discipline, I thought, than those other two ersatz sciences. But alas, I was not my Professor's favorite pupil. I found Kant, frankly, difficult. And, besides that, I was female. So on the whole he ignored my existence, apart from returning my essays unmarked and failing me my end of year examinations—which proved he must have known, somewhere in his stony heart, that I and a couple of others like me, that is to say female, were there in his class. Otherwise he looked through us and round us. This Professor Knox of ours would remark, from time to time, during lectures, that women were incapable of rational thought or moral judgment— a view held by many then and some now—and the young men would nod sagely and agree. And we young women, those being the days they were, did not take offense: we thought that was the way the world was and there was no changing it: we just assumed there was something wrong with us; we could not be properly female—that must be it. We already had evidence of this from our literature classes—a diet of male fiction in which we never saw ourselves—from Kate in *Taming of the Shrew* to *Madame Bovary* to

Tess of the D'Urbevilles, to *Mrs Dalloway* (Virginia Woolf had got into the lists, somehow: but then she had the reputation of having a man's brain in a woman's body—the highest accolade so long as no one was expected to *marry* such a woman), and Professor Knox confirmed it. There was indeed something very wrong with us. We plastered our faces with Max Factor pancake and girdled our hips, and tried our best to look like dolls, and did as our mothers suggested and pretended at parties to be nurses not students, and laughed at male jokes and tried to say nothing sharp or funny on our own account. But it just didn't work. We remained capable of rational thought and moral judgment: our un-femininity kept showing through. "Unfeminine!" A terrible word for what was seen as a terrible state. We cringed beneath the power of it: worse than "shrill"—if you said anything more than once; "aggressive"—if you answered back; because both of those you could do something about—you just shut up and smiled—but "unfeminine"! Oh, it went to the heart of one's naturalness. How we swept and cleaned—we girl graduates—and had babies and showed our garters to escape the insult!

Now by the mid-sixties I began to see the error of not just my but our ways. The myth that women didn't go out to work but stayed home and were supported by their husbands—a myth still believed by some though supported these days by very few statistics—was beginning to wear rather thin. A certain Shirley Conran wrote a famous book called *Superwoman* which explained how to keep every conceivable myth going at once—how a woman—if only she were sufficiently organized—*could* be all things to all men and survive. Be wife, mother, cook, housekeeper, secretary, parlor maid, cleaner, mistress, delphic oracle, and breadwinner and no one notice any shortcoming in any of these areas. I remember beginning to find it odd that at home I had to pretend I didn't go out to work, and at work pretend I didn't have a home. Husbands, though beginning more and more to need their wife's earnings, still felt demeaned by them. "No wife of mine works," was the word on many a proud husband's lips. Meaning, "I am man enough to keep the lot of you. Only a failure lets his wife work." Employers, though needing women's work—then as now female labor costs less than male—felt persecuted by the notion that a woman might ask for time off to look after a sick child or do the shopping. And if you did stay home—what were the rewards? Let me quote you a piece from the first novel I wrote, back in 1966, *The Fat Woman's Joke*, spoken by a certain Esther—an apparently happy housewife, whose comfortable existence was shattered when she went on a diet:

By the end of the week I could see myself very clearly indeed, and it was not comfortable. My home was not comfortable either. It seemed a cold and chilly place, and I could see no point in the objects that filled it, that had to be eternally dusted and polished and cared for. Why? They were not human. They had no importance other than their appearance. They were bargains, that was their only merit. I had bought them cheap, yet I had more than enough money to spend, so where was the achievement? Those old things, picked up and rescued and put down on a shelf to be appreciated, were taking over my whole life. They were quaint, certainly, and some were even pretty, but they were no justification for my being alive. Running a house is not a sensible occupation for a grown woman. Dusting and sweeping, cooking and washing up—it is work for the sake of work, an eternal circle which lasts from the day you get married until the day you die, or are put into an old folks' home because you are too feeble to pick up some man's dirty clothes and wash them any more. For whose sake did I do it? Not my own, certainly. Not [my son] Peter's—he could as well have lived in a tree as in a house for all the notice he took of his surroundings. Not [my husband] Alan's. Alan only searched for flaws: if he could not find dirt with which to chide me, if he could not find waste with which to rebuke me, then he was disappointed. And daily I tried to disappoint him. To spend my life waging war against Alan, which was what my housewifeliness amounted to, endeavouring to prove female competence—which was the last thing he wanted or needed to know about—what a waste of time this was! Was I to die still polishing and dusting, washing and ironing; seeking to find in this my fulfillment? Imprisoning Alan as well as myself in this structure of bricks and mortar we called our home? We could have been as happy, or as miserable, in a cave. We would have been freer and more ourselves, let's admit it, in *two* caves.

These days I must say, for many a woman, chance would be a fine thing. Just to be allowed to stay home and dust—but I was younger then. And "work" for the majority of women means part-time, low-paid work, often un-unionized, which breaks every "place of work" regulation, in cafés, factories, shops, laundries, the catering trade. The hands which serve you, you will notice, are mostly female or, if not female, dark. And though it has always seemed to me that if women had economic power, they could at least choose the direction their lives took, the economic power of women is never great enough. Two thirds of the world's work is done by women, according to UN statistics. Ten percent of the world's wealth is owned by women, and that figure hasn't altered in the last three decades. We scrabble forlornly, I think in my worst moments, against an immovable wall, made of prejudice, habit, and our own natures. And what is this battle for justice, fairness? Perhaps only the child's perennial complaint, the whine: "it isn't fair." Perhaps that's all we're doing, whining.

Listen to this piece—poor Esther: the nonworking wife, her children have left home, and her husband is more interested in his young secretary than in her:

I am finished. I am over. It is very simple, really. I am a woman and so I am an animal. All women are animals. They have no control over themselves. They feel compelled to have children—there is no merit in it, there is no cause for self-congratulation; it is blind instinct. When I was a girl I searched for a man to father my children. My eye lighted on Alan. I had my child. Now the child is grown up and I have no further need of the man. I shuffle him off. And he has no need of me, because women age faster than men, and I am no longer fit mother for his possible children. Let him get more if he can, and start the whole thing over again with someone else. That's his affair, not mine. The drive is finished in me. I am dried up. I am useless. I am a burden. I wait to die. I am making myself feel hungry again.

And she eats, because that's the only pleasure left to her. Or listen to this bit, which appears just after the husband observes that the male-female war is hotting up (this was 1966, remember) and she says she wishes she had been born a man. (One often heard that said by women in those far-off days. Not now, so much.)
    Esther to Alan:

"Men are always accusing women of being unfeminine, and at the same time making sure that the feminine state is as unendurable as possible. You leave your dirty socks around for me to pick up. And your dirty pants. It's my place to pick them up, because I'm a woman. And if I don't, you accuse me of being unfeminine. It's my place to clean up your cigarette ash from the coffee cup where you've ground out your cigarette. I am only fit to serve you and be used and to make your life pleasanter for you, in spite of such lip service as you may pay to equal rights for women. You may *know* I am equal, with your reason, but you certainly don't *feel* that I am."
    "Quite the suffragette."

And that, in those days, was one of the worst things a man could think of to say about his wife. Suffragette. By implication, shrill, aggressive, violent, unreasonable things. (These days, of course, "feminist" has replaced suffragette as a term of abuse, in some circles.) And the other is the accusation, posed as a question. "Tell me, do you hate men?" (That, then as now, is what women aren't supposed to do: their duty being always to forgive and forget. And it does sound an unnatural sort of thing to do, I suppose, to hate men.)
    A few years later, in 1972, I wrote a book called *Down Among the Women*. What a place to be, I complained. Yet here we all are by accident of birth, I said; sprouted breasts and bellies, as cyclical of nature as our timekeeper the moon, and down here among the women we have no option but to stay. What I wrote then still applies: more's the pity.

There will now be a short intermission. Sales staff will visit all parts of the theatre, selling for your delight whale-fat ice-cream whirled into pink sea

waves at two shillings, or ten new pence, the plastic cone; at the apex of each
you will find wedged a stiff syrupy strawberry. Or if you prefer, try a hot dog
from our foyer stall at only two shillings and sixpence, or thirteen new pence;
dig your teeth into the hot pink rubber sausage. The bread is hygienic and
aerated (did you know?) with that same substance which creates the foam on
your daily detergent.

Truly, yes, truly delicious. Or at any rate, all right by me. Time was when
the children had rickets. More hens in the country now than people. Free-range
for the hundreds, or battery for the millions, you make your choice. I know
which I make. A good woman knows that nature is her enemy. Look at what
it does to her. Give her a packet of frozen fish fingers any day, and a spoonful
of instant mashed potato, and a commercial on the telly to tell her it's good.
We swallow the lot, we mothers, and laugh.

Down here among the women, or up, up, up, in the tower blocks; those
rearing phalluses of man's delight.

But I had it in for men. Listen:

Down here among the women you don't get to hear about man maltreated;
what you hear about is man seducer, man betrayer, man deserter, man the
monster.

What did we hear last week, during our afternoons in the park?

Man leaves his wife, young mother of four. She is waiting to go into hospital
for her cancer operation. He returns from a holiday abroad, stays a couple of
hours, and leaves for good, saying, by way of explanation, he is tired of being
married. He probably is, too.

Man runs off with secretary the day his son brings home his first girlfriend.

Man leaves home while his wife's in hospital having the baby. She comes
home to an empty house and unpaid bills. Yet he visited her in hospital,
brought her flowers and grapes . . . no one can understand it.

And listen to this bit:

A well-dressed woman passes. I don't know her. She is middle-aged and
hatchet-faced. She is talking to herself, mutter, mutter. She is angry. She wears
a flowered hat. I think I know what she wants. She wants to hang, flog, behead,
draw, quarter, stone, shave, guillotine. She wants her revenge. If she came
across a flasher she would have him publicly castrated and wield the knife
herself.

I am sure her house is clean. I am sure there is not a speck of dust anywhere.
The cleaner the house the angrier the lady. We are the cleaners. We empty the
ashtrays which tomorrow will be filled again. We sweep the floors which tomorrow will be dusty. We cook the food and clean the lavatory pans. We pick
up the dirty clothes and wash and iron them. We make the world go round.
Someone's got to do it. When she dies it will be said of her, she was a wonderful
wife and mother. She cooked a hundred thousand meals, swept a million
floors, washed a billion dishes, went through the cupboards and searched for
missing buttons. She muttered but we will miss her.

Down among the women, we don't like chaos. We will crawl from our
sickbeds to tidy and define. We live at floor level, washing and wiping. If we

look upward, it's not towards the stars or the ineffable, it's to dust the tops of the windows. We have only ourselves to blame.

"Yes, God," we say, "here's your slippers and your nice hot dinner. In the meantime, just feed us, keep us, fetch the coal and say something nice while you're about it."

Man seems not so much wicked as frail, unable to face pain, trouble and growing old.

And that I fear still holds. These days I would say it applied to women too. I would say men and women both behave as badly as they are allowed to behave, but society allows man a little more than it does woman. It is as much to do with conditioning, role-playing, as with gender. In *The Hearts and Lives of Men*, a more recent novel, I notice I have this to say about a very difficult artist painter.

If men are like children, as some women say, it is certainly more true in this respect than others, that they are happier when obliged to behave, like little guests at a birthday party, strictly run.

By the mid-seventies we'd progressed; I could look back at my student days and see Kant and Professor Knox both in a different light. I could now maintain it was Kant's fault, not mine, that I failed properly to understand him. I would say that if language failed to represent meaning, then there was no meaning: I was reading the ravings of a madman: obviously I couldn't make sense of it. Not my failing, his. What's more he was a very male madman; the main trouble with Kant was that he was a *man*. As was Professor Knox—and now I could dismiss him too on that account, and no doubt as unjustly as once he had dismissed me. Gender must be no excuse for bad behavior.

In the fifties and sixties we women thought if we were unhappy it could only be our fault. We were in some way neurotic, badly adjusted—it was our task to change ourselves to fit the world. We would read Freud, Helene Deutsch, Melanie Klein (these last two at least being moderately relevant to our female condition), bow our heads in shame in the face of our penis envy, and teach ourselves docility and acceptance. As the seventies approached and we failed to achieve these ends, the great realization dawned—we must change not ourselves but the world! It was not we who were at fault, with our mopes and sulks and hysteria and murderous premenstrual rages, it was the world. The world was male. It was only natural, living as we did in a patriarchal society, that we would behave in such a way. So we stopped placating (that is to say smiling) and set out, scowling, to change the world. We worked upon that, not upon ourselves. We became radical separatist, lesbian feminists, or subsections of such, and weren't really nice at all. We stamped hard on male toes, and we liked each other but it was a rare man who liked us. And if he did we despised him for his softness—I remember the fate of the New Man who looked after the crèche while the women had their meetings—how he would be spurned by the booted foot of passing feminists.

In the mid-seventies I wrote a novel—*Praxis*. My protagonist was ambivalent about the new women. Here she bemoans her fate and their nature:

I, Praxis Duveen, being old and scarcely in my right mind, now bequeath you my memories. They may help you: they certainly do nothing to sustain me, let alone assist my old bones clamber out of the bath.

Last night, doing just that, I slipped on the soap and cracked my elbow. This morning the pain was such that I took the bus to the hospital instead of the park.

My erstwhile sisters, my former friends: I did what you wanted, and look at me now!

You have forgotten me.

Two years in prison have aged me two decades. I should not regret the new grey wiriness of my hair, the swollen veins in my legs, the huddling lumpiness of my figure, the faded look in my watery eyes. But I do, I do. The eyes of the world look quickly past me, beyond me, and I am humiliated.

My fingers are stiff and sore with what I suppose to be arthritis. Writing has become painful. But I will write. I am accustomed to pain. And pain in the elbow, the fingers and, since my abortive journey to the hospital, pain in my stamped-upon toe, is nothing compared to that pain in the heart, the soul, and the mind—those three majestic seats of female sorrow—which seems to be our daily lot.

I do not understand the three-fold pain: but I will try. Perhaps it serves a useful purpose, if only as an indication that some natural process is being abused. I cannot believe it is a punishment: to have a certain nature is not a sin, and in any case who is there to punish us? Unless—as many do—we predicate some natural law of male dominance and female subservience, and call that God. Then what we feel is the pain of the female Lucifer, tumbling down from heaven, having dared to defy the male deity, cast out for ever, but likewise never able to forget, tormented always by the memory of what we threw away. Or else, and on this supposition my mind rests most contentedly, we are in the grip of some evolutionary force which hurts as it works, and which I fear has already found its fruition in that new race of young women which I encountered in the bus on the way to the hospital this morning, dewy fresh from their lovers' arms and determined to please no one but themselves. One of the New Women trod me underfoot and with her three-inch soles pulped my big toe in its plastic throw-away shoe (only I, unlike her, cannot afford to throw anything away, and am doomed to wear it for ever) causing me such fresh pain that when the bus broke down and we all had to be decanted into another, I lost heart altogether, abandoned the journey and limped home.

The New Women! I could barely recognise them as being of the same sex as myself, their buttocks arrogant in tight jeans, opening inviting, breasts fall-ing free and shameless and feeling no apparent obligation to smile, look pleasant or keep their voices low. And how they live! Just look at them to know how! If a man doesn't bring them to orgasm, they look for another who does. If by mistake they fall pregnant, they abort by vacuum aspiration. If they don't like the food, they push the plate away. If the job doesn't suit them, they hand in their notice. They are satiated by everything, hungry for nothing. They are what I wanted to be; they are what I worked for them to be: and now I see them, I hate them. They have found their own solution to the three-fold pain— one I never thought of. They do not try, as we did, to understand it and get the better of it. They simply wipe out the pain by doing away with its three centres—the heart, the soul and the mind. Brilliant! Heartless, soulless, mindless—free!

Listen, I have had good times. It is only on bad days that I regret the past and hate the young. I helped to change the world. I made life what it is for those lovely, lively, trampling girls on the bus.

Look at me, I said to you. Look at me, Praxis Duveen. Better for me to look at myself, to search out the truth, and the root of my pain, and yours, and try to determine, even now, whether it comes from inside or from outside, whether we are born with it, or have it foisted upon us. Before my writing hand seizes up, my elbow rots, my toe falls off.

In the meantime, sisters, I absolve you from your neglect of me. You do what you can. So will I.

These days the new women, or so I hope, take a slightly more moderate line. We can see there may occasionally be room for personal self-improvement: we may have to work upon ourselves as well as on the world: accept that neurosis does exist, that it is helpful to examine our motives and obsessions, to try to distinguish between rightful anger and paranoia and so forth. Some of us manage better than others. I have a friend who writes stage plays about the awful behavior of men in general and middle-aged middle-class men in particular. When middle-aged middle-class theater critics berate her plays, she is indignant and astonished. She's like a woman who, divorcing her husband, expects her husband to agree that she is right to divorce him and is quite upset when he doesn't. But he's behaving so selfishly, she complains: so mean, so bad-tempered! Of course he is, you reply. That's why you divorced him: so why the surprise? But she doesn't see it. Sexism in reverse is flying high, I fear. I don't feel sorry for men on this account—they own the theaters, the printing presses, and the TV studios—but sometimes I do feel a little guilty.

In the late seventies I remember going to a women's meeting in London on "New Definitions of Women." I went with Beryl Bainbridge. Someone from the floor (and there'd already been a heated discussion: why were we on the platform, they on the floor? Quite right, we said, we'll change places, but they wouldn't) someone from the floor said, "How are we to define woman in the light of our new self-knowledge?" and Beryl said,

"Why, women are people who have babies," and I had to practically rush her out of the building in a plain wrapper, so great was the outrage. And then I wrote a novel called *Puffball*, which was a kind of gynecological textbook as well as a novel, in which I suggested women were at the mercy of their hormones, their instincts, and became almost as suspect for my views as Beryl Bainbridge was for hers. "Liffey," I wrote—she being my heroine—"Liffey, like most other women, never cared to think too much about what was going on inside her body. She regarded the inner, pounding, pulsating Liffey with distaste, seeing it as something formless and messy and uncontrollable, better unacknowledged. She would rather think about and identify with the outer Liffey. Pale and pretty and nice."

Later, I'm pleased to say, the world caught up with me. Feminists began to take up the Mother Goddess, earth magic; fecundity became an okay word. To be part of nature, nearer to nature, to hear the rhythms of the seasons—and so forth. I remain pretty skeptical about this part of it. I have always seen "nature" as inimical to women; nature kills you. Left to her own instinctive devices, a woman has babies, more and more babies, and is dead by thirty. And as Marie Stopes pointed out—in a world without medicine, our way of supervising nature—with every pregnancy your chances of dying from it double.

And with the having of babies, what's more, comes helplessness. Liffey, in her book, loses her money, through sheer little-girl inattention, and begins to understand that

She was not, as she had thought, a free spirit, and nor was he: that they were bound together by necessity. That he could come and go as he pleased; love her, leave her as he pleased: hand over as much or as little of his earnings as he pleased; and that domestic power is to do with economics. And that Richard, by virtue of being powerful, being also good, would no doubt look after her and her child, and not insist upon doing so solely upon his terms. But he could and he might: so Liffey had better behave, charm, lure, love and render herself necessary by means of the sexual and caring comforts she provided.
Wash socks, iron shirts. Love.

And perhaps on the whole it is not so terrible a fate to wash socks, iron shirts, love. Though I do say to women now—with a clear eye on the statistics of our society—if you have a baby the bottom line is this: you must be prepared to raise it single-handed and support it single-handed. Anything else is an optional extra, a bonus.

I don't think I could write *Puffball* now. The world moves on. Magic and childbirth are not what they were. My latest novel, *The Cloning of Joanna May*, is about a woman who manages to be not just in two places at once, like Superwoman, but five—thanks to the male technology of reproduction. We can't be frightened of the future, I say: it's the past that destroys us.

Sometimes I think there is simply a body of human suffering in the world—emotional suffering—and the sum of it never alters: it just gets handed round from this group to that. I can see it is certainly the women's turn to do the handing around, but it is not something to be relished.

The men of New York, in a recent poll, announced themselves almost to a man as antifeminist, but went on to say they all believed in equal pay, equal parenting, equal rights, and obligations to domestic life. Feminism is alive and well and living in our hearts, if you ask me, and taken as a matter of course in most contemporary novels: the only thing wrong with it is the word itself, which continues to frighten: as if it were a big black stamping feminist boot on the fragile plant that is man's love for woman, woman's love for man. I recently did an English version of Ibsen's *A Doll's House,* and those concluding words still ring true. One day, one day, Nora said to Torvald, Torvald to Nora, "the miracle will happen. You and I, wife and husband, woman and man, will talk and work and love on equal terms."

And I still believe in that miracle. I would add, I believe they could still do so in a perfect society: that if we seize the political and social energy, the desire for change, that now convulses the whole world, we could build ourselves a utopia, but that's another matter.

FAY WELDON

New York, April 2, 1990

Of Birth and Fiction

I looked through my itinerary last Saturday as I sat on the early train. I board it at 7:50 in the morning: it leaves from a small station in the middle of a field in greenest, darkest Somerset, in England, where crows caw and buds burgeon. We have had a very early spring in England. It doesn't make us grateful: we just worry about the ozone layer. I was on my way to Heathrow, from whence Los Angeles, San Francisco, Minneapolis, Chicago, and, finally, thankfully, here. And I observed that morning that I was to speak at the New York Public Library this evening, and I saw moreover the subject was to be "Of Birth and Fiction."

Now what possessed me, I thought. What did I mean? What bizarre procreative or literary process did I have in mind? It is true that women in my novels often give birth, as do women in real life. It is true they often have children, not necessarily very nice children: as often just occasionally happens in real life—at which point mothers get blamed.

But then Mothers always get blamed, even more in real life than in fiction. Mothers get blamed, I notice, for generic male behavior. If husbands behave badly around the house it is because their mothers failed to teach them better, not because their fathers failed to set a proper example. "I blame his mother. . . ." But these are the nineties: I understand, just four months into the new decade, that it's to be all about loving and understanding one another. So I will stop blaming other people for blaming mothers. We are all to hold hands, nation with nation, empire with empire, socialism with capitalism, generation with generation, writers with readers, men with women. We have no alternative. War and sex have both become dangerous. We must learn to like one another. So I will say nothing

bad about men. We must not, in the nineties, blame others, whom we must
see as persons first and of a certain gender second, for being the nation-
ality, the race, the creed, or the sex they are. We must not drop bombs on
anyone, or utter foul words about anyone: in fact we must improve ourselves and high time too.

Of Birth and Fiction.

Was I talking about the creative instinct? I used to be struck, when
speaking to American women, with how they assumed that the having of
babies and the writing of poetry, or fiction, the painting of pictures, did
not go together. That you could not have babies and art too. Not just because of the time, energy, and money spent on rearing children, but for
some other, vaguely mystical, reason. There was simply not enough creativity, talent, to go round: if what there was went into the making of babies
then there would be none left to write books, paint pictures, nail the vision, fix the inspiration on to the page, the canvas, the piano, whatever. It
seemed a wrongheaded extension of the sop that used to be thrown to
women in the old days: women have babies, they used to say, men have
art. We all have to create something; any woman can have a baby, the feeling was: takes a man, a genius, to make something where there was nothing there before, something that will illuminate our lives. Babies add to
life: they just make more of it: that's the women's part. The genius, the
male genius, explains it. How old-fashioned that seems now. Men are fathers too. There's no avoiding it. Babies can grow *in vitro*, outside wombs.
You need an egg, some sperm, a nice warm broth, and lo, life begins! A
whole new personality; a dash of this, a dollop of that, emerges. Grandma's
eyes, Uncle Jim's temper, Daddy's teeth. Birth isn't what it was. Mothers
provide wombs, it's true, wherein a fetus of much-disputed legal owner-
ship can grow: but the feeling still is, well, anyone could do it. Mothers
"bond"—but even that has clinical, dismissive overtones. Even a baby
duckling bonds with the mother, waddles after it: nothing special—just
instinct. The only comfort I can find in this changing situation—and why
is it that somehow situations never seem to change in the female's favor?—
is that to say men have art and women have babies now seems an impossible thing to say.

I always found the opposite was true. I have four children. Sometimes,
looking back on this irrational enterprise, I think I had them because I
found I wrote best just before and after their births. Was this true, or self-
delusion? My mother, also a novelist, was prescribed estrogen when she
was seventy-five and at once started writing again with great gusto. "Estrogen," she said. "That's all it is. Novels are to do with estrogen." Perhaps
she had me for this very reason.

Of Birth and Fiction . . . I thought, since I was on my way to New York, that I would ask Gina Barreca what I meant. She is a professor of literature at UConn: she is my deconstructionalyst. Writers have them, nowadays, as other people have analysts. Gina referred me to a short biographical sketch I once wrote on the subject of Rebecca West, one of our great writers in the first half of this century. Rebecca West had a baby, out of wedlock, by H. G. Wells. Gina said that here I had permanently and properly linked the bringing to birth of fiction with the bringing to birth of a child—and a very literary child at that—Anthony West. "Compose yourself," I said, addressing this woman writer who was in the pangs of giving birth. That, said Gina, is what writers do, they compose themselves; other people just narrate themselves. Listen:

Rebecca, there is life the other side of love. If only you could hear me. Perhaps you can? Perhaps through doubt, fear and pain comes a flickering sense of exultation, of future; the intimation that fate has you marked: that its plans are already made, unalterable. For this is the sense the future must have of the past, and it is this very awareness I am trying to broadcast back to you. *It is all going to be all right.* Your lungs will stand it, you won't tear apart, the pain will pass, and be forgotten. The shame will be faced and conquered. The baby is lovely, healthy, robust, will even grow up to be a writer. As is his father. As are you.

Breathe deeply. Compose yourself. You are not in as difficult a position as many of your contemporaries. You are not helpless. You can (just) earn your own living, by writing. Your lover's wife, seen by a self-deluding posterity (and indeed by her husband, once she is dead) as a saint, for putting up with his infidelities and being so accommodating, even kind and chatty, to his lady friends, has no such option. She is complaisant because she has to be, she has no alternative: she does not *earn.* And so what if her husband wrongs her? Women in your day cannot divorce men for adultery: though men can divorce women for the offense. The double standard is enshrined in law. For your information, the law is presently to change and wives will be permitted to take offense at infidelity, and start their own divorce proceedings. And then later changes will bring us up to our present, when human sexual behavior is accepted with a shrug and a sigh; and matrimonial blame, for good or bad, no longer allocated by the courts. This one guilty—that one innocent. But the lot of the divorced and dependent wife is still not happy, in my day as in yours. Socially isolated, reduced in circumstances, relying for her comfort and security on the strength of a husband's guilt—except for the grudging assistance of an unwilling state. What has changed?

And back there at the beginning of the century, you, the mistress, unmarried and young, and she, the wife, married and in her middle years, both live in a milieu particularly distressing for women. You have no moral power. The trouble is that in the artistic, literary, and intellectual circles in which you move, men have discovered Free Love, the Life Force, as the way forward to the future. Free Love for men, that is, just not for wives, daughters, and sweethearts. Men look for, and claim, Life Mates, but marry pretty housewives, as usual. What's more, eugenics are all the rage—the my brains and your beauty syndrome—and beauty resides in the younger women. So let's transmit the Life Force! It's our duty, not just our desire. Older women are having an even harder time of it than usual, as lofty statements all but drown the creaks and groans of riven homes.

and

But too late now. It's 5 August 1914. You can't afford to know it, just at the moment. Very well. Put it from your mind. Lie back on your feather pillows, in their stiff white cotton slips, the draw-sheet ready, the midwife back from the kitchen; lie back and think, if you can, of love.

But how can you, for more than a minute or two? I know, I know. Here you must lie in dreary Hunstanton—you, accustomed to cities: to Edinburgh, where you were reared; to London, where you had such early, instant success—because this is where your lover has decided you will live! And he is supposed to be here, and he isn't.

The rhythm of the pains gets more insistent, your body convulses—what is this; is this the Life Force? The light of the sun spreading a monstrous flower of pain against burning, closed eyelids: is this your destiny? Oh yes indeed, what else, indeed it is; your body is not yours: they are right in what they say: this is indeed the Life Force, and it's killing you. (It's not, you know. Merely the transition from the First to Second Stage. You know so little, so very little: terms such as First Stage, Second Stage, Three Fingers Dilated, are not in common currency, not even in the midwife's handbook: not fit knowledge for a woman, on 5 August 1914—midnight has come and gone—for how can the soul, the spirit, triumph if the body is too well understood?) All is ignorance, all is faith: all is terror, and you are mystified, and you are hurting, and all you understand is pain, anguish, punishment, and the war is breaking out and your lover is not even here, and it's Too Late!

Push, Rebecca, push, and good for you! Of course you did all these things. Lied, deceived, loved and lost. I'm glad you were deaf to common sense, conventional morality, and indifferent to—though always conscious of—social disgrace. The Life Force was with you and the baby was—is, for here he is. Pain stops: reason asserts itself—worth it all! New life, new energy. Perfect, and perfectly helpless. There is something here that will love and not argue—at least not for a time. Something which can be the flawless recipient of love, as no grown man can ever be.

There now, it's over. Lie back, be well, and now you can indeed think of love. The church bells are ringing: and if not because Anthony is born but because war has broken out and the whole nation must be roused to hate, never mind.

How is it possible for people to live and love and be happy in such a wicked world? Or, conversely, how can the world be peaceful and happy, when it has such wicked people in it? Forget it. Go to sleep.

Of Birth and Fiction. Writers are always a little suspicious of their deconstructionalysts, as patients are of analysts. Perhaps there's a simpler explanation. I merely wanted to bring the subject around gracefully to The

Cloning of Joanna May, this novel that Viking is just publishing, in which the whole business of birth takes a fictional twist; the kind of fictional twist indeed that real life so often these days takes, whether it's to do with sex, or the weather, or reproductive techniques. Now I understand my cunning, when the organizers of this event rang my secretary Jane and asked "what is her talk entitled" and Jane put the call on hold and looked across the room and asked "what is the talk about?" and I said, "Why, Of Birth and Fiction, of course." I meant to talk about *The Cloning of Joanna May*.

Some hopeful readers do see the book as science fiction. No such luck, I say, this kind of thing is happening all the time, all around. Science Speculation takes it to the limits of doubt. It is the duty of writers, I say, to take these social implications on board. What I really mean is, how extraordinary, what a wonderful thing to write about: you need never be finished. Whole onion layers of plot and purpose to be peeled away, and yet more to come. I bit off more than I knew. Just as Joanna May had a piece bitten out of the back of her neck, by her ex-husband Carl, who was a dab hand at genetic engineering, and knows full well that cells taken from the back of the neck, good fresh bloodless tissue, are particularly rich in DNA.

Joanna May is about a woman of sixty who discovers that thirty years ago, unbeknownst to her, she was cloned. This Joanna May, divorcée, childless, wealthy, lonely, discovers one day that she has four identical twins walking around the world. Suddenly, a family. Sisters, perhaps. Or are they daughters? They are younger than she is. Would they see her as mother, just because she was older? Would they grant her more wisdom, because she was sixty: or less, because she was older, understanding that the world itself gets wiser year by year, so that to have been born earlier is a positive disadvantage when it comes to wisdom? Clones, they are, at any rate. Replicas of Joanna May. Joanna May, given another chance; another stab at life, born to a different world, a different strata of society, a different education: Joanna May if only. . . .

Joanna May is shocked at the discovery. Taken aback. These are her views when she hears what her ex-husband did to her.

The world turned upside down. I went to Carl's office to have it out with him, but he had it out with me, and took some living cells from my neck, what's more: the kind of good fresh bloodless tissue that's rich in DNA: he could grow all kinds of me from that—he's right. Ugly, headless, always miserable, always in pain: five-legged, three-headed, double-spined: every leg with perpetual cramp, all heads schizophrenic, and spina bifida twice over. If he wanted, if he could persuade them to do it, that is—and he is a Director of Martins Pharmaceuticals, isn't he, and a benefactor of this and that: an interesting experiment, he'd say, a favour. You do this for me and I'll do that for you. Would they? Snip and snap, create a monster? Not if Carl May put it like that, probably not, but if he said, humbly, in the cause of knowledge, just let's see if we *can*, just let's see. Only the once, then never again. (For once is ethical, twice is not.) Then you never know. They might. But what should *I* care; what is it to do with me? 'I' wouldn't suffer. The 'you's' might. Poor distorted things . . .

The world turned upside down: inside out, round and about; fire burn and cauldron bubble: bubbling vats of human cells, recombinant DNA surging and swelling, pulsing and heaving, multiplying by the million, the more the merrier: all the better, the more efficiently for biologists and their computers to work upon the structure of the living cell, the blueprints of our lives, decoding the DNA which is our inheritance. A snip here, a section there, excise this, insert that, slice and shuffle, find a marker, see what happens, what it grows: record it, collate it, work back and try again. Link up by computer to labs all over the world. Bang, goes Mr. Nobel's gun, and off they go, false starts and fouling, panting and straining, proud hearts bursting to understand and so control, to know what marks what and which—and better it. This DNA, this double helix, this bare substance of our chromosomal being, source of our sameness, root of our difference—this section gives us eyes, that segment of this section blue eyes: take it away and presto, no eyes—laid bare the better to cure us and heal us, change us and help us, deliver us from AIDS and give us two heads. And all of it glugging and growing in a culture of *E. Coli*—the bacteria of the human colon, tough, fecund, welcoming, just waiting around all that time to do its stuff at our behest—toss it, turn it, warm it, start it; nothing stops it. Well why not?

I, Joanna May, beautiful and intelligent in my prime, now past it, am a woman plus repetitions, taken at my prime. Carl's fault, Carl's doing.

I am horrified, I am terrified. I don't know what to do with myself at all, whatever that means now. I don't want to meet myself, I'm sure. I would look at myself with critical eyes, confound myself. I would see what I don't want to see, myself when young. I would see not immortality, but the inevitability of age and death. As I am, so will they become. Why bother? Why bother with them, why bother with me? What's the point? I can't bear it. I have to bear it. I can't even kill myself—they will go on. Now night will never fall.

Of Birth and Fiction.

I wrote another book, also published by Viking, *The Hearts and Lives of Men*. A much simpler, more humane, instructive kind of novel, with a cliff-hanger on every page and a heroine called little Nell, who was the fruit of love, not biological engineering, new reproductive techniques. There seemed to be trouble there too. I have a word to say about her birth.

Reader, I am going to tell you the story of Clifford, Helen and little Nell. Helen and Clifford wanted everything for Nell and wanted it so much and so badly their daughter was in great danger of ending up with nothing at all, not even life. If you want a great deal for yourself it is only natural to want the same for your children. Alas, the two are not necessarily compatible.

Love at first sight—that old thing! Helen and Clifford looked at one another at a party back in the sixties; something quivered in the air between them, and, for good or bad, Nell began. Spirit made flesh, flesh of their flesh, love of their love—and fortunately, and no thanks to the pair of them, it was, in the end, for good.

But that was back in the sixties, the age of innocence. What a time that was! When everyone wanted everything, and thought they could have it, and what's more had a right to it. Marriage, and freedom within it. Sex without babies. Revolution without poverty. Careers without selfishness. Art without effort. Knowledge without learning by rote. Dinner, in other words, and no dishes to clean up afterward. "Why don't we do it in the road?" they cried. Why not?

Ah, but they were good days! When the Beatles filled the airwaves and if you looked down you discovered you had a flowered plastic carrier bag in your hand and not a plain brown one, and that the shoes on your feet were suddenly green or pink, and not the brown or black your forebears had been wearing for centuries. When a girl took a pill in the morning to prepare her for whatever safe sexual adventures the day might bring, and a youth lit a cigarette without a thought of cancer, and took a girl to bed without fear of worse. When the cream flowed thick into *bouef en daube* and no one had heard of a low-fat/low-protein diet, and no one dreamed of showing starving babies on TV, and you could have your cake and eat it too.

Those years when the world lurched out of earnestness and into frivolity were fun indeed for Clifford and Helen, but not, when it came to it, for little Nell. Angels of gravity and resolution need to stand around the newborn's crib, the more so if the latter happens to be draped in brilliant psychedelic satin, not sensible white, washable, ironable cotton.

But love, in that novel, certainly had something going for it. Nell, the child of love, was good—no matter how bad her parents, the lovers, were.

And I had a word or so to say about abortion:

Abortion is sometimes necessary, sometimes not, always sad. It is to the woman as war is to the man—a living sacrifice in a cause justified or not justified, as the observer may decide. It is the making of hard decisions—that this one must die that that one can live in honour and decency and comfort. Women have no leaders, of course; a woman's conscience must be her General. There are no stirring songs to make the task of killing easier, no victory marches and medals handed around afterwards, merely a sense of loss.

And I was prepared in that novel to give practical advice as well. Never have your baby on Christmas Day, I said, and meant it.

Christmas is not a good time to have a baby. The nurses drink too much sherry and spend their time singing carols; the young doctors kiss them under the mistletoe; senior surgeons dress up as Father Christmas. Helen gave birth to Nell unattended, in a private ward, where she lay alone. Had she been in the ordinary public ward at least one of the other patients would have been there to help; as it was, her red light glowed in the nurses' station hour after hour, and no one noticed.

I had one of my children eight days before Christmas and that was bad enough. There were paper streamers in the bathroom and roaches in the bath.

Children often don't come out too well in my novels. I stifle one in *Praxis*, mock them in *She-Devil*, give them away in *The Heart of the Country*. But I do love little Nell immoderately in *The Hearts and Lives of Men*. I see her as the hope of the heart, the whole future. Having come to the conclusion that really I must never write another novel with the words heart, or life, or loves ever again, I put my trust in *Joanna May* and a more clinical approach. I am not automatically against reproductive technology: I am not convinced that having babies by chance, or at any rate by sexual selection left in the hands of overemotional, rash, and unwise individuals, is the best possible way forward. Looking round the world, I am not convinced that nature is very good or very wise. Nature simply is.

In *Puffball*, which I wrote after the birth of my fourth and final child, in 1977, hoping to capture some of the extraordinary feelings and emotions of pregnancy, which are, by a margin, even more extraordinary than the sensations engendered by writing a novel, I said this of nature:

What is nature, after all, for living creatures, but the sum of the chance genetic events which have led us down one evolutionary path or another. And although what seem to be its intentions may, in a bungled and muddled way, work well enough to keep this species or that propagating, they cannot be said always to be desirable for the individual.

And men, sensibly, are discouraged by society from doing what is natural: e.g., fighting, raping, killing one's enemies, trampling the vanquished underfoot. Women are encouraged so to do: nurturing, comforting, having babies, dusting, cleaning. But I forget it's the nineties. I must try to soften out these difficulties, make them unbumpy—like those new tar-softening machines which soften out the potholes in the road. They don't exactly mend the road, or fill in the holes: you just don't notice them so much because the edges are smooth. That's the nineties for you, I predict.

Nature sets us in motion, Nature propels us. It is as well to acknowledge it.

And by Nature we mean not God, nor anything which has intent, but the chance summation of evolutionary events which, over aeons, have made us what we are: and starfish what they are, and turtles what they are: and pumpkins too, and will make our children, and our children's children what they will be, and an infinitesimal improvement—so long, that is, as natural selection can keep pace with a changing environment—on what we are. Looking back, we think we perceive a purpose. But the perspective is faulty.

We no longer see Nature as blind, although she is. Her very nature is imbued with a sense of purpose, as the name of God used to be. God means us. God wills us. God wants for us. We cannot turn words back: they mean what we want them to mean: and we are weak; if we can not in all conscience speak of God we must speak of Nature. Wide-eyed, clear-eyed, purposeful Nature. Too late to abandon her. Let us seize the word, seize the day; lay the N on its side and call our blind mistress ɀature.

But you see the path I am on? Carry on fighting, and you end up with Joanna May. The children of reason, not love. Well, it is a fascinating journey.

I cannot quite give up, renounce the magic. Asked what the favorite of my novels is, I always say *Puffball*, without even thinking. I think because of these few lines.

Liffey sat on the ground and turned her face towards the mild sun. She felt a presence: the touch of a spirit, clear and benign. She opened her eyes, startled, but there was no one there, only a dazzle in the sky where the sun struck slantwise between the few puffy white clouds which hovered over the Tor.
"It's me," said the spirit, said the baby. "I'm here. I have arrived. You are perfectly all right, and so am I. Don't worry." The words were spoken in her head: they were graceful, and certain. They charmed. Liffey smiled, and felt herself close and curl, as a sunflower does at night, to protect, and shelter.

In *The Cloning of Joanna May* I take birth away from women, and hand it over to men: as they are of course busy doing for themselves in the real world. I went to see a most respected professor of Egyptology in Uppsala in Sweden, whom I had heard was engaged in cloning a mummy. I thought it must be just a story. But he was trying to, in conjunction with a genetic clinic in East Germany. They were piecing together such chromosomal fragments they could, retrieved from still-living human tissue eight thousand years old: they reckoned they were 80 percent of the way toward bringing a child to birth that had the genetic makeup of an Egyptian child in the great days of the Egyptian dynasties. He told me they'd stopped research because of public pressure, but I think it was more likely for lack of funds. And the funding will be back soon, perhaps already is. Good or bad? I don't know. Children get born without license: is it the unalienable right of the individual to reproduce not quite himself, but half himself, no matter what his or her nature, temperament, or circumstances, or just something we'd rather not think about? While Carl May, benefactor of mankind or evil genius, depending on your point of view, just gets on with it! How can we trust such a person as Carl May to bring about the new world? Listen to his views on nuclear technology:

The next day Carl May took part in a TV programme about the Chernobyl disaster and the question of the threat or otherwise of radiation, which seemed to so absorb the nation. He took an aggressive and positive line, as suited both

his whim, his business interests and the future of the nuclear industry; all of
these being pretty much the same.

He said he doubted very much the story of 2,000 dead and large areas laid
waste and desolate, never to grow a blade of grass again. He deplored the scare
stories in the media that death was raining down from the skies all over the
world. He drank a glass of milk front of camera, and said there was more to
fear from cholesterol than radioactivity. He said he thought the death toll would
be more like thirty-five—very modest for a major industrial accident (though
of course tragic for those concerned: families, etc.) and naturally there would
be a statistically calculable increase in cancers in those countries subject to
fallout but certainly no more than would be produced by atmospheric pollu-
tion consequent upon the continued burning off of fossil fuels. These things
had to be balanced.

Look, Carl May said, this argument that we should all live as long as we
possibly can is barmy: who wants to live an extra five years in a walking frame
anyway? Better an earlier death, be it cancer or heart attack, than a later one.
It was an old-fashioned sentiment which favoured length of life over way of
life, quantity over quality. You found it the other end of the spectrum, when
it came to how societies regarded birth: the old school, emotional, religious,
said no contraception, no abortions, let the disabled live: the more life the
better, regardless of quality of life. A younger, more reasonable, generation said
no, let's have quality not quantity. Freely available birth control, worldwide
family planning, sterilizations, vasectomies on demand, terminations all but
compulsory for those diagnosed before birth as handicapped, every child a
wanted child—and so forth, Carl May said, while Friends of the Earth, a
Bishop and the Minister of Energy tried to get a word in edgeways.

Friends of the Earth managed, "What about childhood cancer? Leukae-
mia?" and Carl May replied briskly if this nation really cares about the lives
of its children it will stop driving about in cars—how many get killed a year
on the roads!—and increase family allowances: if it cares about cancers in the
old it will ban cigarette smoking and free hospitals for the potentially healthy
and those who have not brought their troubles on themselves.

Now look, said Carl May, people will work themselves up into a state about
anything, especially if it's new. They thought the building of railway lines
would destroy the nation, they thought TV would destroy its culture, they
thought vaccination killed. ("They were right, they were right," muttered the
Bishop.) Nothing much to fear from radiation, compared to other dangers, compared to crossing the road, compared to smoking. A burst of intense radiation
could kill you, sure. So could an overdose of aspirin. Nuclear power stations
were, if you asked him, even more crippled by safety regulations than they
were by the unions, and that was saying something. The unthinking and un-
informed always fear an unseen enemy. From reds under the bed to radiation
in the head, the public gets the wrong end of the stick, is ignorant and hysterical and impossible.

He stopped. Everyone in the studio was startled; even the camera crews
were listening.

The trouble is, reason alone is too hard a couch on which to bring to birth
babies, or novels, or the future. We need a softer, kinder, altogether muzzier

and more emotional approach. Or we might as well, like Carl May, be dead of soul: like Joanna May, wonder how, if she can be cloned, how she can ever die: how night will ever fall.

This, as I say, is the penalty of thinking one day, when I read in my Sunday paper a report from a Canadian laboratory which said that the cloning of human beings was possible but there was no call for it, "but that's absurd—I'd like to be cloned: while one of me was out talking, the other one could be at home writing." And then trying to turn that simple thought into a novel and discovering that, far from being simple, it was probably the most complex subject I had ever tackled; the sum, as it were, of all the novels that had gone before. The next one sets off on an entirely different tack, but that's another story.

FAY WELDON

January 15, 1990

When the Writer Visits the Reader

I told my family I was leaving home at the weekend to go to Amsterdam. "Why?" they said. "Because I'm going to deliver a lecture," I said. They saw that as no good reason for leaving home. I am a writer. A writer, they believe, sits at home at a desk, like Hardy or Jane Austen, and sends a manuscript off by post, has a short argument about money with the publishers, and by magic a book appears, to general acclamation. "Why are you delivering this lecture?" they asked. "What's it about?" "It is about why I am delivering the lecture," I was obliged to reply. I assured them that by talking to an audience I might be able to define and refine my views on the subject, and give a better answer on my return. I suspect, as they do, that I try too hard to justify my actions; that the truth of the matter is that I just like to stand on platforms and hear the sound of my own voice. Time was—and they preferred that time—when I was too nervous to open my mouth in public. Now, they say, I can scarcely be stopped. There is some truth in this, too.

I wonder whether here in the Netherlands you have the same tradition of the Sunday sermon in church as we do in Britain? This begins to sound remarkably like a sermon. The kind of thing the vicar would say—relating the greater to the lesser, the universal to the personal. Perhaps, now so few of us go to church, we just all miss sermons. Perhaps, in the absence of vicars, it's left to writers to stand up in public and speak, while others gather together to listen? Perhaps that's why I'm here. I will try this one on my family. But experience has made them shrewd. I don't think it will work.

Now there are, of course there are, a host of perfectly understandable reasons why writers should make speeches on literary and even political matters. It is good for sales if a writer has what the publishers call a high profile—or so their publishers tell them. What's good for sales is good for publishers, for booksellers, and so must be good for writers. Yet the royalty on every paperback is so small, it is hardly an adequate motive for traveling abroad, addressing groups of readers, academics, fellow writers: writers would be more profitably engaged if they were actually writing, I suspect, than talking about themselves. But profit is simply not the point. We have to face it. I am continually persuaded that those connected with the world of ideas, of fiction, of the imagination—publishers, booksellers, writers—are not primarily motivated by money. Readers, certainly, are not. Where is the profit, I ask you, in financial terms, in reading a novel? I think we also often hide, abashed, almost embarrassed by our own idealism, our own romanticism, behind the familiar shelter "I only do it for the money."

Even when I worked in advertising, that most cynical and, allegedly, greedily cold-hearted of professions, I never quite believed the copywriter's plea, "I do this terrible thing for the money." Most people did it, so far as I can see, because they loved every minute of it. I certainly did.

I do not stand here, believe me, because I want or need the fee. I do it because the time has come to discover why I do it, and so perhaps even to decide finally to stop doing it, and I think if I talk it out with you, I might find out. Stay home, say my family, and make supper: I long to do so. Go out, say the publishers, and some instinct in me, raise your profile high, talk to your readers. Why you might even find out what they want. Not, of course, they add hastily, being nervous of the high literary moral stance of the writer, that you should ever give the reader what the reader wants: heaven forfend that you should ever alter what you write for the sake of the market; it's just, well, helpful to remind yourself that the reader is real, not a figment of the writer's imagination. It is certainly easy for a writer to forget the reader, believe he or she writes for publishers, editors, critics—

Perhaps I just want to get out, to have a decent conversation. But this is a fairly one-sided conversation, isn't it? I talk. You listen, though later you will be required to ask questions. Certainly you will be given no opportunity to interrupt me. Perhaps that is what I want—to talk and not be interrupted. That certainly never happens at home. But I can do that on the page, with less trouble. On and on, using a literary skill to keep your attention: forbidding you to leave the page: using the device of a story to keep you reading while I impose my view, my vision of the world upon you. The world's like this, I say, and that: you'd better believe it. And I prove my point by instructing my invented characters to behave this way

and that, by way of demonstration. Unfair tactics. No documentary pro-
ducer would be allowed to do it. Yet I get away with it. Why? What is a
novel but a pattern composed of lies, exaggeration, polemics, and false
instances? Yet how I love to write them and to read them. I would pay for
the privilege of doing it: it still rather astonishes me that I am not required
to pay for the luxury. I suspect people ought only to get paid for doing what
they do not want to do: then money would have a purpose and a meaning.
It is this feeling in writers, a kind of gratitude to fate for having given them
this gift, that makes them so easily exploitable; why we have to have agents
to protect our rights; why we are so ready to regard our publishers, who
are our business partners, as our friends, believe our editors must know
better than we do; why I belong to the Writers Union, the Society of Authors, why I struggle for better contracts for writers, which I also do for no
payment, and frequently suggest to writers, women writers in particular,
that they should take courses in nongratitude, in the same way as, in their
own self-interest, they will take courses in karate. Because you feel grateful to fate is no reason to say to a publisher, give me a rotten deal.

I look at my list of activities over the previous year and discover I have
done many, many things apart from actually writing. I've judged a whole
succession of literary prizes: the Whitbread Fiction Prize, the GPA Irish
Prize, the Peninsula Prize, the Mail on Sunday first-paragraph-of-a-novel
award. This is a kind of subprofession. It means you get to read and discuss novels with other people who are also easily tempted to read and
discuss them: it means you find out how the minds of your fellow judges—
usually lucid, frequently ingenious, often willful people—work; you learn
a lot from those who have actually studied literature, as I have not: my
own qualifications are in Economics, not much help, one might think. I
find out from this group analysis of a text all kinds of things about what
makes a novel "good," what makes a novel "best." It shows you the kind
of novel you don't want ever to write: the kind of novel you wish you had
written: it obliges you to be not merely reader, but judge; to be persuasive
in your enthusiasms. How can you tell which is the best book? people ask:
how dare you sit in judgment? to which all you can reply is—the book
that wins, say the Booker Prize, is not the "best" book, only time will tell
you that, but the book best fitted to win this year's Booker Prize, and someone has to be prepared to say so. Someone, somewhere, has to make what
is called a "value judgment" or we will all drift into a sea of polite and
easy acceptance of the pretentious and the dull. I understand well enough
why I accept invitations to act as a literary judge. It is flattering to be asked.
I like to read contemporary novels. I like not to have to pay for them. I like
to meet my fellow judges. I love talking about novels. I love to dress up for

award dinners; I love the buzz and excitement of the occasion, the sense of literary scandal brewing: I am prepared, for the sake of these things, to be reviled and derided by those who think I've done it hopelessly wrong. Besides which, I believe I am usually right—and time tends to prove me so—and I have become quite good at it with practice, and it is always very pleasurable to practice a skill, especially one not many have the opportunity or privilege to develop. I am always much reassured by the degree of unanimity of choice in any panel of judges, the first five or six on the short list are usually a matter of consensus—the winner and runner-up hotly contested—and the next down, the third favorite, very often gets the prize because the supporters of numbers 1 and 2 won't give way. It is this compromise choice, the book that upsets nobody, that the experienced judge tries to keep in its proper place. The "Mail on Sunday" pays in bottles of wine. Is that a good idea? My family quite likes that one.

I see from my list I've done three residential writing workshops—two in New Zealand, one a four-day general fictional course, one a screen-writing course; and, a week after I came back from there, a five-day course in novel writing at the Arvon foundation in Devon, which I tutored with a certain Penelope Fitzgerald: an excellent novelist. Now I don't believe you can teach the ungifted to write: I think you can save the gifted a year or so practice time, and that this is worth doing. In any such group of apprentices you will find one or two potentially professional writers: the rest you can help, as it were, find themselves through writing. Writing as therapy is not such a bad idea. The writing of fiction is a training in empathy, even more acutely than is the reading of fiction. It does no one any harm. When I say reading does no one any harm, I sometimes wonder. I am surprised by the number of people who say that though they read Stephen King, they won't keep a Stephen King novel in the house. It seems to them altogether too powerful as an object, to carry with it dark and elemental powers. It is what Stephen King aims for, and what he succeeds in only too well, excellent writer that he is. Whether he "should" or not is another matter. "Should" applies to writers as much as to doctors, or politicians, anyone who interferes with the lives of others, let us not suppose it doesn't.

It has become customary for novelists, screenwriters, poets of standing, to tutor—or facilitate: the NZ word—these classes. Again, why we do it is unclear to me. It takes up valuable time and energy, and pays very little money. We do it because funding in the Arts, in Britain as elsewhere, is starved of money: if you do it, you must do it for the love of it, and so many of us go out and try and teach others, from the desire to pass on a craft from generation to generation, to impart enthusiasm, to share common ground, to try to detect, perhaps, where craft stops and art begins. As I say, it is exhausting. You must, in reading the work of beginners, cherish the good, expunge the bad, while hoping to heaven you can tell what is good and what is bad. You must resist the temptation to make other people write as you do; you must realize that what you see as a weakness may in fact be a strength—I don't like to see more than two adjectives in a row: I will say, well, if a noun needs an adjective, that adjective had better take its time in a phrase, or a sentence, all to itself—only to have brought to me an Iris Murdoch novel in which she uses eighteen adjectives in a row. You learn not to teach rules. You hate the other teachers of creative writing who've had a go at your pupils, distorting their vision and wrenching their style out of shape. No doubt they think the same of me. Penelope Fitzgerald and I came to the conclusion we had a maternal view of language, we want to nurture the potential of someone else's novel, almost as much as our own. Because you can't bear to see a sloppy sentence without wanting to clean it up: as if it had some kind of existence outside its writer: carried in itself the potential for perfection; it is your simple duty to do what you can to help it on its way, in the same way as if you see a drowning man, you feel it is your duty to jump in and save him. You may not do it but you know you should.

When last in New Zealand, the country where I was brought up, though not born, I conceived it as my duty to bring NZ writing to the attention of the world. I chided my pupils there, many of them already published in NZ, for their insularity; I pointed out that they could no longer hide behind their geographical remoteness: the fax, I said, made the whole English-speaking world one land, and that included all those nations who now have English as a second language. You are not writing for three million, I told them, but for a thousand, thousand million, and you should behave accordingly, write accordingly, and change your publishers accordingly. I was, I think, outrageous in my presumption. They were very good about it, but probably quite glad when I flew off.

I noticed there that the young writers, brought up on visual narrative, in film and TV, were much more at ease writing screenplays than prose: took to it, if encouraged, like ducks to water. I came to the conclusion that the peculiar and distinctive character of the NZ short story, in which no person or place is ever described, but simply somehow occurs—so that the reader, being denied any helpful detail, can only assume the middle: middle class, middle age, middlish temperament: how boring writing can become—is because the young writer, film reared, sees his story rather than hears it: all too easily loses the art of transferring the train of his, her thoughts from his own head into another by way of pen and paper: he, she, uses pen and paper because film is so expensive and impractical, but the natural inclination is just to point a camera, and let the eyes of the viewer, not the mind of the reader, do the work. New Zealand produces many fine writers: some unseen, unacknowledged social pressure, in a country where people fear to be odd, somehow drags it out of them: drives them to it. In New Zealand, you decide, the aim is to be "normal"—those who can't manage it take to the pen, being too self-controlled to take to the bottle.

Personally I tend to write first, think later. To teach others "creative writing" helps define the thought that comes too late for one novel, in time, unconsciously, to help the next. To teach is also to learn. I never set out to be a writer: circumstances forced me into it: a mixture of indignation at the ways of the world, and marvel at the ways of its inhabitants, and practical necessity, led to a fictional and apparently endless outpouring of words on paper, shuffled somehow into form, shape, space; of some apparent literary value and even commercial significance to publishers. I never wanted to be a "writer"—though presently found myself writing— but once you begin the need to get it right becomes obsessive: the contact with other writers, would-be writers, or published writers, those who, like you, attempt to scale this unscalable mountain, membership of some arcane and secret society of mad enthusiasts, and to be taken to task by them. Contact with the reader can be frightening: the creature of your imagination made flesh, sometimes critical, sometimes admiring: but this too seems a duty. Yes, of course they buy books, pay for books: it is in your interest to meet them, read to them. But you want to know what they think, what they look like, what makes them laugh: they have to let you into their heads, by the million. It is a small courtesy to them to allow them into yours, just for a little while. I offer all that's there for inspection: it seems only fair.

In 1984 I found myself writing a book called *Letters to Alice*, a kind of blend of literary analysis, a feminist view of history, autobiography, and downright lies, as some of us call fiction. An epistolary not-quite novel. It was Letter 5 of this book that inspired the organizers of this Conference to ask me to speak to you; so I will read you extracts from it. At the time I took the view that the writer leaves home, travels abroad, makes speeches, gives tutorials, not in the interest of increased sales, not motivated by greed or vanity, nor a sense of public duty, nor in service to his/ her art—any of which I can and have put forward to you, and my family, as a possible explanation as to why I stand here in front of you this evening, but simply because it puts off the day when (I) have to start writing the next novel, I quote:

I create the same distractions for myself—visits to friends, consultations with publishers, TV producers and so on—as I create before embarking on a new novel or play. Some writers classify the delaying process as research, and get advances from publishers and grants from Arts Councils to do it but I (I like to think) know it for what it is, an uneasy mixture of terror, idleness and a paralysing reverence for the Muse which, descending, prevents the writer from putting pen to paper for an intolerable time; till something happens—a change in the weather, an alteration to the pattern of dreams—which makes it possible to begin.

North Queensland lives by its wits and its physique—it gives no credence to writers, especially women; what use imagination when a crocodile advances or the locusts get the sugar-cane? You need a flame thrower and a helicopter, not a novel. Down in Canberra things are very different. It is a city of astonishing artifice and astonishing beauty. Once it was a barren plain, an indentation in the dusty desert: now it is striped by tree-lined avenues—the trees imported by the hundred thousand from Europe, over the years—in pretty, idiosyncratic suburbs where house prices define the status of the occupants, and when you change houses you change your friends, willy-nilly—and dotted by swimming pools, and graced by tranquil man-made lakes. It is a place of final and ultimate compromise: it exists only because Sydney and Melbourne could not agree where the seat of Australia's government was to be, and so invented this place, somewhere in between—but rather nearer Sydney. It has handsome new buildings; a High Court where the courts are like theatres and judges and criminals play to an audience; the prettiest, leafiest, and most savagely, suicidally conspiratorial university in the world, the ANU—and it has *readers.*

I talked to them last night. I read to them. I read from *Puffball*—or rather I read *all Puffball,* leaving out the bits difficult to précis. A potted novel: a Reader's Digest version. Once I was too horrified to open my mouth in public—my heart raced and my voice came out in a pitiful mouse-squeak—but now I enjoy haranguing hundreds.

It is practice, only practice, and learning to despise and put up with your own fear that works the transformation—which I tell you, Alice, just in case you suffer yourself from that terror of public speaking which renders so many women dumb at times when they would do better to be noisy. And if you are in a Committee meeting or at a Board meeting or a protest meeting, speak first. It doesn't matter what you *say,* you will learn that soon enough, simply *speak.* As for the windows to be opened, or closed, or cigarette smokers to leave, or no-smoking notices to be taken down—anything. The second thing, you say, later, will be sensible: your voice will have the proper pitch, and you will be listened to. And eventually, even, enjoy your captive audience.

Here in Canberra, this fictitious place, this practical, physical, busy, restless monument to invention, they love books and they love writers. Different cities call out different audiences. In Melbourne the audience is middle-aged and serious; in Sydney middle-aged and frivolous; here in Canberra they are young, excitable, impressionable and love to laugh. They want to know: they ask questions. They nourish you, the writer, with their inquiries, and you fill them with answers; right or wrong, it hardly matters. It's always wonderful to find out that there is a view of the world, not just the world: a pattern to experience, not just experience—and whether you agree with the view offered, or like the pattern, is neither here nor there. Views are possible, patterns discernible—it is exciting and exhilarating and enriching to know it. You need not agree with the person on the platform, but you discover that neither do you have to agree with friends and neighbours: that's the point. You can have your own view on everything—and this, particularly in a place such as Canberra, is liberty indeed. And it is why, I think, increasingly, any seminar on Women and Writing, or Women Writers, or the New Female Culture, or whatever, is instantly booked up—by men as well as by women—and readings by writers, and in particular women writers—are so popular. At last, it seems, there is some connection between Life and Art, the parts do add up to more than the whole: we always thought it! We discover—lo—we are not alone in the oddity or our beliefs. Our neighbour, whom we never thought would laugh when we laughed, actually does.

It puts, of course, quite a burden on the writer, who is expected to direct all this mental theatre, to be seen as an Agony Aunt as well as the translator of the Infinite, and the handmaiden to the Muse, and may not have realized, on first putting pen to paper, where it would all end. But we have our royalties to give us some worldly recompense: our foreign sales, our TV rights, and so on. Like the real Royalty, it does not become us to complain.

Jane Austen and her contemporaries, of course, did none of this. They saved their public and their private energies for writing. They were not sent in to bat by their publishers in the interest of increased sales, nor did they feel obliged to present themselves upon public platforms as living vindication of their right to make up stories which others are expected to read. Imagine Jane Austen talking at the Assembly Hall, Alton, on "Why I wrote *Emma*." But times, you see, have changed, and writers have had to change with them. When the modern reader takes up a "good" novel, he does more than just turn the pages, read and enjoy. He gratifies his teachers and the tax payer, who these days subsidizes culture to such a large extent, in every country in the world; he gives reason and meaning—not to mention salary—to all those who work in Arts Administration and libraries and Literature Foundations, and Adult Education and the publishing, printing and book distribution trades—nothing is simple, you see, nothing: nothing is pure and by virtue of the pressure put upon the reader to read, the burden of the writer is that much the greater. If your writing has any pretensions to literary merit, you *must* appear, you cannot shelter behind the cloak of anonymity: you have to be answerable, although you would rather stay home knitting, or dipping a horrified toe into the dangerous coral seas of the uncultured North. It won't do: you have to come down to Canberra: you want to come down to Canberra. Somehow, it is registered as duty. You're lucky, moreover, if they pay your fare.

But I myself am reader as well as writer: I write, I sometimes think, the book I want to read that no one else has written. It is part of the fellowship of the reader, that what you want to read, and therefore write, a lot of others want to read too. Because you, in your reading, keep pace with them. I think many writers of contemporary fiction feel, as I do, that we are all engaged in the same act, this producing of alternative realities, examples of existence that the real world has neglectfully failed to produce: we advance along the same front, some a little ahead, some lagging behind, but all bound for the same destination.

I am talking, I am aware, of the advanced end of the writing process, when the written language is used for the purpose of invention, to create what is not already in existence, rather than as a means of simple communication: to write down and hand on to others what in a simpler, basic environment—the cave family's caveat in 5000 B.C., a grunted—"Careful, honey, there are wolves out there!" by A.D. 2000, in our complicated world, has become a written notice, "Beware mud on road." We believed in our innocence that the written language would be available to everyone. But it isn't so. And in the developed West, here in the Netherlands as across the water in Britain, we begin to notice the alarming number of people who can't do it, can't cope, can't read "Careful, mud on the road," and will end up in a ditch because of it. It worries and upsets us. How have we failed? How are we to keep our societies literate? A U.N. Campaign for Literacy? More money, better teachers? Less film and television? Perhaps if the children didn't watch, we think, didn't have the information they need to understand the world from the screen, why, they'd have to read! And certainly, I suppose, for all practical purposes, it's best they should read. We're told in England that our great educational reforms in the nineteenth century were brought about so that a largely illiterate peasant population would be persuaded to become an urban proletariat: would be able to read the instructions on machinery; even more important, trained to accept that the natural pattern of work is from morning to eve, six days a week; steady, not sporadic: that a man and woman must get up and get to work, rain or shine. in illness or health, to make his master's living. This was the purpose of school. Not education. Discipline. The truant officer who chases and terrifies the errant schoolchild—the taking of the register morning and afternoon, such a feature of our schools even now, has induced in generation after generation what we now refer to blithely as "the protestant work ethic." I fear it has more to do with profit than with ethic.

But the machinery has become so complicated, hasn't it? The computer, not the chain saw. We expect of our simpler citizens what we expect of the most sophisticated, somehow feeling that we're trying to be fair. We pay our workers by check not by money in the hand. We offer them financial help but only if they fill in a form. We insist on literacy.

I don't think we need see television and film as evil; something that prevent the young from reading as much as they should. The child has an appetite for fiction: we've all observed that. The bedtime story, with its beginning, its middle, its end, and its moral, puts a shape upon the chaos of real events: the child craves it. The child is born with a sense of justice, a longing for fairness, which the real world makes nonsense of. The child sees well enough that good is not in fact rewarded or evil punished. That the greedy, not the good, grow rich. That the cunning, not the deserving, live the longest. If the child turn to TV or film for its moral and purposeful tales, so be it. Educators don't like it: commerce controls the product, not the educator. The adult is horrified at the violence of, say, Indiana Jones—not for himself, of course, but for the child, whom he is determined will remain a tender, trusting plant—whom he loves to tempt with gentle, pretty books, full of laughing children and happy families—saying, look, this is, if not quite the truth, at least what there is to aspire to—read, goddamm you, believe what I say, even in my absence. It's written down. It must be true. The child yawns and turns away, saying this is not truth. I may not read, but already I know the world. I know brutality, humiliation, frustration. You are telling me lies, so why read? I'll just watch Indiana Jones, thank you; it accords with my experience of the world—not the kindly loving denatured world of the middle-class schools, but the violent, terrible, funny, energetic, exciting one outside. I'll get by somehow, without reading.

We observe the unhappiness of the illiterate and think the answer must be to render him/her literate. Of course we must do what we can. Let me dance and froth about at the far end of the scale, chattering about literature: what about those down the other end, who need such infinitely complex skills today to so much as get them through a supermarket safely, let alone an airport? Who couldn't tell a novel from a bus timetable? Perhaps we should concentrate a little less on rendering our simpler citizens fit for our complex, contemporary society, a little more on returning our society to a simplicity that makes it fit for all of us to live in. Unless we do, I fear that more and more of our citizens will decide they simply can't keep up, and opt out of literacy, along with civilization itself.

Infidelity

There's what ought to happen, and what does happen, and they're different.

There's love eternal, couples walking hand in hand into the sunset of old age, and you and I know how seldom that happens, and how we go on hoping against hope that it will.

There are theories of life and there's real life, and a great black tearful pit in between which it's all too easy to fall into. So be careful about the theories, because it can take years to climb out of the pit, and to women years are precious. And besides which, the climb so often has to be done in the glare of public opinion—if only what your mother, his brother, her wife, and the friends and neighbours are saying—and the glare wreaks havoc with the complexion and ages you no end.

So if anyone tells you it's okay to have an affair, that it will enrich your marriage, don't listen. Or at any rate if you do, if you're meeting this man and out of hours, be careful, be secret, tell no one. And if you want to cry to the world I'm happy, it's so wonderful, I'm in love—don't do it. The penalty for illicit love is the closing of the lips (even as the legs open, I was going to add, but this may be too vivid, albeit poetic, an image for *Allure*, and almost is for me) but it is this very punishment which heightens the adventure, makes the drive of the other into the soul, your receptivity to his, so powerful.

After all this heady talk, you married women may well start fluttering your lashes, catching the eye of the taxi driver, your best friend's husband, your gynaecologist, your Congressman, indeed your President, but don't blame me. I'm not saying it isn't worth it: I'm just saying be very, very careful. Or you'll be like poor Alex in *Fatal Attraction*, his wife appearing with a gun when all you'd ever wanted was a bit of acknowledgment: someone to say love matters. Let me say it for you, it does. Stop being so unhappy: get out of his life, find another, or you're dead.

There's how people ought to be and how people are, and they're different. There's how to be happy in twelve easy lessons, and how it feels to be you. There's *The Erotic Silence of the American Wife* and *Backlash* and *Madame Bovary* and *Women Who Love Too Much*, and there's how it is to lie alone, night after night, while your life passes by: or know that your husband is in that creature's bed: or the blissful relief of lying where normally your best friend lies, in her bed with her husband, because she always seemed to be so much happier than you, and you were envious. There's the triumph of finally prising your so-boring mother and father apart, of wrecking someone else's marriage—your parents', metaphorically—so that you win, and then moving on, smiling sweetly. There's all kinds of truths no one wants to know about, because they're painful, or don't show you up in a good light, so you'd rather forget. There's you in the good photograph with your makeup on, as you like to be, and the snapshot of you you hate the more because others say how like you it is, and you can't believe it. That overweight, smirking idiot looking more like your own mother than you ever believed possible. Enough to drive you into the arms of your neighbour's husband, anyone's, come to that.

There's the early morning you in front of the mirror, patting on the moisturiser, trying new foundation, making the most of your eyes with browns and greens and the season's shades, pencilling in the lip-liner— see the curve of the mouth, the sensuous line where lip meets non-lip— narcissus personified, or should it be narcissa? This face, this person, can it be me? Can this be the one I love? Perfect love?—and there's you crammed up on the train on the way to work, protecting your person from grotesque others; you listening fearful to the footsteps which follow you home, can this be true love or attack? The lover with red roses or the rapist on a date? That sensuous line between the two which no amount of pencilling can ever properly delineate. It's forever getting smudged to your disadvantage. Try another lip-liner: perhaps sharper, softer, deeper, brighter. Read *Allure* to see which one's best for you. But always keep the alleged self, the made-up self (notice the pun?) one step ahead of the real self, which you keep hidden from the world, and quite right too.

There's *How to Find Your True Self*, and what you discover your true self
to be: a banshee wailer on the telephone, when love goes wrong, full of
hate and anger, a fishwife, a harridan, out of control and further in love,
and the more you shriek and the fouler your language, the further love
departs, but you can't stop, because the desire to hurt is greater than the
desire to be loved. But you can't see it. You think evidence of your distress
will work upon the other. But of course it doesn't. Just because when you
were a baby, roaring and spitting out your passions, your mother came
running to soothe you and love you, cuddle you and kiss you, doesn't mean
there's anyone out there to do it now. Just some man, with his ear a foot
from the phone, yawning and wondering how long this is going to go on,
wanting to get to bed. With whom? Don't ask. It's not you. Accept it.

There's passionate love and there's bored, this-will-do love. There's the
marriage in which the partners say to one another, be sexually free, dear.
All I want is your happiness. Your personal fulfilment. And what that
means, if you ask me—well, I'm telling you: bending your ear: what
chance do you have?—is that neither of them can be bothered to care.
Either they don't have any imagination, just don't envisage what the other
two do, or murmur—the movement of limbs, the entwining of spirits, the
entering of bodies, one within the other—or if they do envisage it and
simply don't care, and think it doesn't matter, who wants them anyway?

If a husband says to you, "get it out of your system," you might as well
leave him now. If he's not jealous he's not worth having: if he lets you get
away with it, you'll despise him for life. You'll just use the poor defeated
creature like a fetch-and-carry lapdog. "Fetch me my bag, dear," "you
haven't poured my drink, dear" signals to the world you have the upper
sexual hand. Where's the challenge in that? Hand-in-hand into the sunset,
all you like, but who wants to hold that hand? It's cold and it's clammy
and it's only in yours because it never had the energy to wrench itself away.
And you'll know it.

There's how the scene ought to go, and how the scene does go. Let me
play it for you the way it would if we were all the self-aware, civilised,
understanding people we ought to be when we've finished our *Twelve Steps
to Self-Understanding* and have taken to heart Dalma Heyn's *The Erotic Silence of the American Wife* and stirred our wifely selves up with a little
sexual love and passion outside marriage.

Our cast: Dean and Louella. They've been married five years. She's at
the office; he calls from home.

DEAN: Hi, Louella. You too busy to talk a little?

LOUELLA: Never too busy for you, sweetheart.

DEAN: Okay, because I've just played the answerphone and there's this conversation on it between you and Bob. I think it was recorded by accident.

LOUELLA: (after a little pause while she rapidly thinks back) Bob?

DEAN: Yeah, Bob. Your sister Frieda's husband. Look, I'm really sorry for listening in. I don't want you to think I'm prying into your personal stuff, but there may be one or two things here need talking about. What say I take you out for dinner tonight?

LOUELLA: Great, Dean! Where shall we go?

DEAN: I could pick up your little black number from the cleaners, and come by the office and we could go to Arabella's. They do great vegetarian dishes. I'll see about the babysitter.

LOUELLA: I'd really love that, Dean. You're right, we do have one or two things to talk about.

At Arabellas, they sit opposite each other. Candles flicker in their concerned, self-aware faces. They eat quiche and drink mineral water.

DEAN: So you really can manage to love two men at once?

LOUELLA: Dean, there is so much love in my heart, of course there's room for both of you. You are my husband. He is my lover. He gives me such a wonderful new sense of self—we American wives can hardly find the words to express what we feel in these extra-matrimonial relationships! I read it in Dalma Heyn.

DEAN: I understand that, Louella. I don't want to undermine your feelings in any way, believe me. I don't want to undervalue your experiences. I don't want you to feel I'm putting any aspect of your eroticism under attack. I just want us to use this love affair of yours to build up our marriage, make the feeling between us stronger. Enrich both our lives. Speak to me, Louella! I don't want you to fall silent, as you American wives so often do, according to Dalma. I've read it too.

LOUELLA: I just can't get over your listening in to that phone call.

DEAN: You know how these things are, Lou. Try and forgive me. He was talking about what you were doing with your mouths, and your toes, and I kinda got interested. I never did any of that stuff. I didn't know American husbands did.

	I guess you'd have listened if I'd been talking like that with Frieda.
LOUELLA:	I'd have tried not to, Dean.
DEAN:	Well, I accept that. I failed. What bugs me most is that I may have failed you as a husband, somehow restricted your personal growth and not been sensitive enough to your womanly moods. Has that been the trouble?
LOUELLA:	I guess it has, Dean. But I've got to take responsibility here too. I might not have shown myself as a good wife, you see, and, what with one thing and another, that hasn't kept the sex between us all that exciting.
DEAN:	I guess adultery must be life-enhancing.
LOUELLA:	It is, it is, Dean. Not only that, I've been able to deal with the logistics of my affair with Bob so well, it's improved my self-image, just as Dalma describes.
DEAN:	Yes, I really admire you for that.
LOUELLA:	I reckon I'm so clever I could almost get to the White House.
DEAN:	Let's make that your ambition, sweetheart. How about Secretary of State? Handling all these complex and dangerous emotions, which your lust for Bob must have revealed to you, would make you a whizz at Foreign Affairs.
LOUELLA:	What I love about you, Dean, is your sense of humour. Because I do love you, more and more, now I see Bob too. I feel so comfortable in our bed; warm and safe and in a way the sheer familiarity of our surroundings makes the sex with you more focused; I can actually concentrate better on my erotic responses with you than with Bob, as Dalma points out.
DEAN:	I'm really pleased to hear that, Lou. One way and another, I'm glad this has happened. The American wife must be able to take her place standing next to her husband, unafraid and equal in the fight for erotic freedom within marriage.
LOUELLA:	Thank you, Dean.
DEAN:	Thank you, Louella.
BOTH:	Hand in hand into the sunset!

Whereas actually what actually happens is this. There you are, working away at your desk, hugging to yourself last night's secret meeting with Bob. There's a bang and a crash in reception and a sound of breaking faxes, telephones and computer screens, and shouting. You go and see that it's your husband Dean, out of control, and he's making a dash for you to strangle you and being held back by your boss and two colleagues. His language and manners are violent and obscene. You gather that he has overheard your long early-morning conversation with Bob, which he sometimes manages between Frieda leaving for work and his getting the kids to school. The only way to get Dean to leave the office is to go home with him, though you're frightened for your life. So far as your boss is concerned your job is on the line anyway: your mind hasn't been properly on your work lately; you are given to understand that your resignation is now expected. Dean thinks that you losing your job is no worse than you deserve, and you needn't think he's going to support you either. You may quote Dalma Heyn at him all you like, he takes no notice. Dean goes out on a drinking binge: to pick up as many hookers as he can. Why not, he says, and when you murmur about AIDS he says he hopes you get it: him getting it would be a small price to pay. You're shaking and trembling, but thank God Bob rings. Bob loves you and you love Bob—it must be all right. Only it appears that Dean has called Frieda, and Frieda is very distressed, and Bob can't forgive himself for what he has done to her and he is ending the affair there and then. You can't stand the empty apartment and the desolation and go home to your mother, leaving a note for Dean saying how sorry you are and begging his forgiveness. Your mother isn't very nice to you either. Frieda *is* your sister and you have muddled up family relations no end by sleeping with her husband. Did you intend to be your nephew's stepmother as well as their aunt? Over the next couple of weeks you and Dean have endless phone calls (while your mother complains about the cost) in which you humiliate yourself and beg for forgiveness and Dean demands full physical details of what went on: the whens, the wheres, the whats, the hows, while he consults all your friends as to whether or not to have you back. By this time you realise you really and truly love Dean, and are blurting out stupid things like, "I thought if you found out I'd had an affair you'd want to work on our marriage, make it better, wonder where you'd gone wrong," and you realise you unconsciously wanted to be found out and stopped, which is no doubt why you left the message on the answerphone in the first place. (No such thing as an accident!) And you even say, "because there has been something wrong lately—I know there has been—I even wondered if there was another woman—but that was just stupid, wasn't it?" And then you get a formal letter from Dean's lawyers saying you have committed adultery and your joint bank account is frozen. He has left the matrimonial home. And your best friend then tells you Dean has been having an affair with your sister Frieda for the last two years and has moved in with her. And that Bob has left town with the girl you thought just came to walk your sister's dog, but in retrospect obviously not. And you're left with nothing. And, for all you read sections of *The Erotic Silence of the American Wife* aloud to your mother, this just doesn't seem somehow to *connect* with real life. Your mother blames you, of course. Well, you are the older sister, and ought to know better.

Because there's what ought to happen, and what does happen, and they're different, and that's why you have to be careful not to fall into the black pit in between.

I'm not saying *don't*, frowsty old me, it might not turn out like that, with any luck it won't, I'm just saying be careful. I'm saying if society has declared adultery to be "bad," it may not be because God and the neighbours say it is "bad," morally wrong, but because society has observed that wives will forgive husbands who have affairs—someone has to provide the roof over the head: the children need their poppa; it's not that she wants to forgive him; but what can she *do*?—but that husbands are less likely to forgive their wives' infidelity—men *do* and women are done unto, and somehow it seems more personal, more intimate, and perhaps is, when women are done unto; and husbands can be tempted to use shock-horror as an excuse to get out of a fundamentally boring and expensive domestic situation. A familiar marriage, that is. So run through a worst-case scenario before you embark upon your adventures, or at least make sure your job is safe.

The penalty for discovering your erotic self may be extreme. So watch it.

The interests of men and women in domesticity overlap, as I keep saying, but don't coincide. When men woo, they're at their best. Then it's all red roses, kind words, and soul caring for soul. This is the time—I hate to say it so crudely—for marriage settlements, and why we need divorce laws. Because ex-husbands have a real, primitive problem when it comes to supporting women and children who aren't under their noses: if the woman isn't in the bed, cooking the food, providing comfort, solace, and emotional security, and the children aren't frolicking around his feet, he cannot really see why he should support and provide for them just because he once did. The prisons are full of genuinely puzzled alimony-defaulters who find the expectations of the law bizarre. Why pay for something which isn't there? Takes a well-trained New Man to accept the notion that an ex-wife has financial and emotional needs which relate back to the pattern of her life with him, and that there's no such thing as an ex-child.

Because we don't *want* things to be the way they are, doesn't mean they're not. (It does mean more training for more men, more of the time;

more pouring of old wine into new bottles: perpetual prodding, reminding, refining on the part of women: less appreciation of the macho, less acquiring of other women's men. Your flirtation is her sorrow.)

So you succumbed: so you believed you were safe; you fell into a tempting bed, frolicked and played, were discovered in infidelity and your whole world collapsed. Your family is dismayed, and so are hers: you feel naked and afraid: your self esteem is shattered. Take a deep breath, take some Vitamin B, go shopping—the season's colours, you'll find, are ——— and ———, skirt lengths are disappointingly long, but you can always flash a bit of bosom. (Gossard's Wonderbra lives up to its claim, if agony of soul has rendered you wraith-like and meagre of body) Start all over again. Of course. What next? That is to say, who next? And may you live to walk hand-in-hand into a rosy sunset, guilt-free.

FAY WELDON

January 1991

On the Reading of Frivolous Fiction

These days I divide novels into four convenient groups—the good good novels, the bad good ones, the good bad novels, and the bad bad novels. The good good books are the ones that have stood the test of time: the mills of literature grind slowly, as they say, but extremely sure: they're the classics. It is no penance to read them. *Madame Bovary* or *Vanity Fair* or *Tom Jones*: as with a Shakespeare play, you may resist going, you may fidget while you're there, but you're glad you've been. If only because you join in the communion of your common heritage: by some kind of osmosis, absorb the resonance of the past, make the present seem the richer.

It is the bad good books that are unendurable; that, posing as literature, can put a reader off forever. A novel? Oh, I once read one of those. The ones that aspire to literature, that defy you to read on: these are the writer-centered not the reader-centered ones, which say to the reader, "Look at me the writer, what a clever writer I am, how sensitive, how perspicacious, how much better than you the reader." Or the ones, written by a good writer—such as Walter Scott—who seems to have somehow lost his knack and be writing on, and on, and on—

Remember, always, as you embark on a novel, the rights of the reader. One: you are allowed to skip. There is an art in skipping. The more you read, the better you get at it. Just as when a friend talks and you switch off because you know what's to be said next: that's all skipping is. Two: you are allowed not to finish novels. You don't have to get the value, as it were. There is no duty here. I meet too many people who say, "I'll read this, but I have to finish that first." And they sigh. Why? If it's a pain, why finish it? It is the writer's failure, not yours, if you don't want to. Throw it away, give it away, leave it on the train, the bus: don't clutter your bookshelves with it. Books are disposable. You've probably got hold of one of the bad good ones, masquerading as a good good one. Enough to put you off for ever.

Be Not Ashamed, that is the other thing I keep wanting to say to the culturally nervous. The good bad books can be terrific. *Hollywood Wives,* Mills and Boon, the thriller, the horror, the sci-fi romp: it is true they take you out of the real world, but what's the matter with that? The real world isn't so hot. Read the bad good books while you gather strength for the good good books: the illumination of the vision, the shift of focus in the psyche that the good good book provides is strong stuff. You can't be open to it all the time. But every book you read, every book you enjoy, and in enjoying assess, makes the relationship between you and the printed page easier, more natural, until it's like breathing.

Take a parallel from the cinema: no shame in going to *ET,* to *Ghost,* to *Arachnophobia:* you know they're not Bertolucci's *1900:* you know they're frivolous: you know the level on which they operate. The important thing is the opening of the mind to invention, the exercise of the imagination. As it is with films, so it is with fiction. The frivolous can be fantastic.

INDEX

UNIVERSITY PRESS OF NEW ENGLAND
publishes books under its own imprint and is the publisher for Brandeis University
Press, Brown University Press, University of Connecticut, Dartmouth College, Middle-
bury College Press, University of New Hampshire, University of Rhode Island, Tufts
University, University of Vermont, Wesleyan University Press, and Salzburg Seminar.

Library of Congress Cataloging-in-Publication Data
Fay Weldon's wicked fictions / edited by Regina Barreca.
    p.   cm.
Includes bibliographical references and index.
ISBN 0–87451–642–0.
    1. Weldon, Fay—Criticism and interpretation. 2. Women and
literature—England—History—20th century. I. Barreca, Regina.
PR6073.E374Z65   1994
823′.914—dc20   94–20493